*What former Roman Catholic
priests and nuns are saying about*

The Gospel According to Rome

This book is an absolute must for pastors, soul-winners, and Catholics searching for the truth! A valuable resource providing a clear comparison of scriptural truth and the doctrines of Roman Catholicism.

—Wilma Sullivan
Former Sister of Mercy

The Gospel According to Rome is tenderly written, scripturally sound, scrupulously fair, and historically accurate. This is a book for all those who genuinely love Roman Catholics.

—Bartholomew F. Brewer
Former Discalced Carmelite
Priest

I wish I had read this book 20 years ago! It would have turned me to the Bible as the source of truth by which to live. It would have freed me from doctrines and practices that neither satisfied me nor gave me life.

—Bob Bush
Former Jesuit Priest

The Gospel According to Rome presents Catholicism with fairness and great accuracy. The author draws from current Catholic documents including the new *Catechism of the Catholic Church*. It is refreshing to find that there is neither distortion nor ridicule but carefully researched information. This book will be of great service to both Catholics and non-Catholics who are interested in comparing Catholicism with biblical Christianity.

—Mary Kraus
Former Franciscan Sister

In 1983, as a Catholic priest, I searched in vain in Christian bookstores for something written about my Church. I wanted to read something by someone who knew Catholicism well and who also knew the Bible. Since that time, I have known many others who have made similar quests only to return equally frustrated.

The book I longed for is now in your hands. With compassion, care, and clarity, James McCarthy gives a message that is long overdue. *The Gospel According to Rome* is not only clear and well documented, but in it you will also feel the heartbeat of Catholicism.

—Richard Bennett
Former Dominican Priest

The carefully researched and organized Roman Catholic doctrines presented in this book are exactly what I was taught and then taught to others during my 20 years of preparation and practice as a Catholic priest. The comparison of these dogmas with the Word of God gives this excellent book a special value. I highly recommend it to all who are interested in understanding Roman Catholicism.

—Joseph Tremblay
Former Priest of the Oblates of
Mary Immaculate

The Gospel According to Rome provides both a panoramic view and an incisive analysis of Roman Catholicism. Having served nine years as a cloistered nun, I especially appreciate this book's liberating message. May God use it to His glory!

—Rocío Pestaña Segovia
Former Franciscan Nun

The GOSPEL ACCORDING to ROME

JAMES G. MCCARTHY

HARVEST HOUSE PUBLISHERS
Eugene, Oregon 97402

Correspondence or requests for additional material on this topic should be sent to: Good News for Catholics, Inc., P.O. Box 595, Cupertino, CA 95015, USA.

THE GOSPEL ACCORDING TO ROME

Copyright © 1995 by James G. McCarthy
Published by Harvest House Publishers
Eugene, Oregon 97402

Library of Congress Cataloging-in-Publication Data

McCarthy, James G., 1952–
    The Gospel according to Rome   / James G. McCarthy
      p. pm.
    Includes bibliographical references and indexes.
    ISBN 1-56507-107-7
      1. Catholic Church–United States–Controversial literature.
    2. Catholic Church. Catechismus Ecclesiae Catholicae.   I. Title.
BX1770.M35   1995
238'.2–dc20   94-41023
                                           CIP

Printed in the United States of America.

00 01 / BC / 12 11 10 9 8 7 6 5

Cross References to
Catechism of the Catholic Church

The Gospel According to Rome is indexed to the 2865 numbered paragraphs of the *Catechism of the Catholic Church*. For example, [26] indicates that related information can be found in the *Catechism*, paragraph 26. A superscripted bracketed number following a quotation identifies the source of the quote as the *Catechism*. For example: "We begin our profession of faith by saying... ."[26] We suggest that you get a copy of the *Catechism of the Catholic Church* and refer to it whenever you seek additional explanations of Roman Catholic doctrine.

Contents

Foreword

What is the true gospel? For five hundred years that question has divided Roman Catholics and Protestants.

Today Catholics and evangelical Protestants are joining forces in the political arena to fight together against abortion, homosexuality, and other threats to society's moral fabric. Several leaders on both sides have suggested that the moral issues we agree on are more important than the doctrinal differences that divide us. They say Protestants and Catholics ought to lay aside doctrine and embrace one another as true brothers and sisters in Christ.

No matter how noble the motives for such a proposal may be, we must return to the harsh reality that what divides Catholics and Protestants is a disagreement over what constitutes *the true gospel*. That simply *cannot* be viewed as an unimportant matter. The Apostle Paul wrote to the church at Galatia:

> I am amazed that you are so quickly deserting Him who called you by the grace of Christ, for a different gospel; which is really not another; only there are some who are disturbing you, and want to distort the gospel of Christ. But *even though we, or an angel from heaven, should preach to you a gospel contrary to that which we have preached to you, let him be accursed.* As we have said before, so I say again now, if any man is preaching to you a gospel contrary to that which you received, let him be accursed (Galatians 1:6-9, emphasis added).

Before we pronounce Catholics and Protestants all brothers and sisters in Christ, we must deal honestly with the question of whether one side or the other proclaims "a different gospel." Whoever is guilty of this is accursed—anathematized by the the very Word of God. It is not a triviality that can be laid aside and ignored.

Both Catholics and Protestants have historically understood the magnitude of the difference between their separate belief systems. Because it goes to the very heart of the gospel, the difference is so great as to constitute two wholly distinct religions. If one is true Christianity, the other cannot be. That has been the nearly unanimous view of Catholics *and* Protestants since the dawn of the Reformation.

We must realize that the moral opinions shared by Catholics and evangelicals are *not* more important than the doctrinal issues that divide us. The gospel is a matter of the utmost consequence—certainly far more weighty in the scope of eternity than even the greatest moral and political concerns of the moment.

Such a position may seem shocking or antiquated to those who think Protestant-Catholic tensions should be relegated to the dark ages. After all, we live in more enlightened times—don't we?

But far from an enlightened age, ours is an era of unprecedented spiritual ignorance. Many "Protestants" have no concept of what the gospel message is. A recent survey disclosed that half of those who say they are "born again" cannot identify John 3:16. Many of those surveyed defined *gospel* as "a style of music."[1]

At the same time, many Catholics have no idea what the Roman Catholic Church teaches. I often speak to Catholics who tell me the doctrine of the Church has changed dramatically since the sixteenth century. Both Catholics and Protestants are often confused on this point. Many suggest that there is no longer any basic difference between official Roman Catholic doctrine and evangelical Protestant belief.

The facts to the contrary are clear and extremely well documented. The Catholic Church first spelled out her differences with the Protestant Reformation in the 1500s at the Council of Trent. Every subsequent Church Council has reaffirmed the Canons and Decrees of the Council of Trent. Those pronouncements stand even today as the official position of the Church. And the gospel they describe—the gospel according to Rome—is antithetical to the gospel proclaimed by historic evangelicalism.

This book offers a trustworthy antidote to an age of spiritual ignorance. Both Catholics and evangelicals will appreciate the clear and systematic way it presents Roman Catholic teaching. The relevant Scriptures are set alongside the teachings of the Catholic Church to allow the reader to make the comparison.

Catholic apologists usually complain—and often rightly so—that Protestant treatments of Church teachings tend to be caustic, unfair, or inaccurate. This book carefully avoids such pitfalls. It is a comprehensive guide to Roman Catholic beliefs, based on Catholic sources, well documented, objective, and wholly without rancor. Catholic teachings are carefully examined in light of Scripture, which speaks for itself.

Jim McCarthy has a gift for making difficult concepts clear. His work is organized in a format that is easy for the reader to follow. It avoids being too technical, making the book especially helpful to the lay reader. And above all, McCarthy writes with a deep love for the Lord, for the truth, and for Roman Catholics. This is evident throughout the book.

Whether your background is Catholicism or Protestantism, this book will increase your understanding of both Scripture and Roman Catholic doctrine. Best of all, it shines the clear light of Scripture on the narrow way of truth.

—*John MacArthur, Jr.*
Pastor-Teacher
Grace Community Church
Sun Valley, California

THE FOCUS

Why This Book?

My family are Catholics, Irish Catholics, as far back as anyone can remember. Both of my parents hail from the Emerald Isle, each from devoutly religious families of eight children. Three of my uncles entered the priesthood and two of my aunts the convent.

My parents immigrated separately to the United States following World War II. There they met, married, and raised eight children. All were baptized. All were confirmed.

On Sundays the McCarthy family filled an entire pew. On weekdays we were represented in virtually every grade of the local parochial school. Catholic high school naturally followed. So did Catholic weddings, usually conducted by one of the uncles who was a priest. My own wedding was performed by four priests—my three uncles and our local pastor.

I thank God for the wonderful family He has given me. I appreciate the education I received from teachers who really cared—especially the Sisters of the Holy Names. They instilled in me an awareness of God and the importance of spiritual priorities. Despite their best efforts, however, I did not know God or the biblical way of salvation.

A turning point came when a friend invited me to a home Bible study sponsored by a small Christian church. There I learned of the finished work of Christ and of God's free offer of salvation. After studying the Bible for several months, I trusted Christ as my Savior.

Two years later I left the Roman Catholic Church. It was the most painful decision I have ever had to make. But when I became convinced that the teachings of the Catholic Church could not be reconciled with Christianity as taught in the New Testament, I realized that I had no alternative.

I have written this book because I owe a debt, a debt of love to my Catholic family and friends and the millions of sincere Catholics whom they represent. My motivation in writing is the same desire that Paul had for his kinsmen:

> Brethren, my heart's desire and my prayer to God for them is for their salvation. For I bear them witness that they have a zeal for God, but not in accordance with knowledge.

> —Romans 10:1,2

To the Catholic Reader

Why should you read this book? Because it contains important information from the Bible about the Roman Catholic Church that you need to know. Each week during the Mass you are asked to proclaim with the priest: "We believe in one, holy, catholic, and apostolic Church" [811]. As a Catholic, you have been taught that the Roman Catholic Church alone manifests these four divine marks [811-870]. The Church is *one* in that all its members hold to the same faith, submit to the authority of the Pope and bishops, and participate in the same liturgy and sacraments [813-822]. It is *holy* in its calling, goals, sacraments, sacrifice, and fruit [823-829]. It is *catholic* in that it extends back in time to Christ and in space over the whole earth [830-856]. Finally, the Church is *apostolic* because it was founded by the apostles, it teaches what the apostles taught, it has the apostles' successors as its bishops, and it has the apostle Peter's successor as its Pope [857-865]. Since the Roman Catholic Church alone manifests these four characteristics, it alone is the true Church instituted by Christ. Or so you have been told, and, if you are like most Catholics, so you have believed.

But is this actually the case? Have you ever seriously investigated the claims of the Roman Catholic Church? Before entrusting your immortal soul to the keeping of the Church, be sure you can answer the following questions:

- Is Roman Catholicism the faith received from Christ?
- Does the Roman Catholic Church actually extend back to the time of Christ?
- Does the Church have a legitimate claim to the teaching, ruling, and sanctifying authority of Peter and the apostles?
- Are the sacraments of the Church able to make a person holy and acceptable to God?
- Does the Roman Catholic way of salvation lead to heaven?

This book answers these questions by documenting what the Roman Catholic Church teaches on important issues relating to salvation, worship, devotion, and authority. It then analyzes these doctrines and demonstrates from the Bible why the Roman Catholic Church is not the one, holy, catholic, and apostolic church founded by Christ.

My hope is that you will prayerfully read this book and carefully consider the claims of your Church, its doctrines, and your own relationship with God.

To the Non-Catholic Christian Reader

Since the Second Vatican Council, the leadership of the Roman Catholic Church has been increasingly concerned at the ever widening spectrum of religious beliefs and practices being embraced by Catholic clergy and laity alike. To address the problem, in 1985 an extraordinary synod of bishops meeting in Rome proposed the creation of a single catechism, originally referred to as the *Universal Catechism*, for the worldwide Roman Catholic Church [10]. The goal was to provide a summary of the essential and basic teachings of the Church, and thereby help standardize the teaching of the Roman Catholic faith in the third millennium [11]. Written by a commission under the direction of Joseph Cardinal Ratzinger and approved by Pope John Paul II in 1992, the Church released the English translation of the book in 1994 under the title *Catechism of the Catholic Church*.

Now for the first time in modern history, Catholics and non-Catholics alike have available to them in a single volume an official explanation of the Roman Catholic faith. Consequently, the publication of the new *Catechism* presents a unique opportunity to understand Roman Catholicism and to compare it to Christianity as found in the Bible.

To aid non-Catholic Christians such as yourself in achieving this goal, I have written *The Gospel According to Rome*. In this book I have sought to organize and simplify the beliefs and practices of Roman Catholicism, emphasizing those doctrines that I believe are of greatest importance to readers like you. Material has been drawn both from the new *Catechism* and directly from the sources it quotes. Throughout this book you will also find extensive cross-references to the *Catechism*.

My purpose in writing is to help you to grow in your understanding not only of Roman Catholicism but also of the Catholic people and their spiritual needs. In the epilogue of this book, titled "The Junction," you will find some suggestions to assist you in communicating the wonderful gospel of our Lord Jesus Christ to Catholics.

Additionally, in many ways Catholicism is a fitting expression of the "way which seems right to a man" (Proverbs 14:12). I think you will find through this study that there is a little bit of Roman Catholicism in each of us. It is my hope that this book will help you to eliminate unbiblical ideas from your own thinking, to understand better the basis of your own relationship with God, and to grow in your love and appreciation of Christ, who alone offers full and free salvation.

Finally, if you are a former Catholic, studying the doctrinal roots of your upbringing in the light of Scripture should be a liberating experience. As the Lord Jesus promised His disciples, "You shall know the truth, and the truth shall make you free" (John 8:32).

The Sources

This book is an examination of the teachings of the Roman Catholic Church. The standard of measure will be the Bible. The question at hand will not be "Who is right, Catholic or Protestant?" but "Is Roman Catholicism right when measured by Scripture?"

This book is divided into four sections:

- Part One: Salvation
- Part Two: The Mass
- Part Three: Mary
- Part Four: Authority

The introductions to each chapter are designed to give you a feel for what it is like to be a Catholic. Through them you will attend several sacraments and be a silent observer at historic events that have shaped the Roman Catholic Church. An explanation of the Church's teaching in one doctrinal area will follow. This is presented from Roman Catholic sources without criticism or analysis so that you can clearly understand the Church's position. As you will see in these sections, some of what Roman Catholicism teaches does have a sound biblical basis.

Other Roman Catholic doctrines are clearly unscriptural. These will be the topic of the final section of each chapter, "A Biblical Response." There those aspects of Roman Catholicism that distort or contradict Scripture will be examined and compared to biblical truth. At the end of each of the four sections you will find a summary of these errors.

Though individual Catholics may vary widely in their apprehension and expression of the Roman Catholic faith, it is important to remember that there is only one official Roman Catholic faith [172-175]. By definition it is the beliefs and practices held by the Roman *Catholic* Church, the *whole* or *general* Church [830]. It is the faith contained in Scripture and Tradition as interpreted by the Roman Catholic bishops under the leadership of the Pope, the Bishop of Rome [76, 85-87, 182, 888-892, 2039].

The focus of *The Gospel According to Rome*, therefore, is mainline, traditional Roman Catholicism as taught by the popes and bishops and recorded in official Church documents. Special emphasis will be given to the modern expression of that faith as found in the new *Catechism of the Catholic Church*, the documents of the Second Vatican Council, and current liturgy. On major points, quotations will be provided so that you can judge the matter for yourself. These have been selected from the most authoritative sources available, starting with the new *Catechism* itself.

The Catechism of the Catholic Church

This is the first officially published catechism of the Roman Catholic Church in over 400 years. Pope John Paul II described it as a "compendium of all Catholic doctrine" and "a point of reference" to guide in the preparation of instructional material.[2] The Pope said, "The Catechism sets forth once more the fundamental and essential contents of Catholic faith and morality as they are believed, celebrated, lived and prayed by the Church today."[3]

The Decrees of the Ecumenical Councils

The Roman Catholic Church recognizes 21 universal councils. It considers the decrees of these councils to be authoritative definitions of the Roman Catholic faith [884, 891]. Their place in Roman Catholic theology can be seen in the new *Catechism of the Catholic Church,* which cites these councils over a thousand times. Most of these references are to the last three councils: the Council of Trent (1545-1563), the First Vatican Council (1869-1870), and the Second Vatican Council (1962-1965).[4]

Papal Documents

Popes have published numerous official papers down through the centuries. Most clarify doctrines and practices, restate long-accepted beliefs, or address pastoral needs within the Church. Occasionally a Pope passes judgment upon a disputed question. In such cases the matter "... cannot be any longer considered a question open to discussion among theologians."[5] The Church teaches that papal documents are authoritative, for when a Pope officially publishes his teaching, he speaks as the representative of Christ on earth.[6] The Catechism of the Catholic Church makes 256 references to pontifical documents.

The Code of Canon Law

Canon Law contains the rules and norms that govern the Roman Catholic Church. The revised Code of 1983 contains 1752 laws. Topics range from the authority of the Pope and bishops, the obligations and rights of Catholics, guidelines for the sacraments, the establishment of tribunals, and penalties for offenses against religion and the Church. The Catechism cites Canon Law 197 times.

The Liturgy of the Church

The Church refers to the public worship and practice of the Roman Catholic faith collectively as the *liturgy* [1069-1070]. In Catholicism, it is through liturgy—what the priest and people do when they come together—that the Church preserves and conveys its official doctrines

[1074-1075]. The liturgy, therefore, is an authoritative source of Roman Catholic doctrine [1124-1125, 2663].[7] The new *Catechism of the Catholic Church* cites the liturgy 114 times in the course of explaining the Roman Catholic faith.

The Roman Catechism

Also called the *Catechism of the Council of Trent*, Pope Pius V ordered the publication of this guide to the Roman Catholic faith in 1566 [9]. Since then it has served as the most authoritative catechism of the Catholic faith. The new *Catechism of the Catholic Church*, which cites The *Roman Catechism* 27 times, will now serve in that capacity.

Summa Theologica

Using a system of logic developed by Aristotle, Thomas Aquinas, a Dominican friar (c. 1225-1274), was the first to consolidate into a single theological system the traditional teachings of the Roman Catholic Church. His greatest work, the *Summa Theologica*, is the classic explanation of Roman Catholicism. The Church values the writings of Aquinas so highly that at the Council of Trent the bishops had before them on an altar three groups of writings to guide them: the Scriptures, the decrees of the popes, and the *Summa Theologica* of Thomas Aquinas. His teaching dominated Catholic thought well into the twentieth century. Even today the Church requires that seminary students be taught dogmatic theology "with St. Thomas as their teacher in a special way."[8] The *Catechism of the Catholic Church* cites the *Summa* 48 times.

Other Catechisms and Theology Books

There are many excellent books by Catholic authors that accurately summarize and explain the Roman Catholic faith. Those used here to present the Roman Catholic faith have all been declared free of doctrinal or moral error by an official representative of the Church and printed with the seals *Nihil Obstat*, meaning Nothing Objectionable, and *Imprimatur*, Let It Be Printed.

❖ PART ONE ❖

SALVATION

How do Roman Catholics hope to get to heaven? Does the average Catholic think he or she will make it? What role do the sacraments play in attaining eternal life? What is the purpose of penance and purgatory?

Part One will examine the Roman Catholic way of salvation. This section is structured on five fundamental beliefs of the Roman Catholic faith:

- ❖ Infants receive grace through the sacrament of baptism (Chapter 1, *Infant Justification*).
- ❖ Adult converts to Catholicism receive grace through the sacrament of baptism after proper preparation (Chapter 2, *Adult Justification*).
- ❖ Sacraments and good works increase grace in the soul; cooperation with grace preserves grace in the soul (Chapter 3, *Increasing and Preserving Justification*).
- ❖ Grace is lost through mortal sin, but can be regained through the sacrament of penance (Chapter 4, *Rejustification*).
- ❖ Eternal life is attained by dying in a state of grace (Chapter 5, *Final Destiny*).

In this section you will also get a sense of what it is like to be a Catholic. You will meet Joseph Lorente and follow his life from infancy through death. You will attend his baptism and first holy communion. When he falls from grace as an adolescent, you will join him in the confessional booth as grace is restored once again. Finally, you will be with him as a mature adult in the last hours of his life.

You will also meet Rosa, a convert to Catholicism. From her life, you will learn what it is like to become a Catholic as an adult.

◆1

INFANT JUSTIFICATION

Joseph, 18 Days Old

"What name do you give your child?" asked Father Fiorelli with a smile.

"Joseph," replied Mr. and Mrs. Lorente.

Raising an open hand and gesturing toward the sleeping infant, Father Fiorelli inquired further, "What do you ask of God's Church for Joseph?"

"Baptism and eternal life," came the rehearsed response.

Father Fiorelli, robed in festive colors, paused for a moment to survey the happy family before him. He enjoyed baptisms, especially when families that he knew well like the Lorentes were involved. Father Fiorelli had baptized each of their other four children, and had taken great pleasure watching them grow up. Today he would baptize their latest addition, Joseph.

Opening an official guide titled *The Rite of Baptism for Children in the Roman Ritual*,[9] Father Fiorelli continued, "You have asked to have your child baptized. In doing so, you are accepting the responsibility of training him in the practice of the faith. It will be your duty to bring him up to keep God's commandments as Christ taught us, by loving God and our neighbor. Do you clearly understand what you are undertaking?"

"We do," responded the parents.

The priest turned to an aunt and uncle who had been chosen by the family to serve as godparents, and asked, "Are you ready to help the parents of this child in their duty as Christian parents?"

"We are," they answered dutifully.

A Scripture reading followed from the third chapter of the Gospel of John. It concluded with Jesus' words: "Unless one is born of water and the Spirit, he cannot enter into the kingdom of God."

A prayer of exorcism came next. In it Father Fiorelli petitioned God to protect the child from the powers of darkness and set him free from original sin. He then anointed Joseph with oil and led the family into the parish baptistry.

Once everyone had reassembled around the baptismal font, Father Fiorelli continued the rite:

> My dear brothers and sisters, God uses the sacrament of water to give His divine life to those who believe in Him. Let us turn to Him, and ask Him to pour His gift of life from this font on this child He has chosen.

Looking up to heaven, Father Fiorelli prayed:

> Father, look now with love upon Your Church, and unseal for her the fountain of baptism. By the power of the Holy Spirit, give to the water of this font the grace of Your Son. You created man in Your own likeness: cleanse him from sin in a new birth to innocence by water and the Spirit.

Touching the water, the priest continued:

> We ask You, Father, with Your Son to send the Holy Spirit upon the water of this font. May all who are buried with Christ in the death of baptism rise also with Him to the newness of life. We ask this through Christ our Lord.

Father Fiorelli next reviewed with the Lorentes and the godparents their responsibilities in raising Joseph in the Catholic faith. Then, following a renunciation of sin, the priest asked them to profess with him the Catholic faith, "Do you believe in God, the Father Almighty, Creator of heaven and earth?"

"I do," each of the parents and godparents responded.

"Do you believe in Jesus Christ, His only Son, our Lord, who was born of the Virgin Mary, was crucified, died, and was buried, rose from the dead, and is now seated at the right hand of the Father?"

"I do."

"Do you believe in the Holy Spirit, the holy Catholic Church, the communion of saints, the forgiveness of sins, the resurrection of the body, and the life everlasting?"

"I do."

"This is our faith. This is the faith of the Church. We are proud to profess it, in Christ Jesus our Lord."

"Amen," came the unified response.

"Is it your will that Joseph should be baptized in the faith of the Church, which we have all professed with you?"

"It is," they responded.

Father Fiorelli instructed Mrs. Lorente to position Joseph over the baptismal font. Then, as the priest poured water upon the infant's forehead, he pronounced, "Joseph, I baptize you in the name of the Father, and of the Son, and of the Holy Spirit."[10]

Father Fiorelli then instructed the Lorentes to dress Joseph in the white baptismal garment that they had brought with them. This symbolic action was to portray the new holy state of Joseph's invisible soul. As they dressed the child, the priest continued:

> Joseph, you have become a new creation, and have clothed yourself in Christ. See in this white garment the outward sign of your Christian dignity. With your family and friends to help you by word and example, bring that dignity unstained into the everlasting life of heaven.

A candle, symbolizing the faith now alive in Joseph's soul, was then lit for him. This was followed by a song, the praying of the *Our Father*, and a formal blessing which concluded the ceremony.

Later, everyone regathered at the Lorente home to celebrate Joseph's baptism, his first step on the long road leading to Roman Catholic salvation.

Original Sin Through Adam
[385-421]

The Roman Catholic Church teaches that every newborn child must be baptized to remedy a deadly spiritual disease [403, 1250]. The Church traces the problem back to the Garden of Eden.

When Adam and Eve ate the forbidden fruit, they committed the first human sin, the *original sin* [397-400, 416]. By this transgression they became the objects of God's wrath and subject to the power of Satan and death [1006, 1008, 1018].

Original sin also refers to the effects of Adam's sin upon his descendants [396-409, 417-419]. Every newborn child comes into the world with original sin on his or her soul and alienated from God [400-406, 416-417].

The Church teaches that God sent His Son to remedy this problem [389, 410-412, 599-630]:

> Him God put forward as an expiation by his blood, to be received by faith (Romans 3:25), for our sins, and not for ours only, but also for the sins of the whole world (1 John 2:2).
>
> —Council of Trent[11]

This does not mean, however, that every person is automatically saved:

But though *he died for all* (2 Corinthians 5:15), yet not all receive the benefit of his death, but only those to whom the merit of his passion is imparted.

—Council of Trent[12]

Justification Through Baptism
[403, 1213-1284, 1987-2020]

According to the Roman Catholic Church, an infant receives the benefits of Christ's death through the sacrament of baptism [790, 977, 1214-1216, 1227, 1250-1252]:

Holy Baptism is the basis of the whole Christian life, the gateway to life in the Spirit, and the door which gives access to the other sacraments. Through Baptism we are freed from sin and reborn as sons of God; we become members of Christ, are incorporated into the Church and made sharers in her mission: "Baptism is the sacrament of regeneration through water in the word."

—*Catechism of the Catholic Church* [1213]

The Church teaches that through baptism a child is:

- rescued from the power of Satan
- freed from original sin
- made innocent and stainless before God
- born again
- given the gift of divine life
- made a partaker of eternal life
- made a temple of the Holy Spirit
- made a member of Christ's body
- welcomed into the Church
- committed to being raised in the Roman Catholic faith

Limbo

Limbo is the classic Roman Catholic answer to the question: What happens to infants who die before baptism? Thomas Aquinas, the greatest theologian of the Roman Catholic Church, reasoned that infants don't deserve to go to hell, for "of all sins original sin is the least, because it is the least voluntary."[13] Yet, according to Roman Catholic theology, without baptism no one can see God. So where do deceased unbaptized infants go?

Some of the Church's theologians have proposed that there must be a place for unbaptized infants somewhere between heaven and hell. They call it *limbo*, literally meaning *on the border*. They describe it as a place of

During the sacrament of baptism, the priest explicitly states each of these effects [1234-1245, 1262]. Two are particularly important [1262, 1987].

The Removal of Original Sin
[977-978, 1250, 1263, 1279, 1673]

Roman Catholicism teaches that baptism removes original sin, the guilt inherited from Adam. The priest expresses this belief in the prayer of exorcism, saying, "We pray for this child: set him free from original sin...."[14] The Church says that a baptized child is immaculate and guiltless before God. Should the child die at that moment, his or her entrance into heaven would be unhindered.

The Reception of Sanctifying Grace
[374-384, 1265-1266, 1279, 1999, 2023-2024]

According to Roman Catholic theology, when God created Adam and Eve, He gave them a supernatural gift: participation in divine life. As a result, they enjoyed constant communion with God [376]. The Church calls this gift of divine life *sanctifying grace* or *deifying grace*

natural happiness, but something short of heaven, for God is not there.

In modern Catholicism, limbo is, as the saying goes, "in limbo." It is neither an official dogma of the Church nor a denied belief. In discussing the fate of unbaptized infants, modern Catholicism usually entrusts their souls to the mercy of God, making no mention of limbo. This is the approach taken by the new *Catechism* [1261, 1283]. Nonetheless, even today, when a Catholic persists in asking where unbaptized infants go when they die, the answer usually comes back, "Limbo."

[1999]. It made Adam and Eve holy and just before God [375, 384]. At least, that is, until they sinned [379].

When Adam and Eve disobeyed God, they lost divine life in their souls, "the grace of original holiness"[399] [390, 399]. They died spiritually and became unholy and displeasing in the sight of God. Furthermore, their sin doomed their descendants to inherit their fallen condition. Consequently, every child comes into the world devoid of sanctifying grace and in a state of original sin, being inclined toward evil and subject to suffering and death [400-406].

The Roman Catholic Church teaches that only baptism can remove original sin and restore divine life to the soul [405]. The priest states this belief during the rite when he asks God to " ... pour His gift of life from this font on this child.... "[15] The Church describes the pouring of divine life into the soul as the *infusion of sanctifying grace* [1266, 1996-1997, 1999, 2023]. *To infuse* means *to pour in.*

Through this infusion, the child's soul, which was spiritually dead because of Adam's sin, becomes alive [1213, 1228, 1239]. Intimate participation in the life of God is established by the agency of the Holy Spirit [1129, 1227, 1265, 1988]. The infant is spiritually reborn, adopted as a child of God, incorporated into the Roman Catholic

Church, and brought into a *state of grace* [1267-1270, 1279, 1996-2004].

According to the Roman Catholic Church, with the infusion of sanctifying grace come the *gifts of the Holy Spirit* and the *theological virtues*, most notably charity [1812-1832]. Catholic theology, therefore, often equates being in a state of grace with having charity in one's heart or soul.

The theological term used by the Church for the spiritual transformation brought about by baptism is *justification* [1987-1995, 2019-2020]. Roman Catholicism defines justification as—

> ...a transition from that state in which a person is born as a child of the first Adam to the state of grace and of adoption as children of God through the agency of the second Adam, Jesus Christ our saviour.
>
> —Council of Trent[16]

Baptism justifies a child by removing the guilt of original sin and by infusing into the soul sanctifying grace [654, 1987, 1999, 2019]. For this reason Catholic theologians also refer to sanctifying grace as *justifying grace* [1266].

The Church teaches that Christ "... merited justification for us by his most holy passion on the wood of the cross, and made satisfaction to God the Father on our behalf"[17] [1992, 2020]. This merit "...is applied to both adults and infants through the sacrament of baptism duly administered in the form of the church."[18] Baptism is therefore the "instrumental cause"[19] of justification, the means by which justifying grace is applied to the soul [1227, 1239, 1254, 1987, 1992, 2020].

Baptism, however, does not deliver a child from the temporal consequences of sin, such as the weaknesses of the human nature and an inclination to sin. Neither does it guarantee that the child will attain to eternal life as an adult, for baptism is only the first step in the Roman

Catholic plan of salvation [405, 978, 977, 1254-1255, 1257, 1264, 1426].

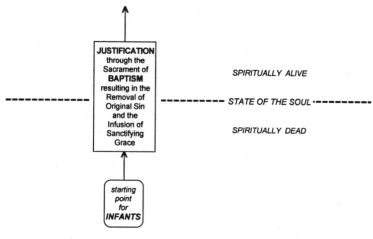

Figure 1:1
Infant Justification

A BIBLICAL RESPONSE

The Roman Catholic Church annually baptizes about 16 million children under the age of seven years old. Most are only a few weeks old. As they grow up, the Church teaches these children that original sin has been removed from their souls and divine life resides within them. Consequently, most Catholics go through life confident that they are right with God and on the road that leads to heaven. Their confidence, however, is unwarranted, for the Scriptures teach that lost sinners are justified by faith, not baptism.

Biblical Justification
Is by Faith Alone

The New Testament word for *justification* is from a root meaning *upright, just,* or *righteous.* To *justify* means to show to be righteous or *to declare to be in a right state.*

According to the Bible, justification is a divine act: "God is the one who justifies" (Romans 8:33). Biblical justification is an act of God in which He declares an unworthy sinner to be righteous in His sight (Romans 4:3).

Biblical justification is more than the acquittal or forgiveness of sins. It includes a positive reckoning in which God credits to the sinner's account "the righteousness of God" (Romans 3:22). From that point onward God views the individual as "in Christ" (Ephesians 1:3-14).

Biblical justification has been made possible by the death of Christ. On the cross, the Lord Jesus took our guilt that we might receive His righteousness:

> He [God] made Him [Christ] who knew no sin to be sin on our behalf, that we might become the righteousness of God in Him [Christ].
>
> —2 Corinthians 5:21

The Bible says that God justifies "the one who has faith in Jesus" (Romans 3:26). The gospel is preached. Some, being persuaded that it is true, place their trust in Christ to save them. These believers God justifies, declaring them righteous in His sight.

Justification *by faith* is the consistent teaching of Scripture: "For we maintain that a man is justified by faith" (Romans 3:28); "Abraham believed God, and it was reckoned to him as righteousness" (Romans 4:3); "Therefore having been justified by faith, we have peace with God through our Lord Jesus Christ." (Romans 5:1).

The Roman Catholic Church, on the other hand, teaches that justification is by the sacrament of baptism. Catholic theologians attempt to show a biblical basis for this belief by citing Scriptures which speak of baptism in the same context as the new birth, forgiveness, or salvation. They then identify baptism as the cause of those effects.

Such indirect methods, however, can never negate the clear and explicit teaching of Scripture that justification is by faith. (See Appendix A, *Infant Baptismal*

Justification, for an examination of the primary biblical texts used by the Roman Catholic Church in support of its position.)

The Sacrament of Faith

Though the Roman Catholic Church insists that baptism is the "instrumental cause"[20] of justification, it agrees that the Bible teaches that faith is necessary for justification:

> Believing in Jesus Christ and the One who sent him for our salvation is necessary for obtaining that salvation.... Without faith no one has ever attained justification... .
>
> —*Catechism of the Catholic Church*[161]

The Church objects to criticism that faith is missing in infant justification, explaining that baptism is "the sacrament of faith" [1992] [161, 1236, 1253]. An array of explanations is offered to demonstrate how this can be so [1231, 1250-1255, 1282]:

- The infant enters into the life of faith through baptism.
- The faith of the priest, parents, and god-parents justifies the infant in baptism.
- The baptism of a helpless infant expresses the need for free, unmerited grace.
- Parents would be withholding an essential blessing from their child if they did not baptize him or her shortly after birth.
- Faith is related to and dependent upon the community of believers. Infant baptism portrays this, for the parents promise to raise the child in the Catholic faith.
- Faith is not a single decision but a process. Baptism provides strength and illumination for lifelong growth in faith.

• Catholics renew their profession of Christian
faith twice each year as part of the Eucharistic
liturgy.

None of these rationalizations, however, addresses
the root problem: *The infant is incapable of exercising
saving faith.* The notion that parents or the priest can
believe on behalf of the child is unbiblical. Each individual must decide for himself (John 1:12,13). Defenses
arguing that faith is a process or that Catholics renew
their profession as adults are irrelevant in proving that
infants are justified the moment they are baptized.

Wonder-Working Water

The Roman Catholic Church counters by saying
that what is irrelevant is the infant's lack of personal
faith. It is the sacramental action of the rite of baptism
that removes original sin and infuses sanctifying grace.
The proper performance of the rite produces a result
that is independent either of the worthiness of the priest
or of the faith of the child [1127-1128, 1239].[21] This almost
magical concept of baptism is expressed in the ritual
itself. The priest invokes God to empower the water,
saying, "By the power of the Holy Spirit give to the water
of this font the grace of your Son"[22] [1217-1218, 1238]. There
is no biblical precedent for such a prayer.

Emergency baptism is another practice that shows
the alleged wonder-working power of the sacramental
waters. Since the Church teaches that baptism is necessary for salvation, the possibility of an infant dying
before receiving the sacrament must be guarded against.
The Church requires Catholics to baptize an infant in
danger of death without delay. An abbreviated rite can be
used. If neither a priest nor a deacon is available, any
Catholic may baptize the dying child [1256, 1284]. The
Church asks Catholic doctors, nurses, and other medical
and social workers to be prepared to perform emergency
baptism.[23] Catholic medical professionals have even
been known to baptize unborn infants in peril within the
womb by use of a syringe!

If Justification Is by Baptism...

Why didn't Jesus baptize anyone (John 4:2)?

Why did Jesus tell the repentant thief on the cross, who was never baptized, "Truly I say to you, today you shall be with Me in Paradise" (Luke 23:43)?

Why did Cornelius and those who were with him receive the Holy Spirit before they were baptized (Acts 10:44-48)?

Why did Paul say, "For Christ did not send me to baptize, but to preach the gospel" (1 Corinthians 1:17)?

Why is baptism left out of so many verses explaining salvation, such as "For I am not ashamed of the gospel, for it is the power of God for salvation to everyone who believes" (Romans 1:16)?

A False Hope

The sincere motives of Catholic parents in having their newborn infants baptized are beyond question. Nevertheless, the practice is unbiblical. Parents cannot decide for their child that he or she will receive God's gift of salvation and be born again. The Bible teaches that each individual must make his or her own choice:

> But as many as received Him, to them He gave the right to become children of God, even to those who believe in His name, who were born not of blood, nor of the will of the flesh, nor of the will of man, but of God.
> —John 1:12,13

Infant baptism misleads Catholics as to their true spiritual condition and need by producing a false hope. Early in life Catholic children are taught that baptism has removed their original sin and infused them with sanctifying grace. The Church even provides tangible proof that the sacrament has been properly executed by issuing each child a baptismal certificate.

In this way Catholics grow up convinced that they already have a right relationship with God and are on the road that leads to heaven. But their hope, as we have seen, is without biblical support. Their baptismal certificates are worthless in the eyes of God, for their faith is not in the Savior, but in a sacrament and in the minister of the sacraments, the Roman Catholic Church.

❖2

ADULT JUSTIFICATION

Rosa, 23 Years Old

As she waited for the evangelistic crusade to begin, Rosa started to have second thoughts about having come. It wasn't her idea in the first place. She had heard advertisements for the crusade on the radio, but never gave it a second thought. Then Katie, a friend from work, invited her. Caught off guard and trying to be courteous, Rosa said she would go. Now, feeling terribly out of place, she wished she had declined, but it was too late to do anything about it.

And so, seated with Katie in the second deck of the city's stadium, Rosa decided to make the best of it. Anyway, this might be the opportunity she had wanted to get to know Katie better. Rosa had always admired Katie's good attitude at work and her reputation as a serious Christian. Maybe this would be her chance to find out why she was so different.

Finally the crusade began. The choir sang and an athlete told the story of how he had become a Christian. Then the evangelist began to preach.

Only then did Rosa's misgivings about coming to the crusade vanish. She had never heard anything so captivating or convicting. Tears began to trickle down her cheeks. She tried to compose herself, but couldn't.

After the evangelist concluded his message, he invited everyone who wanted to receive "God's free gift of salvation" to come down to the field in the center of the stadium. Rosa didn't really understand what it was all about, but whatever it was, she wanted it. Her life was empty and filled with disappointments.

As the choir sang *Just As I Am*, Rosa started down, determined to get right with God. As she walked, she noticed Katie bowing in silent prayer.

Down on the field the evangelist reviewed for Rosa and those with her the way of salvation. He then asked the group to join him in prayer.

As soon as the prayer was over, a young woman with an armful of literature approached Rosa. "Hi, I'm with the crusade. Can I direct you to one of our counselors?" she asked.

"I'm not sure," Rosa replied.

"Do you have a church?"

"Not really," Rosa answered, "All my family are Catholics. We seldom went to Mass, and I was never baptized. I would like some help, though. I'm not sure where I stand with God."

"I'll find someone who can counsel you," the young woman promised as she swung around and scanned the long row of tables set up along the perimeter of the field. "You should talk to that counselor in the black turtleneck shirt," she said pointing to a man sitting behind a table about 20 yards away. "Come on, I'll introduce you."

As they approached, the man extended his hand and greeted them, "Hi, I'm Father Pablo Fernandez from Saint Mary's Church." Then, realizing that Rosa was Hispanic, he added, "¿Cómo se llama?"

Rosa hesitated. Bitter memories of Catholicism in Mexico were holding her back. But then she thought about how the evangelist had promised that salvation could be hers that very day. Rosa also thought of Katie, still up in the stands. *I want the joy that Katie has*, Rosa thought to herself. *Katie brought me here. I can trust her.*

Rosa reached out and took the priest's hand, answering, "Me llamo Rosa."

Father Pablo opened the crusade materials and began to explain them. When he was finished, he had Rosa fill out a response card.

"Rosa!" said Father Pablo enthusiastically, looking at the address on the card, "you're living in my parish. Come visit me sometime and I'll tell you more. The Church has a new program designed for people just like you."

The following Sunday, Rosa visited Father Pablo's church. After Mass he enrolled her into the *Rite of Christian Initiation of Adults*, an 11-month program of spiritual development and study. "Upon your successful completion of this course," Father Pablo promised Rosa, "next Easter Sunday I will baptize you into the Roman Catholic Church."

Rosa was disappointed. She had thought that the priest was going tell her how to be saved. All week she had been singing a stanza from the hymn she had heard at the crusade:

> Just as I am, and waiting not
> To rid my soul of one dark blot,
> To Thee whose blood can cleanse each spot,
> O Lamb of God, I come! I come![24]

Now the priest was telling Rosa that she would have to wait almost a year! *But if this program is what it takes to prepare to receive God's gift of forgiveness*, Rosa thought to herself, *I'll do it!*

Steps Leading to Adult Justification
[1229-1233]

Unlike newborn infants who are to be baptized without delay, adults seeking justification in the Roman Catholic Church must undergo extensive preparation [1232]. Four steps are involved: cooperation with first actual grace, faith, good works, and the sacrament of baptism.

First Actual Grace
[153-155, 1989, 1993, 1998, 2000-2001, 2018, 2021-2022, 2024]

According to Roman Catholic theology, it is God who takes the initiative in the justification of adults [1998]. The Church teaches that "...justification in adults takes its origin from a predisposing grace of God through Jesus Christ...."25

When God reaches out to a person, He freely bestows what the Church calls *first actual grace*. This is a helping hand that enables an individual to seek God and prepare, or dispose, his soul for baptism and justification. The Church calls this actual grace, because good *acts* are its goal.

Once the sinner receives first actual grace, he must decide whether or not he will yield to its influence [1993, 2002]. If throughout his lifetime he persists in rejecting this grace, he will die in a state of sin and suffer the eternal consequences. On the other hand, if a sinner agrees to cooperate with first actual grace, he will begin to perform *salutary acts*. These are human actions performed under the influence of grace that lead to justification. The first is faith.

Faith
[144-184]

After proper instruction, an adult preparing for justification must [161, 183]—

> ...believe to be true what has been divinely revealed and promised, and in particular that the wicked are justified by God by his grace through the redemption which is in Christ Jesus.
>
> —Council of Trent26

The Roman Catholic Church describes this faith as *theological* or *confessional* faith [1814]. It is the firm acceptance of the major doctrines taught by the Church as summarized in creeds. Giving assent to these creeds is the first response of cooperation with actual grace [155]. The second is good works.

Good Works
[1247-1249, 1815-1816, 2001-2002]

Roman Catholicism teaches that adult candidates for baptism must prepare their souls by performing good works [1247-1248]. The seeking sinner must "...make preparation and be disposed by a movement of his own will...."[27] This preparation is accomplished through faith and various acts of virtue:

> ...acknowledging that they are sinners, they turn from fear of divine justice, which profitably strikes them, to thoughts of God's mercy; they rise to hope, with confidence that God will be favorable to them for Christ's sake; and they begin to love him as the fount of all justness. They are thereby turned against sin by a feeling of hatred and detestation, namely by that repentance which must occur before baptism. Finally, when they are proposing to receive baptism, they are moved to begin a new life and to keep God's commandments.
>
> —Council of Trent[28]

Baptism
[1214-1284]

The final requirement for adult justification is baptism [1254]. As we saw in the previous chapter, the Roman Catholic Church teaches that baptism is the "instrumental cause"[29] of justification [1227, 1239]. It removes original sin and infuses sanctifying grace into the soul [1262-1266]. According to the Church, the amount of sanctifying grace, the grace that justifies, which baptism infuses into the soul, varies from one person to the next depending on God's generosity and the individual's prebaptismal preparation.[30]

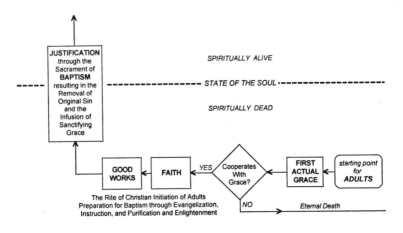

Figure 2:1
Adult Justification

The R.C.I.A.

[1232-1233, 1247-1249, 1259]

Though the Council of Trent (1545-1563) defined the Roman Catholic doctrine of justification, it did not establish a specific course of preparation for adults seeking to be justified. In 1963 the Second Vatican Council addressed this deficiency, ordering the restoration of an ancient tradition by which candidates prepared for baptism [1232]. Known as the *catechumenate*, the program instructed candidates, called *catechumens*, in the basics of faith and virtue [1230].

The modern catechumenate is called the *Rite of Christian Initiation of Adults* (R.C.I.A.). Under the most recent guidelines, published in 1983, adults prepare for baptism by a three-phase process of 1) evangelization, 2) instruction, and 3) purification and enlightenment.[31]

Evangelization

This first phase is more accurately called the *precatechumenate*. It is a time of inquiry in which the Church introduces interested persons to the Roman Catholic religion. The candidates have an opportunity to ask questions and then decide if they wish to convert to Roman Catholicism.

To assist the candidates in their preparation, a program coordinator assigns a sponsor to each candidate. The sponsor assists the candidate in his preparation and the Church in evaluating the progress of the candidate.

The Church considers candidates ready to move on to the second phase of the R.C.I.A. when they can give initial evidence in their lives of:

- an understanding of the fundamentals of Catholic teaching
- the practice of spiritual living
- repentance
- prayer
- fellowship with the Catholic community

Instruction

The Church formally promotes qualified candidates into the instructional phase of preparation in a ceremony called the *Rite of Acceptance to the Order of Catechumens.* Appropriately, this rite begins outside the entrance to the Church. After greeting the candidates, the officiating priest exhorts them to walk in God's light, saying:

> This is the way of faith along which Christ will lead you in love toward eternal life. Are you prepared to begin this journey today under the guidance of Christ?
> —*Rites of the Catholic Church*[32]

Each candidate responds, "I am."

Following this commitment, the sponsors make the sign of the cross on the forehead of each candidate. The candidates are thereby admitted to the catechumenate and the celebrant prays:

Lord, we have signed these catechumens with the sign of Christ's cross. Protect them by its power, so that, faithful to the grace which has begun in them, they may keep your commandments and come to the glory of rebirth in baptism. We ask this through Christ our Lord.

—*Rites of the Catholic Church*[33]

The celebrant next invites the catechumens and their sponsors to enter the church. Once inside, the ritual continues with prayers and optional rites of exorcism, the renunciation of false worship, the giving of a new name, and the presentation of a cross.

This begins the second phase in preparation for Catholic justification. The purpose of this phase is growth:

The catechumenate is an extended period during which the candidates are given suitable pastoral formation and guidance, aimed at training them in the Christian life. In this way, the dispositions manifested at their acceptance into the catechumenate are brought to maturity.

—*Rites of the Catholic Church*[34]

The catechumenate is a time of formal instruction in the doctrines and practices of the Roman Catholic religion. Teachers explain how to live a moral life. Specifically:

...the catechumens learn to turn more readily to God in prayer, to bear witness to the faith, in all things to keep their hopes set on Christ, to follow supernatural inspiration in their deeds, and to practice love of neighbor, even at the cost of self-renunciation.

—*Rites of the Catholic Church*[35]

The time required for this transformation varies from one candidate to the next:

The time spent in the catechumenate should be long enough—several years if necessary—for the conversion and faith of the catechumens to become strong. By their formation in the entire Christian life and a sufficiently prolonged probation the catechumens are properly initiated into the mysteries of salvation and the practice of an evangelical way of life. By means of sacred rites celebrated at successive times they are led into the life of faith, worship, and charity belonging to the people of God.

—Rites of the Catholic Church[36]

When ready, the catechumens are presented to a bishop for *election*. In this ceremony—

... the Church judges their state of readiness and decides on their advancement toward the sacraments of initiation. Thus the Church makes its "election," that is, the choice and admission of those catechumens who have the dispositions that make them fit to take part, at the next major celebration, in the sacraments of initiation.

—Rites of the Catholic Church[37]

During this rite the sponsors must testify as to the worthiness of the candidates. The bishop asks the sponsors:

As God is your witness, do you consider these candidates worthy to be admitted to the sacraments of Christian initiation?

Have they faithfully listened to God's word proclaimed by the Church?

Have they responded to that word and begun to walk in God's presence?

Have they shared the company of their Christian brothers and sisters and joined with them in prayer?

—Rites of the Catholic Church[38]

Upon affirmation, the bishop announces to the cat-echumens:

> I now declare you to be members of the elect,
> to be initiated into the sacred mysteries at the
> next Easter Vigil.
>
> —*Rites of the Catholic Church*[39]

From this point on the Church refers to the candi-dates as the *elect*.

Purification and Enlightenment

The third and final phase in preparation for bap-tism is one of purification, reflection, and spiritual enlightenment. Three *scrutinies* are involved:

> The scrutinies, which are solemnly celebrated on Sundays and are reinforced by an exorcism, are rites for self-searching and repentance and have above all a spiritual purpose. The scrutinies are meant to uncover, then heal all that is weak, defective, or sinful in the hearts of the elect; to bring out, then strengthen all that is upright, strong, and good.
>
> —*Rites of the Catholic Church*[40]

This period of purification customarily takes place during Lent, the 40 days preceding Easter, which is considered a season of prayer and penance for the entire Church. On Holy Saturday, the day before Easter, the Church advises the elect to spend the day in prayer, reflection, and fasting in anticipation of baptism. A priest leads the elect in the reciting of the Apostles' or Nicene Creed and the Lord's Prayer as an expression of their faith.

Finally Easter Sunday has arrived. The catechu-mens have successfully completed their long preparation and are properly disposed for justification [1247]. A priest baptizes them in a rite similar to the one for infants. The sacraments of Holy Eucharist and confirmation immediately follow [1233, 1275].

A BIBLICAL RESPONSE

The Roman Catholic Church annually prepares almost two million adults and children over the age of seven for baptismal justification. Tragically, however, rather than leading these people to trust in Christ alone for salvation, the Church leads them away. Through the *Rite of Christian Initiation of Adults*, Roman Catholicism teaches people to approach God through their own righteousness and good works. This stands in direct contraction to the Bible, which teaches that:

- God justifies by grace, not by works.
- God justifies the ungodly, not the righteous.

God Justifies by Grace, Not by Works

Despite Scripture's teaching that God justifies sinners "as a gift by His grace" (Romans 3:24), the Roman Catholic Church says that candidates seeking justification must perform good works [1248-1249]. At the same time, the Church maintains that Roman Catholic justification is a free gift, offering two reasons:

First, explains the Church, good works performed in preparation for justification are done so under the influence of actual grace [1989, 1998].[41] The works themselves, therefore, are works of grace [2001].

The second reason, according to the Church, is that justification cannot be earned [1308, 1992, 1996, 1999, 2003, 2010, 2027]:

> We are said to receive justification as a free gift because nothing that precedes justification, neither faith nor works, would merit the grace of justification ....
> —Council of Trent[42]

In the words of the new *Catechism*:

> Since the initiative belongs to God in the order
> of grace, *no one can merit the initial grace* of for-
> giveness and justification, at the beginning of
> conversion.
>
> —*Catechism of the Catholic Church* [2010]

This means that though a person must have both
faith and works to be justified, neither his faith nor his
works directly earn the blessing of justification.[43] Consequently, the Church's theologians argue, Catholic justification is a gift of God.

Yet the person seeking justification must work hard
and long—"several years if necessary."[44] The R.C.I.A.
requires candidates to demonstrate their conversion by
acts of:

- loving and worshiping God
- praying
- fasting
- loving one's neighbor
- practicing self-renunciation
- obeying the commandments
- bearing witness to the Catholic faith
- following supernatural inspiration in deeds
- confessing the major doctrines of the Church

Telling a person who actually has met all these
requirements that justification is a free, unmerited gift
would be meaningless. Such a person would have every
right to be declared righteous by his own merit. But the
Bible says, "To the one who works, his wage is not reckoned as a favor, but as what is due" (Romans 4:4).
Requiring even one good work for justification makes
justification, at least in part, an earned blessing.

According to the Bible, justification is not earned; it
is a gift. God justifies believers "as a gift by His grace"

(Romans 3:24). If God does something by grace, then "it is no longer on the basis of works, otherwise grace is no longer grace" (Romans 11:6). That is why God does not ask sinners to work for justification but to *believe.* He justifies "the one who has faith in Jesus" (Romans 3:26).

The Roman Catholic Church, on the other hand, maintains that justification by faith without works is heresy:

> If anyone says that the faith which justifies is nothing else but trust in the divine mercy, which pardons sins because of Christ; or that it is that trust alone by which we are justified: let him be anathema.
>
> —Council of Trent[45]

Faith alone, says the Church, is insufficient grounds for justification [1815-1816]:

> If anyone says that the sinner is justified by faith alone, meaning thereby that no other co-operation is required for him to obtain the grace of justification, and that in no sense is it necessary for him to make preparation and be disposed by a movement of his own will: let him be anathema.
>
> —Council of Trent[46]

Aware that Paul repeatedly lists faith as the only required response for justification (Romans 3:26; 3:28; 4:3; 5:1), the Church realizes that its condemnation of justification by faith as a gift demands some further explanation:

> When the Apostle says that a person is justified by faith and as a gift, those words are to be understood in the sense which the perennial consent of the catholic church has maintained and expressed, namely, that we are said to be justified by faith because faith is the first stage of human

salvation, the foundation and root of all justification, without which it is impossible to please God and come to the fellowship of his children.

—Council of Trent[47]

However, there is nothing in Paul's writings (or anywhere else in the New Testament, for that matter) which teaches that faith is merely the "first stage" leading to justification. When the Church calls faith the "first stage" of salvation, and good works the second stage, it ignores the fact that the Scriptures emphatically state that good works have no part in justification:

But to the one who does not work, but believes in Him who justifies the ungodly, his faith is reckoned as righteousness.

—Romans 4:5

According to the Bible, the only requirement for justification is faith.

The Church strongly disagrees and points to the Letter of James as its proof.

You see that a man is justified by works, and not by faith alone.
—James 2:24

Standing by itself, James 2:24 might seem to support the Roman Catholic Church's claim that both faith and good works must precede adult justification [161-162, 1248, 1815]. When the verse is interpreted in its context, however, this support vanishes.

James is writing not to a group of catechumens, but to people already professing to be Christians. But he suspects that some of those who will receive his letter are in fact deceiving themselves. They are living lives of hypocrisy, claiming to be Christians but never having truly experienced the new birth. Hoping that these people will reevaluate their lives, James challenges his readers to moral and consistent living.

James 2:24 is an integral part of a discussion composed of 13 verses (James 2:14-26). The passage opens with two questions that raise a point which James wants his readers to consider: "What use is it, my brethren, if a man says he has faith, but he has no works? Can that faith save him?" (James 2:14). In other words, if someone *says* he has faith, but his life does not show it by good works, does that person indeed have genuine faith? Is he truly saved?

In the verses that follow, James shows that true faith manifests itself by good deeds. A faith that is only talk is "dead" (James 2:17) and "useless" (James 2:20).

James uses Abraham as an example to illustrate that if a person has real faith it will be manifested by good works. To help the reader see this point, James raises another question: "Was not Abraham our father justified by works, when he offered up Isaac his son on the altar?" (James 2:21).

James answers in the affirmative. As recorded in Genesis 22, when Abraham raised his knife to slay his son in obedience to God, his actions declared him to be a righteous man of real and living faith. It is in this context that James concludes: "You see that a man is justified by works, and not by faith alone" (James 2:24).

It is important to note that this verse is not explaining how Abraham was justified *by God*. The chronology of Abraham's life makes this point clear.

As recorded in Genesis 15, when God promised Abraham that his descendants would be as numerous as the stars of heaven above, Abraham took God at His word. The Scriptures say that Abraham "believed in the Lord; and He reckoned it to him as righteousness" (Genesis 15:6).

This was the basis of God's justification of Abraham. The Lord, in response to Abraham's faith, credited righteousness to Abraham's account. God declared Abraham to be righteous in His sight *simply because he believed*. No good works were involved. Paul confirms this point:

> For if Abraham was justified by works, he has
> something to boast about; but not before God.
> For what does the Scripture say? "And Abraham
> believed God, and it was reckoned to him as
> righteousness."
>
> —Romans 4:2,3

More than 20 years later God put Abraham's faith to
the test, commanding him to offer up his son Isaac on
Mount Moriah. As recorded in Genesis 22, Abraham
obeyed God. He passed the test by demonstrating that he
was a man who feared God and would obey Him without
limitation (Genesis 22:12,18). As a result, God swore to
greatly bless Abraham and multiply his seed (Genesis
22:16-18).

Note that in Genesis 22 God did not *justify* Abraham;
He *blessed* him: "I will greatly bless you, and I will greatly
multiply your seed..." (Genesis 22:17). There was no
need for God to justify Abraham, to reckon righteousness to his account, for He had already done so years
earlier (Genesis 15:6).

In James 2:24 James is referring to the second event
in Abraham's life. He is not talking about how Abraham
was justified *by* God unto eternal salvation, but how
Abraham was justified, declared righteous, *before* God
and men. His goal is to help his Christian readers evaluate their lives. James wants his readers to understand that
if they are going to claim to have faith even as Abraham,
then their works of obedience should demonstrate it even
as Abraham's obedience demonstrated his faith. It is a
man's *actions* that *declare* him to be righteous, not mere
talk or a professed faith that is not lived out.

Despite Roman Catholic claims, James 2:14-26 is
not talking about how to prepare one's soul for baptismal
justification. The subject is the *kind* of faith that saves
(James 2:14). The passage is talking about *living* faith as
opposed to *dead* faith (James 2:17). It is about a faith
which is evidenced by good works. James' challenge is:
"Show me your faith" (James 2:18) even as Abraham
showed his.

God Justifies the Ungodly, Not the Righteous

The good news of Jesus Christ is that God receives sinners just as they are. He "justifies the ungodly" (Romans 4:5). That is good news, for until a person is born again and indwelt by the Holy Spirit, he cannot be anything other than what he is: an ungodly sinner in both nature and practice.

For this reason, God does not require sinners to reform their lives before He will justify them. Instead, God calls sinners to repentance (Acts 17:30).

Repentance is a response to the convicting work of the Holy Spirit (John 16:7-11). It is a change of heart and mind affecting an individual's view of both God and himself (Acts 26:20; 1 Thessalonians 1:9,10). The person stops making excuses for his evil conduct. He takes sides against himself and acknowledges his guilt before God. He tells God that he is sorry for his rebellion and that he is willing to submit to the Lord's rightful authority over his life.

Reformation is something else again. To reform means *to change into a new and improved form or condition.* The Bible never tells sinners that they must reform their lives before God will justify them.

Here again the Roman Catholic approach to adult justification terribly misleads people. It tells sinners seeking God that before they can be justified, they must undergo a moral transformation. They must learn "...to practice love of neighbor, even at the cost of self-renunciation"[48] and give "evidence of their conversion by the example of their lives."[49] To be counted among the elect, they must demonstrate that they are "fit to take part,"[50] and "worthy to be admitted,"[51] and that they have "begun to walk in God's presence."[52] Only then, according to the Church, are these seekers properly disposed for justification.

The Church also leads astray those who are seeking justification by pointing them to a *program* rather than *directly to Christ.* The Church teaches people that the R.C.I.A. can bring about "their formation in the entire

Christian life" and initiate them into "the practice of an evangelical way of life"[53] [1248]. The Church teaches that "by means of sacred rites celebrated at successive times" these seekers can come into "the life of faith, worship, and charity belonging to the people of God" [54][1248].

All of this is completely unbiblical. There is no rite or program on earth that can make a person worthy to be counted among the elect. The unregenerated person is a slave to sin (Romans 6:6). He cannot begin to walk in God's presence until Christ comes into his life and makes him a new person (Romans 8:5-11).

A Righteousness of Their Own

By the time a person completes the R.C.I.A. and is baptized, he or she is fully indoctrinated into a lifestyle of approaching God based upon good works and personal righteousness. This is the same deception that kept the Jews of the first century from coming to Christ for salvation:

> For not knowing about God's righteousness, and seeking to establish their own, they did not subject themselves to the righteousness of God.
>
> —Romans 10:3

Christ told the Pharisees, "I did not come to call the righteous, but sinners" (Matthew 9:13). He taught that God is willing to justify only those who first recognize that they are unworthy sinners (Luke 18:9-14). Consequently, participation in the R.C.I.A. is actually detrimental to a person seeking justification. Rather than leading lost sinners to God, it leads them away.

❖3

INCREASING AND PRESERVING JUSTIFICATION

Joseph, Eight Years Old

At the rehearsed signal from Sister Genevieve, Joseph and the entire second-grade class stood and began filing into the center aisle of the church. The boys wore white shirts and white ties. In the opposite pews, the second-grade girls looked like miniature brides in their white dresses and lace veils. In solemn procession and with folded hands, all began marching to the front of the church to receive their first holy communion.

The children had been preparing for this day all year in their daily religion classes at Saint Michael's School. They had learned of sanctifying and actual grace, and of venial and mortal sin. They had studied the role of the sacraments, the Ten Commandments, and the answers to pages of catechism questions.

The previous Thursday, Joseph and the other children had made their first confession to a priest. Now they were ready to receive the Blessed Sacrament through holy communion.

Reaching the front of the church, Joseph knelt down at the altar rail, an ornate marble wall that separated the sanctuary (the holy space around the altar) from the rest of the church. Some 40 children knelt beside him. On the opposite side of the rail stood Father Fiorelli and an altar boy. The priest was giving a host, a consecrated bread wafer, to each child. As Joseph waited his turn, he fixed his eyes on the bright gold objects on the altar.

"The body of Christ," said Father Fiorelli, holding a host directly in front of Joseph's nose.

The quick efficiency of the priest had caught the boy by surprise. In a moment of stunned silence, Joseph felt a heat wave flowing up his neck and burning the tips of his ears. Finally he recalled the proper response, answering, "Amen."

The altar boy accompanying Father Fiorelli slipped a gold platter under Joseph's chin as the priest placed a host on Joseph's tongue.

Joseph rose and returned to his pew. There he bowed his head and began to worship the host as Sister Genevieve had trained him, remembering her repeated warnings: "You must treat the host with supreme respect and adoration." To impress her point, Sister Genevieve had told the class the story of the *Miraculous Bleeding Host*:

> An old woman of Santarem, Portugal, asked a witch for help with her wandering husband. The sorceress promised to help, but demanded a consecrated wafer from the Church as payment.
>
> The old woman was desperate, and so went to Mass and received holy communion. But rather than swallowing the host, the woman secretly removed it from her mouth and wrapped it in her veil. Before she could leave the church, however, blood began to pour from the wafer! The woman ran to her home, leaving a bloody trail behind. There she hid the host in a trunk, thinking she could conceal her crime.
>
> During the night, however, a bright light began to shine from within the trunk right through the wood! In great shame the old woman called for the priest and confessed her sin. He

took the host back to the church and mounted it
in a shrine of gold and glass.[55]

When Joseph first heard the story, he thought Sister
Genevieve was just making it up to scare the class into
behaving. But when she showed the children a photo-
graph of the miraculous bleeding host, Joseph stared in
wide-eyed horror. Thin veins ran through the wafer. At
the base of the host there was a small quantity of coagulated
blood! A shiver went down his spine as he raised a silent
vow to heaven: *O God, I'll never to do anything like that!*

Now Joseph realized that he himself held a consecrated host within his own mouth. Slowly, and ever so
carefully, he swallowed his sacred treasure, making
every effort not to break it.

From that day onward, Sunday Mass and communion would be a regular part of Joseph's life. Several
times each year he would also receive the sacrament of
confession. And when Joseph became 12, a diocesan
bishop would administer to him the sacrament of confirmation.

Despite all these sacraments, however, Joseph would
still not be saved, for, according to the Church, salvation
from the judgment to come is not an event but a process. It
begins with baptism. It progresses through the frequent
reception of the sacraments and through cooperation with
grace. It ends with death and events in the next life.

To understand this process, it is necessary to examine
the Church's doctrines relating to sanctifying grace,
actual grace, the sacraments, merit, and sanctification.

Sanctifying Grace
[1266, 1996-2005, 2023-2024]

According to Roman Catholicism, sanctifying grace
is a gift of the Holy Spirit initially given to individuals
through the sacrament of baptism [1999]. It then "abides

in them,"[56] making them continually holy and pleasing to God [1995, 2000, 2024].

The effects of sanctifying grace upon the soul, therefore, are not a momentary or passing experience, but a constant and abiding one [2000]. The Catholic is said to be *in the state of grace*. This is the customary or habitual state of his soul. For this reason, sanctifying grace is often called *habitual grace* [2000, 2024].

However, though sanctifying grace is a constant influence, it is not a permanent one. Just as Adam lost divine life in his soul through the first sin, a baptized Catholic can forfeit sanctifying grace in his soul through serious, conscious, and deliberate sin. Should this happen, the sacrament of penance can restore sanctifying grace once again, as we shall see in the next chapter.

Actual Grace
[2000, 2024]

According to the Roman Catholic Church, *actual grace* is a supernatural assistance to do good and avoid evil. Actual grace enlightens the mind and inspires the will to perform good works necessary for salvation.

Unlike sanctifying grace, which has a constant influence upon the soul, actual grace is a temporary strengthening. It is the promise of God's helping hand in time of need. It is a momentary aid for a specific action, which passes with the using. Therefore actual grace must be continually replenished. This is accomplished through the sacraments [1084, 1972].

The Sacraments
[1076-1666]

According to Roman Catholic theology, Christ formally established seven sacraments [1113-1114]:

- Baptism
- Penance
- Eucharist

- Confirmation
- Matrimony
- Holy orders
- Anointing of the sick

The Church teaches that these seven sacraments are the primary means by which God bestows sanctifying and actual grace upon the faithful. Each sacrament also provides a special and unique blessing all its own. (See Appendix B for a description of the seven Roman Catholic sacraments.)

The sacraments are said to "contain"[57] grace. They are not merely symbolic expressions of grace that God gives to those who believe. Rather, each sacrament is a *channel* of God's grace, the "instrumental cause"[58] of grace [1084]. God is believed to confer grace upon Catholics by means of the sacraments through the proper performance of the sacramental ritual, "through the sacramental action itself,"[59] "by the very fact of the action's being performed"[1128] [1127-1128, 1131].

To receive grace from a sacrament, a Catholic must be properly prepared. Except for baptism and penance, the Catholic must be in a state of grace; that is, he must already have sanctifying grace in his soul. Preparation also includes a believing heart, reflection, prayer, and sometimes acts of penance. When a person meets these requirements, he is said to be *properly disposed*, or ready for a *valid* or *fruitful reception* of grace through the sacrament. The quantity of grace that the person will receive is proportional to how well he is prepared and to the generosity of God.

The Roman Catholic Church teaches that the sacraments are necessary for salvation [1129].[60] Baptism, or at least the desire of it, is necessary for initial justification [1257-1261, 1277].[61] Penance is necessary for restoration to the life of grace should a Catholic forfeit grace through serious sin. Confirmation, anointing of the sick, and especially Holy Eucharist provide grace needed to avoid sin and do good.

Rosaries, Relics, and Rites
[1667-1679]

What do these three things have in common? Each is a sacred sign of the Roman Catholic Church, called a *sacramental*, intended to bring a spiritual dimension to the events of everyday life [1667-1668, 1670]. Virtually any religious object or action may qualify. Some of the better-known officially sanctioned sacramentals of the Church are:

- stations of the cross
- crucifixes
- scapulars
- miraculous medals
- genuflecting
- lighting candles
- statues
- pictures of the saints
- the sign of the cross
- anointing with holy oil
- holy water
- ashes on the forehead
- ringing bells
- observing holy days
- blessed palms
- blessing of a new car
- the blessing of throats
- exorcisms

The seven sacraments are also object lessons that portray the religious beliefs of the Roman Catholic faith through sacred drama [1074-1075, 1084]. To ensure accuracy, the Church has standardized the liturgy (the words and the actions of the sacraments), and it forbids unauthorized innovation. In this way the sacraments preserve and teach the Roman Catholic faith.

Merit
[2006-2011, 2025-2027]

Roman Catholicism teaches that though sanctifying and actual grace influence a person's will to do good, they do not override it [978]. Therefore, if these graces are to accomplish their intended purpose, the individual must do his part [2002]. Catholics must "cooperate with heavenly grace lest they receive it in vain."[62]

The cooperative work of the individual under the influence of grace results in the performance of good

According to Roman Catholic theology, sacramentals are similar to sacraments, but are not as powerful. Sacraments give sanctifying and actual grace by virtue of the performance of the rite. Sacramentals do not [1670]. Their purpose is to help Catholics prepare for the fruitful reception of grace from the sacraments [1667]. Each has a special purpose and is said to result in one or more of the following benefits:

- the reception of actual grace
- material blessings such as health or safety
- an increased love of God
- a sorrow for sin
- the atonement of the temporal punishment due for sin
- the forgiveness of venial sins
- protection from Satan

works. These works include obedience to the commandments of God and the Church, acts of charity, self-denial, and the practice of virtue.

According to Roman Catholic theology, the performance of good works earns a reward from God. The earned right to a reward is called *merit* [2006].

In Roman Catholicism, merited reward can take various forms. For example, a Catholic in a state of grace can merit an increase of sanctifying grace [2010].[63]

Good works can also merit other blessings [2027]:

> Moved by the Holy Spirit and by charity, *we can then merit* for ourselves and for others the graces needed for our sanctification, for the increase of grace and charity, and for the attainment of eternal life. Even temporal goods like health and friendship can be merited in accordance with God's wisdom.
>
> —*Catechism of the Catholic Church*[2010]

The amount of merit earned is proportional to:[64]

- the kind of work performed
- the quantity of the work accomplished
- the difficulty of the work
- the duration of the work
- the amount of sanctifying grace already in the soul
- the intensity or fervor with which the work is performed

Sanctification
[824-825, 1995-2004, 2012-2016]

Roman Catholic theology teaches that grace inspires the mind and strengthens the will. It encourages a person to continue participating in the sacraments and performing good works. This generates more grace, and the cycle repeats. In this way the Catholic grows in grace and holiness. The Church calls this process *sanctification.*

Sanctification has two goals. The first is *to preserve* the grace of justification received at baptism [1392]. This grace can be lost through deliberate, serious sin. Maintaining grace in the soul until death is essential in order to attain to eternal life [1023, 1052].

The second goal of sanctification is *to increase* or *to perfect* the grace of justification in one's soul [1392]. Through baptism the Catholic receives an initial installment of sanctifying or justifying grace. After baptism this grace in the soul can be increased. In this way the Catholic is "further justified."[65]

The Second Vatican Council listed nine of the most important means by which Catholics are sanctified:[66]

- loving God
- loving one's neighbor
- obeying God's commandments

- receiving the sacraments, especially holy communion
- participating in the liturgy
- praying
- practicing self-denial
- serving others
- practicing virtue

Sanctification begins with baptism [1254]. It proceeds in a lifetime of activity as the Catholic receives the sacraments and performs good works in cooperation with grace. The process is completed only after death, when a person finally enters the presence of God in heaven. Then, and only then, can a Catholic say that he is saved. Until then the Catholic is not *saved* but is *being saved* through a process of sanctification.

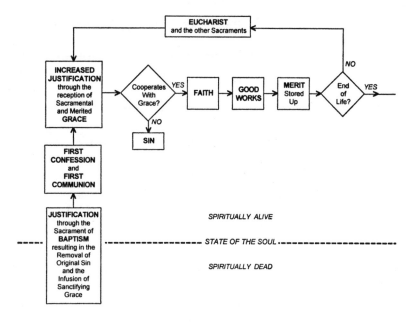

Figure 3:1
Increasing and Preserving Justification

A BIBLICAL RESPONSE

Contrary to the Roman Catholic understanding of sanctification, the Bible teaches that the standing of a justified sinner before God is perfect. Neither justification nor the grace of God toward the justified can be increased by sacraments or good works. The Bible teaches that:

- Grace is undeserved favor, not a merited reward.
- Justification is complete in Christ.

Biblical Grace Is Undeserved Favor

The Bible describes grace as the favorable attitude of God toward an individual. It is a mindset on the part of God, a decision to bless (Ephesians 2:4-7).

Grace is by definition free and unmerited (Romans 11:6). It is the undeserved, unearned favor of God.

The way in which loving parents treat their children illustrates grace. The parents give the children all that they have. They provide food, shelter, clothing, and affection. All this, and much more, the parents give without thought as to whether or not the children have earned the benefits or can repay them.

God's grace is greater still. God shows favor to those who have sinned against Him, to those who not only do not deserve His favor, but who deserve the very opposite (Romans 5:1-11). For these God gave His only-begotten Son. To these God freely offers eternal salvation (John 3:16), adoption as sons and daughters (2 Corinthians 6:18), and "every spiritual blessing in the heavenly places" (Ephesians 1:3). So great is God's grace toward His children that it will take the ages to come for God to "show the surpassing riches of His grace in kindness toward us in Christ Jesus" (Ephesians 2:7).

Roman Catholic sanctifying grace, on the other hand, is something else again. It is something that is "... poured out by the agency of the Holy Spirit in the hearts of those who are being justified, and abides in them."[67] It is—

> ...a divine quality inherent in the soul, as it were, a brilliant light that effaces all those stains which obscure the lustre of the soul, investing it with increased brightness and beauty.
>
> —*The Roman Catechism*[68]

Sanctifying grace is said to raise Catholics to "a supernatural state of being"[69] and to make them "partakers of the divine nature" (2 Peter 1:4).

This concept of sanctifying grace has its origin in a medieval theology that subdivided grace into categories: created or uncreated; of God or of Christ; external or internal; for salvation or for sanctification; constant or temporary; etc. Theologians further classified grace by assigning designations according to its function in Roman Catholic theology, such as *sanctifying grace, justifying grace, habitual grace, actual grace, sacramental grace, sufficient grace, efficacious grace*, etc. Using terminology from Aristotle, the Church's scholars described sanctifying grace as a *quality* of the soul, not a *substance*, but a *created* and *real accident* that inheres in the *soul-substance*.[70]

In moving away from explicit biblical language and definitions, the Church distorted biblical grace beyond recognition. The favor of a loving God for His children became a philosophical abstraction understood only by theologians and clerics.

Not only did the Church obscure the meaning of grace, but it altered its very essence. Grace became the medium of exchange in the Church's merit system: Do work, earn grace. The more grace you have, the harder you work. The harder you work, the more grace you earn. The Church denounced anyone who taught otherwise:

> If anyone says that...the justified person, by the good deeds done by him through the grace of

God and the merits of Jesus Christ (of whom he is a living member), does not truly merit an increase of grace...let him be anathema.

—Council of Trent[71]

All the while, the Roman Catholic Church maintained that merited grace was still a gift of God, for the works that earned the grace, the Church explained, were themselves the product of previous grace.

Nevertheless, the fact remains that Catholics must work to earn grace—a contradiction of terms. Unlike biblical grace, the Church's grace is not free; but if it is not free, it is not grace. Grace cannot be earned by good works; "otherwise, grace is no longer grace" (Romans 11:6).

The Church distorted grace still further by teaching that Christ set up seven sacraments as God's primary means of dispensing grace. Through the sacraments, by the execution of a rite, grace is bestowed "through the sacramental action itself"[72] [1127-1128].

Biblical grace cannot be dispensed like a product from a machine. Neither would the Father, having removed the barrier of sin at such a high cost, now place sacraments between Himself and His children. God wants His children dependent upon *Him*, not sacraments. He offers a *relationship*, not a ritual.

Roman Catholic theology makes people dependent upon the sacraments for salvation and thereby dependent upon the Church [1129]:

...the Church, a pilgrim now on earth, is necessary for salvation: the one Christ is mediator and the way of salvation; he is present to us in his body which is the Church. He himself explicitly asserted the necessity of faith and baptism, and thereby affirmed at the same time the necessity of the Church which men enter through baptism as through a door. Hence they could not be saved who, knowing that the Catholic Church was founded as necessary by God through Christ, would refuse either to enter it, or to remain in it.

—The Second Vatican Council[73]

The belief that sacraments, and thereby the Roman Catholic Church itself, are necessary for salvation has no biblical support [168-169, 824, 845-846, 1227]. The Scriptures say nothing about seven sacraments as the primary channels of God's grace. Neither do they speak of an institution such as the Roman Catholic Church as the administrator of the sacraments.

The Bible teaches that God's grace is offered *freely and directly* to all who trust in Christ:

> Therefore having been justified by faith, we have peace with God through our Lord Jesus Christ, through whom also we have obtained our introduction by faith into this grace in which we stand.
>
> —Romans 5:1,2

God's adopted children "stand" in His grace. They are the constant focus of His unrestrained love and generosity in Christ: "For of His fullness we have all received, and grace upon grace" (John 1:16).

Biblical Justification Is Complete in Christ

Biblical justification is perfect and complete. It is a divine act: "God is the one who justifies" (Romans 8:33). God forgives the sinner and reckons to his account the righteousness of God (Romans 3:21,22; 4:3-8). Henceforth God views the person as "in Christ" and "holy and blameless before Him" (Ephesians 1:3,4). For this reason Scripture refers to all believers as "those who have been sanctified in Christ Jesus, saints by calling" (1 Corinthians 1:2).

Roman Catholic justification is imperfect and incomplete. It begins with the infusion of grace through baptism, and then increases through the other sacraments. The Church teaches Catholics that they can also increase justifying grace in their souls through their works [2010]:

> ... they, through the observance of the com-
> mandments of God and of the Church, faith
> cooperating with good works, increase in that
> justice received through the grace of Christ and
> are further justified. ...
>
> —Council of Trent[74]

Consequently, in Roman Catholicism good works are not only the result of justification, but the cause of its increase. The Church is emphatic on this point:

> If anyone says that justice once received is
> neither preserved nor increased in the sight of
> God by good works, but that the works them-
> selves are no more than the effects and signs of
> justification obtained, and not also a cause of its
> increase: let him be anathema.
>
> —Council of Trent[75]

In contrast, biblical justification cannot increase. Why not? Because biblical justification is the crediting of God's perfect righteousness to the sinner's account (Romans 3:22; 2 Corinthians 5:21). Paul told the Colossians, "In Him you have been made complete" (Colossians 2:10).

For this reason, a Christian trusting in Christ for righteousness does not even try to be further justified. Christ died to save him (Romans 5:8). God has justified him (Romans 8:33). His position in Christ is perfect (Ephesians 1:3-14). His future is secure: "Much more then, having now been justified by His blood, we shall be saved from the wrath of God through Him" (Romans 5:9).

In Roman Catholic theology there is no such thing as a declaration by which God finally and perfectly justifies and eternally saves. Rather, salvation is a road, a race, a journey. It is a process of sanctification by which the grace of justification is preserved and increased.

With anxious concern, Catholics must work to achieve their own salvation. This, says the Church, is the teaching of Philippians 2:12,13 [1949]:

> So then, my beloved, just as you have always obeyed, not as in my presence only, but now much more in my absence, work out your salvation with fear and trembling; for it is God who is at work in you, both to will and to work for His good pleasure.

Despite Roman Catholic claims, the context of this passage makes it clear that Paul is not teaching that Christians must work for their eternal salvation. The Philippians were having problems getting along with each other. Paul exhorted them to be "of the same mind," to maintain "the same love," to be "united in spirit, intent on one purpose" (Philippians 2:2). He told them not to act "from selfishness or empty conceit" (Philippians 2:3). He encouraged them to humbly "regard one another as more important than himself" (Philippians 2:3), and not to look out just for their "own personal interests, but also for the interests of others" (Philippians 2:4).

Paul pointed the Philippians to the Lord Jesus as the perfect example of what he was teaching: "Have this attitude in yourselves which was also in Christ Jesus..." (Philippians 2:5). He concluded: "So, then, my beloved... work out your salvation with fear and trembling" (Philippians 2:12).

Here Paul was exhorting the Christians in Philippi to work out the *consequences* of their salvation. Christ had freed them from sin and given them eternal life. Now, as sons and daughters of God, they were to walk in a manner worthy of their calling.

More specifically, the Philippians needed to work out their salvation or deliverance from the disputes within the church. Paul instructed them, "Do all things without grumbling or disputing" (Philippians 2:14). He even admonished two women by name, Euodia and Syntyche, to stop quarreling (Philippians 4:2).

Paul was not telling the Philippians how to save themselves from hell, work their way into heaven, or earn eternal life. His letters to the Romans and Galatians make it abundantly clear that *it is the work of Christ alone that saves* and that eternal life is a free gift. In his letter to the Philippians, Paul was concerned about the believers' day-to-day holiness. He was exhorting the Philippians to yield their lives to God so that they might be conformed to the image of Christ (Philippians 2:5-11; Romans 8:29).

Paul was speaking of one of the three kinds of Christian sanctification found in Scripture. The Bible teaches that a person is *positionally* sanctified, "holy and blameless" before God (Ephesians 1:4), the moment he trusts Christ and is justified. A Christian is *practically* or *experientially* sanctified as he learns to abstain from evil and walk in the Spirit (1 Thessalonians 4:1-8; Galatians 5:16-26). Every Christian will be *ultimately* sanctified at Christ's coming (1 John 3:1-3). In Philippians 2, Paul is concerned about the Christian's *practical* or *experiential* sanctification.

Sanctification and justification must not be confused. Justification is a declaration of God by which a person is forgiven and credited with the righteousness of God. It is a once-and-for-all event by which a person comes into a right relationship with God through faith in Jesus Christ.

Practical sanctification is a process by which the Christian's moral character and personal conduct come into growing conformity with his legal standing before God. It is a work of God, but one in which the believer must cooperate (Romans 6:19).

Roman Catholicism's misapplication of Philippians 2:12 to eternal salvation shows how the Church's theology confuses justification and sanctification. Roman Catholicism treats them as interrelated processes. Sanctification, as taught by the Church, preserves and increases the grace of justification. The day-to-day life of the Catholic determines his standing before God and ultimately his eternal destiny.

The Work of a Lifetime

For the Roman Catholic, eternal salvation involves a lifetime of doing, working, and striving. The Catholic must keep the commandments of God and of the Church. He must receive the sacraments and perform acts of piety. He must do good works. His eternal salvation depends on all of these.

Behind all this activity is a theology that considers justification an incomplete and fragile condition of the soul. Consequently, there are always more sacraments to be received and more work to be performed. The Catholic must constantly strive to increase and preserve grace in his soul in the hope of one day attaining eternal life.

Biblical salvation, on the other hand, is characterized by rest. Christ has already finished the work of salvation on the cross. Justification is a free and perfect gift of God. The Christian, confident that his eternal salvation is secure (1 John 5:11-13), rests in Christ:

> For the one who has entered His rest has himself also rested from his works, as God did from His.
>
> —Hebrews 4:10

Roman Catholicism knows nothing of resting in Christ. To the contrary, the truest Catholics are the ones who work the hardest. When Saint Bernadette was on her deathbed, she spoke with regret of those who did not understand the need to work to get to heaven: "As for me," she said, "that will not be my case. Let us determine to go to Heaven. Let us work for it, suffer for it. Nothing else matters."[76]

❖4

REJUSTIFICATION

Joseph, 19 Years Old

Stepping into the darkness of the confession booth, Joe closed the door behind him and knelt down. It was an old-style confessional composed of three closet-sized rooms. Father Sweeney, the parish pastor, was already sitting in the center booth. In the left-hand booth an elderly woman was confessing her sins to the priest in a soft whisper. In the right-hand booth Joe waited his turn, silently pondering the bittersweet events of the past week.

Joe's troubles started the previous weekend with the annual college ski trip. He returned to the city from the mountains late Sunday night. Though unprepared for his Monday morning classes, he flopped into bed too worn-out from partying to do anything about it. The next two days flashed by in a rush of catching up. By midweek everything was back under control—everything, that is, except one thing: His conscience was tormenting him.

Joe had missed Mass on Sunday while skiing, but that wasn't the problem. After all, he was traveling, and he didn't know where the Catholic Church was.

The problem was Saturday night. The problem was Cyndy.

Joe had met her early Saturday while on a ski lift. They spent the day skiing together, and then arranged to meet for dinner that evening at the lodge. The rest, well, just happened.

Saturday night was a new experience for Joe—somewhat overdue, he thought. At first he felt strangely pleased with himself, more sophisticated, in the prime of his life. After a few days of reflection, however, guilt was casting a dark shadow over every memory. He had to do something.

"You may now start your confession," said Father Sweeney.

The priest's familiar voice jolted Joe's mind back into the confession booth. Father Sweeney had slid open a wooden panel covering the small window joining the two booths. Tiny holes in the translucent plastic window allowed sound to pass through, but screened out most light. Joe could see the pastor's profile silhouetted on the window as he waited for Joe to respond.

Joe bowed his head, and, making the sign of the cross, began his confession. "In the name of the Father, and of the Son, and of the Holy Spirit. Amen. Bless me, Father, for I have sinned. It has been two years since my last confession."

"That's a long time," remarked Father Sweeney. "It's good that you have returned to the sacrament of reconciliation. I want you to feel free to tell me what is on your heart." Then, with increased formality, Father Sweeney began to recite *The Rite of Penance According to the Roman Ritual*:[77] "May God, who has enlightened every heart, help you to know your sins and trust in His mercy. Let us look on Jesus, who suffered to save us and rose again for our justification." Then, after reading a few verses from Scripture, Father Sweeney paused and added, "You may now confess your sins."

Joe began at a rapid pace, "Forgive me, Father, for I have sinned. I confess that I, I..." he hesitated and stopped. As a boy, Joe had always had a list of sins ready to recite: *I was disrespectful to my mother three times; I lied eight times; I was unkind to my sisters ten times; I stole change from my mother's purse twice....* But this time it was different. This was the first time he had to confess a serious sexual sin.

Joe began again, "I confess that I missed Mass about ten times; I lied four times; I cheated on an exam at school. And ...and I had sex with a girl. Once."

After a long pause, Father Sweeney answered calmly, "Missing Mass is a grave offense. It deprives you of the help you need to avoid sin." Then the elderly priest patiently explained to Joe how neglecting the sacraments had led him to moral failure. He ended with a question, "Do you realize that fornication is a serious sin?"

"Yes, I do," Joe answered sincerely.

"Very well," said the priest in a fatherly tone. "For your penance, I want you to say the rosary. You need to be more diligent in your reception of the sacraments and avoid situations that will lead you into sin. Now make an act of contrition."

Joe couldn't believe it. *That's it?* he thought to himself. *That's all he's going to say?*

Relieved that the worst was over, Joe began to pray *The Act of Contrition*:

> O my God, I am heartily sorry for having offended You. And I detest all my sins because of Your just punishment, but most of all because they offend You, my God, who are all good and deserving of all my love. I firmly resolve with the help of Your grace to confess my sins, to do penance, and to amend my life. Amen.

Raising one arm, Father Sweeney began praying in a liturgical voice:

> God, the Father of mercies, through the death and resurrection of His Son has reconciled the world to Himself and sent the Holy Spirit among us for the forgiveness of sins; through the ministry of the Church, may God give you pardon

and peace, and I absolve you from your sins in the name of the Father, and of the Son, and of the Holy Spirit.

With those words Joe could see from the shadow of Father Sweeney's arm that he was making the sign of the cross. Joe responded with a soft, "Amen."

The priest concluded the rite with a prayer:

May the passion of our Lord Jesus Christ, the intercession of the Blessed Virgin Mary and of all the saints, whatever good you do and suffering you endure, heal your sins, help you to grow in holiness, and reward you with eternal life. Go in peace.

Joe left the confessional without delay and headed for the front of the church. There he knelt down at the altar rail and did his penance.

Ten minutes later the prayers were finished. Joe's conscience was quiet. A dark cloud began to lift. He left the church and headed home.

But as he went, a thought was slowly taking shape in his mind: *That wasn't so bad. Ten minutes of penance. Maybe the sin wasn't so bad after all. It was almost worth it!*

But then again, maybe not, for, according to the Roman Catholic Church, Joe might have lost more than his virginity Saturday night. He might have lost his soul, for Joe's sin was a deadly sin.

Mortal and Venial Sin
[1849-1876]

The Roman Catholic Church teaches that there are two categories of sin [1854]. The first is *mortal sin* [1855, 1874]:

We commit *mortal sin* when we transgress a commandment of God in a serious matter, with

full knowledge, and free consent of the will.
Serious matter is, for example, unbelief, hatred of
our neighbor, adultery, serious theft, murder, etc.
—*Dogmatic Theology for the Laity*[78]

As original sin killed the life of God in Adam, so
mortal sin ends the life of God in baptized Catholics [1855].
That is why the Church calls this kind of sin *mortal*, from
the Latin word for *death*. Mortal sin kills the soul and,
unrepented, brings eternal punishment [1033, 1861, 1874].

The second kind of sin, according to the Church, is
venial sin [1862, 1875]:

> We commit a *venial sin* (one which can be
> forgiven outside confession) whenever we trans-
> gress a commandment of God either in a matter
> which is not so serious, or without full knowl-
> edge, or without full consent of the will...for
> example, deliberate distraction at prayer, petty
> thievery, idleness, white lies, lack of love and gen-
> erosity in small things, etc.
>
> —*Dogmatic Theology for the Laity*[79]

The Church calls these sins *venial*, from the Latin
word *venia*, meaning *pardon*. God will forgive the sinner
of these minor sins if he confesses them to God in prayer
with sincere repentance. Venial sins weaken a person's
spiritual vitality and make the individual more suscept-
ible to greater sins. But unlike mortal sins, they do not
kill the life of the soul or incur eternal punishment [1855].

Roman Catholic theologians compare the manner
in which mortal and venial sins affect the soul to the way
in which illnesses affect the body. Most ailments are
minor. The body's immune system fights them off and
eventually restores health. A venial sin is like a minor
sickness of the soul. It hinders spirituality and lowers
resistance to temptation, but the vitality of the soul sur-
vives [1863].

Mortal sin is a deathblow. It kills the soul as surely as
a fatal disease kills the body. When a Catholic who has

received sanctifying grace through baptism commits a mortal sin, he loses that grace [1861].[80] Though by baptism he had been justified, because of mortal sin he forfeits the grace of justification, or, it might be said, is *dejustified*.[81] He becomes a child of wrath and destined for hell [1033, 1861, 1874]. And just as a dead body has no capacity to restore life to itself, the Church teaches that a soul struck dead by mortal sin cannot revive itself. The sinner must turn to the Church and to the sacrament of penance [1446, 1856].[82]

The Sacrament of Penance
[976-987, 1422-1498]

The Roman Catholic Church teaches that the sacrament of penance reestablishes a right relationship between God and a wayward Catholic. Consequently, the Church also refers to penance as the sacrament of *reconciliation* [1424].

The sacrament of penance has several parallels with the sacrament of baptism [980]. As baptism supplies sanctifying grace to the soul that is dead because of Adam's sin, the sacrament of penance restores sanctifying grace to the soul that is dead because of mortal sin [987, 1446]. Baptism justifies, while penance, it might be said, *rejustifies*. Through it those "who through sin have forfeited the received grace of justification, can again be justified...."[83]

As baptism is necessary for salvation of the infant born with original sin, so penance is necessary for salvation of the baptized Catholic who has committed a mortal sin. However, unlike the reception of baptism, which is relatively simple, the sacrament of penance involves several requirements [1448, 1491].

Confession of the Sin
[1455-1458, 1493]

Catholics often refer to the sacrament of penance as the *sacrament of confession*, or simply *confession*, for in the rite the Catholic discloses his sins to a priest [1424]. The sinner must search "all the folds and corners of his conscience"[84] and confess every mortal sin that he finds. The Church also encourages the sacramental confession of venial sins, but does not require it [1493].

Contrition of the Sinner
[1430-1433, 1450-1454, 1490-1492]

Before the priest will forgive the Catholic guilty of mortal sin, the person must demonstrate sorrow for his sins and a determination to avoid sinning in the future. Catholics usually express this by a prayer called the *Act of Contrition.*

Judgment by the Priest
[1441-1445, 1461-1467, 1485]

Roman Catholicism teaches that though only God can forgive sins, He has willed to do so through the Church [1441-1445]. Consequently, in the sacrament of penance it is the responsibility of the priest to judge the sinner. The priest may first ask several questions to establish the circumstance of the sin and to measure the person's guilt. He then determines if the sinner is truly sorry and determined not to repeat the sin. Based on this information, the priest decides whether or not to pardon the sinner.[85]

Absolution by the Priest
[1441-1445, 1449, 1461-1467, 1495]

If the priest forgives the sinner, and he usually does, he then administers absolution. To absolve means *to set free, to release from the consequences of guilt.* The Church teaches that "...the form of the sacrament of penance, in which its effectiveness chiefly lies, is expressed in those words of the minister, *I absolve you* from your sins...."[86] Absolution frees the person guilty of mortal sin from eternal punishment. Indeed, the Church claims that "there is no offense, however serious, that the Church cannot forgive."[982] This absolution is not simply a declaration that God has forgiven the sinner, but a judicial act of the priest.[87]

Penance by the Sinner
[1434-1439, 1459-1460, 1494]

The final requirement before a sin can be fully forgiven is that the sinner must make satisfaction to God for the sin.

> Raised up from sin, the sinner must still recover his full spiritual health by doing something more to make amends for the sin: he must "make satisfaction for" or "expiate" his sins. This satisfaction is called "penance."
>
> —*Catechism of the Catholic Church*[1459]

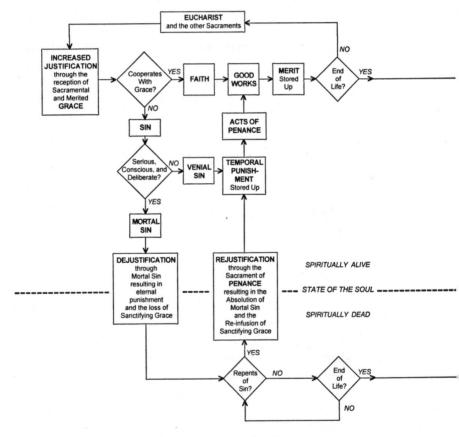

Figure 4:1 **Rejustification**

To assist the person in making reparation for his sin, the priest imposes an *act of penance*. It is selected to be "in keeping with the nature of the crimes and the ability of the penitents."[88] It may take the form of a fast, a charitable gift to the poor, self-denial, service to one's neighbor, or the performance of some devotional exercise [1460]. Usually the penance is to say a certain number of prayers such as the *Our Father* and the *Hail Mary*. (The *act of penance*, the punishment which satisfies for sin, should not be confused with the *sacrament of penance*, the rite of sacramental reconciliation.)

The Roman Catholic Church recommends regular sacramental confession for all Catholics [1458]. Those not guilty of mortal sins should tell their "... venial sins and mention some sin already told in a previous Confession"[89] [1493]. In this way, the Catholic can benefit from the actual grace supplied by the sacrament, and so avoid future sin [1496]. Church law requires Catholics to confess serious sins as least once each year [2042].[90] "Anyone who is aware of having committed a mortal sin must not receive Holy Communion, even if he experiences deep contrition, without having first received sacramental absolution...."[1457]

A BIBLICAL RESPONSE

Since the Second Vatican Council, Catholic clergy and laity alike have been reevaluating the role of the sacrament of reconciliation. Questions concerning the way in which the sacrament is to be administered (individually or as a group), how often it should be received, and even whether the sacrament is necessary at all have resulted in record low participation.

Nevertheless, the Church's official teaching remains the same. The sacrament of penance is "...the only ordinary way by which the faithful person who is aware of serious sin is reconciled with God and with the Church...."[91]

The Scriptures contain no such injunction. To the contrary, the Bible teaches that:

- Confession is to God, not to a priest.
- Satisfaction for sin is in Christ's blood, not in acts of penance.
- All sin is mortal; no sin is venial.

Biblical Confession Is to God Alone

When King David repented of his adultery, he confessed his sin *directly to God*. No priest. No ritual. No sacrament. Just a broken man owning up to his sin before his Maker. He later wrote of the incident in a psalm to God, saying:

> I acknowledged my sin to Thee,
> And my iniquity I did not hide;
> I said, "I will confess my transgressions to the Lord";
> And Thou didst forgive the guilt of my sin.
> —Psalm 32:5

Confession *directly to God* was also the experience of Nehemiah (Nehemiah 1:4-11), Daniel (Daniel 9:3-19), and Ezra (Ezra 9:5-10). Ezra, though a Levitical priest himself, taught God's people to "make confession to the Lord God of your fathers" (Ezra 10:11).

New Testament Christians can also go directly to God with their sins.[92] They go not to a Judge, but to their Father with Jesus at their side: "If anyone sins, we have an Advocate with the Father, Jesus Christ the righteous" (1 John 2:1,2). They go with confidence that God will hear them: "Let us therefore draw near with confidence to the throne of grace, that we may receive mercy and may find grace to help in time of need" (Hebrews 4:16). They go with the promise of God that He will forgive them: "If we confess our sins, He is faithful and righteous to forgive us our sins and to cleanse us from all unrighteousness" (1 John 1:9).

The Roman Catholic Church, on the other hand, teaches that Catholics must confess all serious sins to a priest in the sacrament of penance. This obligation, says the Church, is implied in the judicial authority of the priesthood. Christ gave this power, claims the Church, to priests when He appeared to the apostles, breathed on them, and said:

> Receive the Holy Spirit. If you forgive the sins of any, their sins have been forgiven them; if you retain the sins of any, they have been retained.
>
> —John 20:22,23

The Church teaches that with those words the Lord gave priests the power to judge and to forgive Christians who had fallen into sin [976, 1461, 1485]. The sacrament of penance, it claims, is the rightful application of that authority.

In John 20:22,23, however, the Lord was not speaking to a group of ordained bishops or priests. His audience was a group made up of ten of the apostles with several other disciples. There is therefore no reason to restrict the application to ordained clergy. Additionally, *there is no biblical example of sacramental confession to a priest in the entire New Testament!*

Furthermore, Luke's account of the same event shows that Jesus was not establishing a sacrament of the church, but was speaking of the responsibility of His disciples to proclaim the gospel to the lost:

> He said to them, "Thus it is written, that the Christ should suffer and rise again from the dead the third day, and that repentance for forgiveness of sins should be proclaimed in His name to all the nations, beginning from Jerusalem. You are witnesses of these things."
>
> —Luke 24:46-48

The disciples were to go forth and proclaim the forgiveness of sins through Jesus Christ. They were to be the Lord's witnesses, not the Christians' confessors.

This is the very thing we find the disciples doing in the book of Acts. Peter, for example, proclaimed Christ to Cornelius, saying, "...everyone who believes in Him receives forgiveness of sins" (Acts 10:43). When the Holy Spirit came upon Cornelius and his household, Peter realized that his listeners had believed. He then proclaimed that they were forgiven and accepted by God: "'Surely no one can refuse the water for these to be baptized who have received the Holy Spirit just as we did, can he?' And he ordered them to be baptized in the name of Jesus Christ" (Acts 10:47,48).

There were also occasions when the disciples found it necessary to proclaim the sins of some retained. Simon the magician was one such person. Simon heard the gospel, said he believed, and was baptized. Shortly afterward he revealed his true motive: He thought he could obtain magical powers from the apostles. Peter told Simon he was still in his sins (Acts 8:21,22).

One final point supports the interpretation of John 20:22,23 as teaching that the disciples were to proclaim God's forgiveness as witnesses: John 20:23 uses a significant verb tense. The Lord did not say, "If you forgive the sins of any, their sins *will be* forgiven them." Neither did He say, "If you forgive the sins of any, their sins *are* forgiven them." What He said was, "If you forgive the sins of any, their sins *have been* forgiven them" (emphasis added).

Here Jesus uses the Greek *perfect* tense. "It implies a process, but views that process as having reached its consummation and existing in a finished state."[93] This means that the disciples had the authority to declare forgiveness to those whom God *had already forgiven*.

As for the Roman Catholic interpretation, we might ask how is it possible for a priest to judge an anonymous individual (whom he cannot even see clearly) based on a few minutes' discussion. How can one man look into the heart of another and measure the seriousness of his sin, the degree of his guilt, and the depth of his contrition, and then assign the divine satisfaction for that sin? "Who can forgive sins but God alone?" (Mark 2:7).

Biblical Satisfaction
for Sin Is in Christ's Blood Alone

According to Roman Catholicism, sin has a double consequence: *eternal* punishment and *temporal* punishment [1472]. Mortal sin incurs eternal punishment, banishment from God's presence to suffer in hell *forever*. Every sin, whether mortal or venial, incurs temporal punishment, punishment that lasts for a *limited* period of time.

Temporal punishment, according to the Church, is not simply the natural consequences of sinful and foolish living, as spoken about in the book of Proverbs. Neither is it merely the corrective chastisement of a loving Father, as described in Hebrews 12:4-11. Rather, temporal punishment, says the Church, results from the very nature of sin [1472]. It is a punishment that must be paid even though a sin has been forgiven [1473].

Catholics believe that they can pay for temporal punishment in this life through *acts of penance* or in the next life (as we shall see in the following chapter) through suffering in a place called *purgatory* [1030-1032, 1472].

Acts of penance include saying special prayers, fasting, self-deprivation, giving money to the poor, and accepting the trials and disappointments of life. Some Catholics participate in more extreme forms of penance such as self-flagellation, wearing a hair shirt or spiked chain, crawling on their knees to a shrine or church, or sleeping on a stone floor [1460].

The most common act of penance is the satisfaction for sin that the priest assigns to the Catholic after hearing his confession. This is defined as—

> the voluntary enduring of the penalty imposed by the confessor in order to compensate for the injury done to God and to redeem or atone for

the temporal punishment which is ordinarily due even after sin has been forgiven.

—*Manual of Dogmatic Theology*[94]

The Bible, on the other hand, teaches that when God forgives, He forgives all—not a spot remains:

Though your sins are as scarlet,
They will be as white as snow;
Though they are red like crimson,
They will be like wool.

—Isaiah 1:18

Christ made perfect and complete satisfaction for sin on the cross: "He Himself is the propitiation for our sins" (1 John 2:2).

The Roman Catholic idea that a sinner must pay for the temporal punishment of his sins is equivalent to saying that Christ's blood was insufficient and that therefore God requires more. Furthermore, it turns the sinner, at least in part, into his own savior. He, even as Christ, can "compensate for the injury done to God."[95]

Finally, what is the outcome when a sinner confesses a grievous sin to a priest and then is told that he can atone for the temporal punishment of the sin by doing something as simple as saying a few *Hail Marys* and *Our Fathers*? The sinner can only conclude that sin is not very serious.

All Sin Is Mortal

Just how serious is sin? The Bible teaches that the spiritual consequence of every sin is the death penalty, eternal separation from God in the lake of fire (Revelation 20:14,15): "The soul who sins will die" (Ezekiel 18:4); "The wages of sin is death" (Romans 6:23).

This is not to say that every sin is equally wicked or abhorrent to God. Scripture teaches that some sins are more evil than others and will be judged accordingly (John 19:11; Matthew 10:15). Jesus taught that there will be degrees of eternal punishment in hell (Luke 12:47,48).

Nonetheless, the Lord never distinguished between sins in terms of their ultimate penalty.[96] Jesus taught that every sin warrants eternal punishment in hell. He taught that the sin of anger brings the same punishment as the sin of murder (Matthew 5:21,22), and the sin of lust the same penalty as the sin of adultery (Matthew 5:27-30).

Roman Catholicism, on the other hand, teaches that some sins are "light sins,"[1863] minor infractions of the moral laws of God [1862-1863]. Telling a small lie or stealing something inexpensive is somehow different from telling a big lie or committing grand theft. Small sins, venial sins, do not bring eternal punishment.

Additionally, the Roman Catholic Church teaches that, though venial sins may incline a person toward later committing a mortal sin, not even the regular practice of venial sins warrants eternal punishment. A baptized Catholic who does not commit a mortal sin remains in a state of grace even if he is habitually guilty of a multitude of venial sins [1863].

The Scriptures, on the other hand, teach that if a person's life is characterized by any kind of sin, he should not consider himself a born-again Christian:

> Little children, let no one deceive you; the one who practices righteousness is righteous, just as He is righteous; the one who practices sin is of the devil. . . . No one who is born of God practices sin. . . .
>
> —1 John 3:7-9

The Church even says that if mitigating circumstances exist, not even the gravest sin merits eternal punishment. It teaches that for a sin to be mortal, three conditions must be met [1857-1862]:

- The sin must be serious. The evil act must be a grave offense against God or someone else.
- The sinner must be aware. The one performing the act must have full knowledge that what he is doing is grievously wrong.

- The sin must be deliberate. The sinner must know he can resist the temptation, yet willfully choose to do evil.

Should the sin not meet one of these requirements, it does not merit eternal punishment no matter how evil the act might be.

In practice these conditions become ready-made excuses for lawlessness. Consider, for example, a person who has displayed a low ability to resist a certain sin. According to Roman Catholic theology, his sin may not be completely deliberate: "The freedom of our will can be impeded by our natural disposition, the influence of improper upbringing, internal or external compulsion, or the force of violent and sudden passion."[97] If a person in such a condition were to commit a gravely evil sin, therefore, it is not a mortal sin. Father Melvin L. Farrell shows how this might apply to sexual temptation:

> For example, a habit of masturbation may be temporarily beyond a young person's sincere efforts to overcome. In an unguarded moment, a couple planning marriage may succumb to their passion for each other. A person may have a fixation for homosexual acts which seemingly cannot be controlled. To automatically label all such persons as guilty of mortal sin is unwarranted.
> —*A Catechism for Parents and Teachers*[98]

Consequently, though the Bible teaches that all sins are mortal, the Church teaches that no sin is necessarily mortal. And, though the Bible never mentions venial sin, the Church teaches that every sin could potentially be venial!

An Underestimated Problem

In the Sermon on the Mount Jesus taught, "If your right eye makes you stumble, tear it out and throw it from you.... If your right hand makes you stumble, cut it off and throw it from you...." (Matthew 5:29,30). Why such severe treatment? "For it is better for you that one of the parts of your body perish than for your whole body to be thrown into hell" (Matthew 5:29). The eternal consequences of sin are so horrifying that, if physical mutilation could keep one from sinning, it would be a better alternative than ending up in hell.

God allows the full weight of sin to fall upon the sinner that he might cry out, "What must I do to be saved?" (Acts 16:30). It is the convicted sinner who realizes that he needs a Savior. This is the person who, upon learning the gospel, clings to the cross like a drowning man to a life preserver. This is the person who knows that though he deserves to go to hell a thousand times over, Jesus' blood has made full satisfaction for his every sin: past, present, and future.

Roman Catholic theology, on the other hand, consistently undermines the seriousness of sin and its consequences, most notably by teaching that most sins are not punishable by death.

This is a lie that is as old as the world itself. Soon after God warned Adam and Eve that if they disobeyed Him they would "surely die" (Genesis 2:17), Satan told Eve, "You surely shall not die!" (Genesis 3:4).

This same lie has deceived countless Roman Catholics. As a result, most go through life unaware of the magnitude of their guilt before God. Underestimating their problem, they readily embrace an inadequate and faulty solution: the gospel according to Rome.

FINAL DESTINY

Joseph, 58 Years Old

Though Joseph continued to sleep, his heavy, strained breathing had awakened his wife, Margaret. She turned on a lamp and tried to arouse him, but Joseph would not respond. Margaret studied his breathing: shallow gasps, ten per minute, each punctuated with a deep groan. Frantic, she reached for the phone.

Margaret's first call went to 911, emergency services. "I think my husband is having a heart attack! Please come quickly." After asking several questions, the dispatcher assured her that an ambulance was on the way.

Margaret's second call went to Father Mario Sanchez, the parish priest. Though still half-asleep himself, the elderly priest promised to come immediately.

When the paramedics arrived, Margaret silently retreated to a corner of the room. There she watched as one paramedic began a survey of Joseph's vital signs and the other relayed the information by telephone to a doctor at City Hospital. Margaret didn't realize that Father Sanchez had entered the room until she heard him reciting in a soft whisper the *Rite of Anointing*,[99] the final sacrament.

With a stole over his shoulders and a small vessel of oil in his left hand, the old priest leaned over the bed and anointed Joseph's forehead with the sign of the cross, praying, "Through this holy anointing, may the Lord in His love and mercy help you with the grace of the Holy Spirit." Then, as a paramedic put an IV line into Joseph's right arm, Father Sanchez anointed Joseph's left hand: "May the Lord who frees you from sin save you and raise you up."

Margaret could only stare in unbelief. *This can't be happening!*

Father Sanchez stepped back to allow room for the paramedics to work, and continued with the rite:

> Father, You readily take into account every stirring of good will, and You never refuse to pardon the sins of those who seek Your forgiveness. Have mercy on Your servant Joseph, who has now entered the struggle of his final agony. May this holy anointing and our prayer of faith comfort and aid him in body and soul. Forgive all his sins, and protect him with Your loving care. We ask this, Father, through Your Son Jesus Christ, because He has won the victory over death, opened the way to eternal life, and now lives and reigns with You for ever and ever. Amen.[100]

The paramedics, having done all they could for Joseph, lifted him onto a gurney and into the ambulance. As it sped off, Father Sanchez offered a final blessing while making the sign of the cross: "May the blessing of Almighty God, the Father, and the Son, and the Holy Spirit, come upon you and remain with you forever. Amen."

Joseph died three hours later.

The weeks that followed were filled with mourning. Father Sanchez helped the Lorente family by arranging for the funeral rites. There would be two evening vigils at a funeral home. The family requested that a Rosary be said each night for Joseph. On the third day there would be a funeral Mass followed by a procession to the cemetery and the *Rite of Committal*.

Margaret found comfort in thinking of Joseph's life: *He was such a good man, raised four children, worked hard, and went to Mass. He even received the last sacrament. Surely he will go to heaven.*

Or will he? All his life, Joseph—like so many other sincere Catholics—did what the Church told him to do. But did he do enough? Did he do what God requires? Does the Roman Catholic way of salvation lead to heaven?

Final Perseverance
and the Particular Judgment
[1021-1022, 1051, 1274]

Think of Roman Catholic salvation as a journey down a road, a long road with an uncertain end. The starting point is baptism. The middle section is made up of a lifetime of receiving the sacraments and doing good works. The finish line is death [1682-1683].

For a Catholic, death is the moment of truth. "In death, the separation of the soul from the body, the human body decays and the soul goes to meet God...."[997] There the individual learns whether or not he has attained to eternal life. This is a private and personal event called the *particular judgment*. It is when God decides a person's final destiny [1005, 1013, 1022, 1051].

In order to pass the particular judgment and ultimately reach heaven, a Catholic must die in a state of grace [1010, 1052]. This means that at the moment of death his soul must be in possession of sanctifying grace. In such a case the Catholic is said to have achieved *final perseverance*; he has preserved grace in his soul until the end [161, 1026, 2016].

If a person is devoid of sanctifying grace at the moment of death, however, God will banish the individual to eternal punishment [1022, 1033-1037, 1056-1057]:

> The souls of those who depart this life in
> actual mortal sin, or in original sin alone, go

down straightaway to hell to be punished, but with unequal pains.

—Council of Florence[101]

The Church teaches that no one knows until the particular judgment what his fate will be [1036, 2005].[102] Anyone might commit a mortal sin at the last moment, die in that condition, and be eternally lost. Therefore no living Catholic can say that he *is saved* in an eternal sense. Rather, he *is being saved* as he cooperates with grace. To *be eternally saved*, a Catholic must persevere to the end [161-162, 1026]. According to the Roman Catholic Church, that is what Jesus taught when He said, "The one who endures to the end, he shall be saved" (Matthew 24:13).

Purgatory
[954, 958, 1030-1032, 1054, 1472]

Roman Catholicism teaches that if at the particular judgment God finds a person in the state of grace, the individual's ultimate salvation is ensured [1030]. Before the person can enter heaven, however, the person may need to make atonement for temporal punishment that was not paid for while on earth [1022, 1030, 1682]. Catholics, the Church teaches, must make satisfaction for their sins:

> The truth has been divinely revealed that sins are followed by punishments. God's holiness and justice inflict them. Sins must be expiated. This may be done on this earth through the sorrows, miseries and trials of this life and, above all, through death. Otherwise the expiation must be made in the next life through fire and torments or purifying punishments.
>
> —Second Vatican Council[103]

Some of those who pass the particular judgment go straight to heaven. Baptized infants who died before reaching the age of accountability, for example, are considered free of guilt and temporal punishment. They are pure enough, therefore, to immediately enter heaven and enjoy the *beatific vision*, an intuitive contemplation of God [1023-1029].

Another group that goes straight to heaven are those who have worked hard or have suffered sufficiently on earth. This would apply to some of the heroes of the Catholic faith whom the Church has canonized as saints.

The average Catholic, however, may not be immediately ready for heaven:

> People who have committed many sins, even if they are only venial sins, but who have never done penance by themselves and never tried to gain any indulgences, have a heavy load of punishment to atone for. God, however, is not only merciful, but also supremely just. If this punishment is not atoned for on earth, then he demands that satisfaction be made after death, "down to the last farthing" (Matthew 5:26). For "nothing unclean can enter into heaven" (Apocalypse 21:27). Experience, too, can teach us that most men, at the time of their death, are not good enough for heaven and still not bad enough for eternal damnation. Reason alone, without the aid of revelation, leads us to expect that there must be some means of purifying the punishment due to sin after death. This concept is what we express in the word purgatory. Scripture and tradition both clearly teach that purgatory does exist.
>
> —*Dogmatic Theology for the Laity*[104]

Roman Catholic theologians are not in agreement as to the nature of suffering in purgatory. Some teach that the pain of purgatory is chiefly a sense of loss in being separated from God. Others, following Thomas Aquinas, teach that souls in purgatory suffer intense and excruciating physical pain from fire [1031].

How long a person must suffer in purgatory is not clear, for not only must the Catholic pay for his sins but his soul must be "cleansed after death by cleansing pains."[105] The amount of time required to perform this soul scrubbing varies from one person to the next:

> Some venial sins cling more persistently than others, according as the affections are more inclined to them, and more firmly fixed in them. And since that which clings more persistently is more slowly cleansed, it follows that some are tormented in Purgatory longer than others, for as much as their affections were steeped in venial sins.
>
> —*Summa Theologica*[106]

Catholics still living can help a deceased loved one in purgatory by saying prayers, giving alms, and performing good works [958, 1032, 1475]. The Catholic then offers up these meritorious acts for the poor soul in purgatory. The most effective means of helping the dead, says the Church, is the sacrifice of the Mass [1055, 1689]. Parishioners can ask a priest to say a Mass for the benefit of a person believed to be in purgatory. Normally a small gift of money accompanies the request.

Indulgences
[1471-1479, 1498]

Another way in which the living can help the dead is by acquiring special credits, called *indulgences*, that cancel out temporal punishment [1032, 1471]. Roman Catholicism teaches that the Church has the power to dispense indulgences from a vast reservoir of merit called the *treasury of the Church* [1476-1477]:

> The "treasury of the Church" is the infinite value, which can never be exhausted, which Christ's merits have before God. They were offered so that the whole of mankind could be set

free from sin and attain communion with the Father. In Christ, the Redeemer himself, the satisfactions and merits of his Redemption exist and find their efficacy. This treasury includes as well the prayers and good works of the Blessed Virgin Mary. They are truly immense, unfathomable and even pristine in their value before God. In the treasury, too, are the prayers and good works of all the saints, all those who have followed in the footsteps of Christ the Lord and by his grace have made their lives holy and carried out the mission the Father entrusted to them. In this way they attained their own salvation and at the same time cooperated in saving their brothers in the unity of the Mystical Body.

—Second Vatican Council[107]

Catholics can earn an indulgence from the Church by doing specific acts of piety such as praying the Rosary [1478]. A plenary indulgence, the cancellation of all current temporal punishment, can be obtained by performing special acts with a perfect disposition [1471]. This must be accompanied by reception of the sacrament of confession, holy communion, and prayer for the Pope's *intentions*—that is, his personal prayer requests.

Once a Catholic has acquired an indulgence, he is free to decide how to use it. He can apply it to his own temporal punishment, or by prayer he can apply it to the account of a deceased loved one in purgatory [1479].

Merit and the General Judgment
[678-679, 682, 2006-2011, 2025-2027]

According to the Roman Catholic Church, whenever a person who is in a state of grace does a good work, he earns a reward [2010-2011, 2016]. The right to a reward is called *merit*.

Merit accumulates during a person's life. If the Catholic commits a mortal sin, however, all merit is forfeited. But should the Catholic repent and receive the sacrament of penance, lost merit is once again restored.[108]

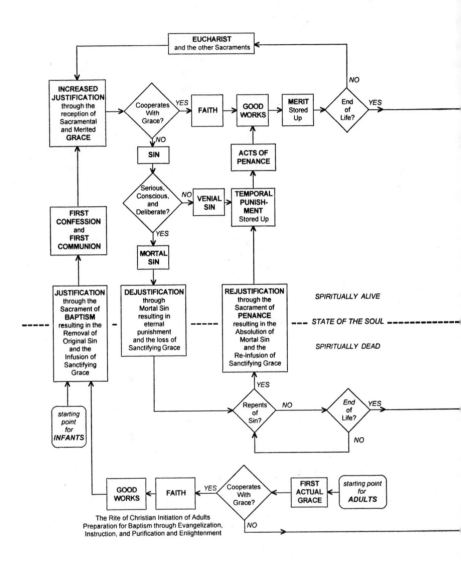

EUCHARIST
and the other Sacraments

INCREASED JUSTIFICATION through the reception of Sacramental and Merited GRACE

Cooperates With Grace? — YES → FAITH → GOOD WORKS → MERIT Stored Up → End of Life? — YES

NO

SIN

ACTS OF PENANCE

FIRST CONFESSION and FIRST COMMUNION

Serious, Conscious, and Deliberate? — NO → VENIAL SIN → TEMPORAL PUNISHMENT Stored Up

YES

MORTAL SIN

JUSTIFICATION through the Sacrament of BAPTISM resulting in the Removal of Original Sin and the Infusion of Sanctifying Grace

DEJUSTIFICATION through Mortal Sin resulting in eternal punishment and the loss of Sanctifying Grace

REJUSTIFICATION through the Sacrament of PENANCE resulting in the Absolution of Mortal Sin and the Re-infusion of Sanctifying Grace

SPIRITUALLY ALIVE

— — — STATE OF THE SOUL — — — —

SPIRITUALLY DEAD

YES

Repents of Sin? — NO → End of Life? — YES

NO

starting point for INFANTS

GOOD WORKS ← FAITH ← YES — Cooperates With Grace? ← FIRST ACTUAL GRACE ← starting point for ADULTS

NO

The Rite of Christian Initiation of Adults
Preparation for Baptism through Evangelization,
Instruction, and Purification and Enlightenment

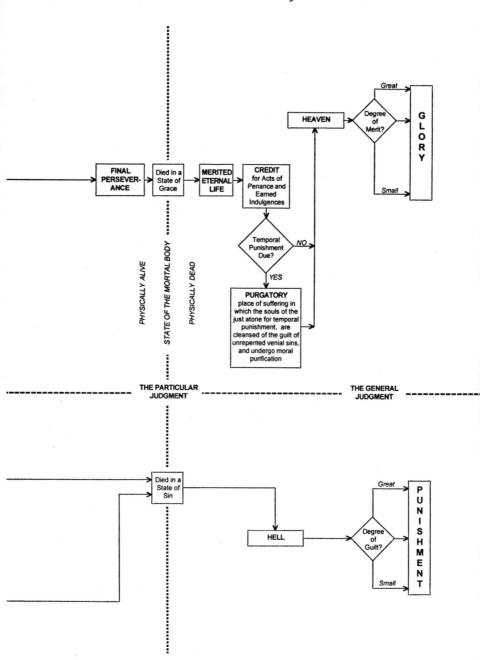

Figure 5:1
The Gospel According to Rome

Merited reward takes three forms in Roman Catholicism:[109]

Increase of Grace
[2010, 2027]

When a Catholic does a good work, the Church teaches that he immediately receives the reward of an increase of grace. This grace further justifies the Catholic. He becomes holier and more pleasing to God. This process of sanctification was discussed in Chapter 3, *Increasing and Preserving Justification.*

Eternal Life
[1022, 1036, 1051, 1821, 2010, 2027]

The Church teaches that upon death each person must face God in the particular judgment [1021-1022]. If God determines that the individual has died in the state of grace, the person obtains "the joy of heaven, as God's eternal reward for the good works accomplished with the grace of Christ."[1821] The Council of Trent stated:

> To those who work well right to the end and keep their trust in God, eternal life should be held out, both as a grace promised in his mercy through Jesus Christ to the children of God, and as a reward to be faithfully bestowed, on the promise of God himself, for their good works and merits.
>
> —Council of Trent[110]

Vatican II stated [1036]:

> Since we know neither the day nor the hour, we should follow the advice of the Lord and watch constantly so that, when the single course of our earthly life is completed, we may merit to enter with him into the marriage feast and be numbered among the blessed....
>
> —Second Vatican Council[111]

Increase of Glory in Heaven
[1038-1041, 1053]

The Church teaches that merited reward also results in an increase of the degree of glory that an individual enjoys in heaven. God does not decide this reward
until the end of the world. Christ will return to earth.
The dead will rise with immortal bodies, and God will
release all who are still suffering in purgatory [988-1004,
1038]. Then there will be a second evaluation of each
person's life. This is the *universal* or *general judgment*
[1038-1041, 1059]. According to Roman Catholic theology,
Jesus described the general judgment in the Gospel of
Matthew [678, 681-682, 1038-1039, 1059]:[112]

> But when the Son of Man comes in His glory,
> and all the angels with Him, then He will sit on
> His glorious throne. And all the nations will be
> gathered before Him; and He will separate them
> from one another, as the shepherd separates the
> sheep from the goats.
> —Matthew 25:31,32

The general judgment is the public proclamation of
the results of the particular judgment and the determination of a person's *total* reward [1039]. It occurs at the
end of the world so that the complete effect of each
person's life upon all of society and history can be calcu-
lated and duly rewarded [1040].

If the person died in a state of grace, Christ will
reward the individual in proportion to his good works
[682]. This will decide the degree of his glory in heaven.

Similarly, if the person died without grace in his
soul, Christ will decide the degree of his punishment in
hell [679].

A BIBLICAL RESPONSE

When asked how they hope to get to heaven, few
Catholics express their faith in terms of *justification,
sanctifying grace, temporal punishment,* or *final perse-*

verance. A typical answer might sound something like this:

> I hope to get to heaven because I believe in God and try to be a good Catholic. I try to be nice to everyone and keep the commandments. I go to Mass and pray. If I sin, I say the *Act of Contrition*— though I've never really done anything all *that* bad. When I die, I think I'll go to heaven. I might have to go to purgatory first, though, if there is a purgatory.

Although the average Catholic has little formal knowledge of the Church's theology, the religious beliefs of most Catholics correspond fairly well to the Church's teachings. Unfortunately, however, the Church's teachings do not correspond well to Scripture. Contrary to Roman Catholic doctrine, the Bible teaches that:

- Eternal life is a free gift, not a merited reward.
- Salvation is secure, not probational.
- Payment for sin is through the cross, not purgatory.

Eternal Life Is a Free Gift

As we have seen, the Roman Catholic Church teaches that there are three forms of merited reward: an increase of grace, eternal life, and increased glory in heaven. The inherent contradictions of earning grace, the first form of merited reward, were discussed in Chapter 3, *Increasing and Preserving Justification*. The third form of merited reward, an increase of glory, is not a uniquely Catholic doctrine. Many non-Catholics also understand the Bible to teach that believers are stewards who will be rewarded for their service (2 Corinthians 5:10; Romans 14:10-12).

As for the second form of merited reward, eternal life, the Church's teaching stands in direct contradiction to the Bible. For though the Bible teaches that God will reward faithful stewards *in* heaven, it never says that He will reward them *with* heaven.

Eternal life is not a reward, but the unmerited gift of God. Jesus, speaking of His sheep, said, "I give eternal life to them" (John 10:28). He promised, "I will give to the one who thirsts from the spring of the water of life without cost" (Revelation 21:6, see also John 4:14; 6:40; 6:47; 17:2; Romans 5:17; 6:23).

Nevertheless, the Roman Catholic Church insists that eternal life is a merited reward earned by doing good [1036, 1051, 2010, 2027]. Just as a Catholic can earn an increase of grace and an increase of glory, he can earn eternal life. The Church denounces anyone who teaches otherwise:

> If anyone says that the good deeds of a justified person are the gifts of God, in the sense that they are not also the good merits of the one justified; or that the justified person, by the good deeds done by him through the grace of God and the merits of Jesus Christ (of whom he is a living member), does not truly merit an increase in grace, eternal life, and (so long as he dies in grace) the obtaining of his own eternal life, and even an increase of glory: let him be anathema.
>
> —Council of Trent[113]

When the Council states here that Catholics can truly merit eternal life, it means that there is an equality between the work performed and the reward received. Aquinas explains this relationship saying that, by the mercy of God, good works which proceed from the grace of the Holy Spirit merit everlasting life *condignly*.[114] According to Aquinas, eternal life is "granted in accordance with a fair judgment."[115]

Roman Catholic theologians contrast condign or well-deserved merit with *congruous* merit. This latter kind of merit applies to cases in which the reward "results from a certain graciousness in the light of God's liberality."[116]

Eternal life, according to the Church, is a truly merited reward. It is merited condignly, not congruously. It is not a free gift which God graciously gives apart from anything man has done to earn it. It is the result of a fair judgment.

To substantiate its claim that eternal life is a merited reward, the Roman Catholic Church cites Paul's Letter to the Romans:

> [God]... will render to every man according to his deeds: to those who by perseverance in doing good seek for glory and honor and immortality, eternal life; but to those who are selfishly ambitious and do not obey the truth, but obey unrighteousness, wrath and indignation.
>
> —Romans 2:6-8

The Roman Catholic Church interprets this passage to say that if a person dies with sanctifying grace in his soul, he deserves to go to heaven because of his good deeds [55]:

> ... it must be believed that nothing more is needed for the justified to be considered to have fully satisfied God's law, according to this state of life, by the deeds they have wrought in him and to have truly deserved to gain eternal life in their time (provided they die in a state of grace).
>
> —Council of Trent[117]

The Bible, on the other hand, teaches that what every man and woman truly deserves is eternal punishment. The good news of Jesus Christ, however, is that God is willing to graciously give those who trust Christ eternal life, a gift that no one deserves! In order that these two truths would not be confused, the Holy Spirit included both of them in one verse:

> For the wages of sin is death, but the free gift of God is eternal life in Christ Jesus our Lord.
>
> —Romans 6:23

With such a clear statement here that eternal life is a free gift, Romans 2:6-8 cannot possibly be interpreted as teaching the direct opposite—that eternal life is a merited reward. A closer look at Romans 2:6-8 reveals the source of the Church's misinterpretation.

In Romans 2:6-8 Paul is addressing the kind of person who considers himself morally superior to others in character and conduct. This moralist, however, is himself practicing the very sins he condemns in others. Paul warns this hypocrite that he will not escape the judgment of God. A day is coming when God "will render to every man according to His deeds" (Romans 2:6). Those who do good—the biblical evidence of new life (John 15:8) will receive honor and eternal life. Those who do evil—the biblical evidence of an unregenerated heart (1 John 3:7-10)—will receive wrath and indignation.

Note that Paul does not say God will render to every man honor or wrath *because* of his deeds. That would make good works the *cause* of eternal life, as taught in Roman Catholicism. Rather, Paul says that God will render judgment *according* to how a man has lived. This means that there will be a relationship of *correspondence* between how a person lives and the outcome of his judgment. Those who practice good—evidence of true spiritual life—will receive good from the Lord. Those who practice evil, such as the hypocritical moralist Paul is addressing, will receive wrath and indignation.

Roman Catholicism, on the other hand, teaches that God gives eternal life to people *because* of their good works, to those who deserve it:

> It is a universally accepted dogma of the Catholic Church that man, in union with the grace of the Holy Spirit must merit heaven by his good works....we can actually merit heaven *as our reward*.... Heaven must be fought for; we have to earn heaven.
>
> —*Dogmatic Theology for the Laity*[118]

What About Good Buddhists?

If, as the Church claims, God acknowledges the good works of Catholics for salvation, what about the good works of Jews, Muslims, Hindus, Buddhists, or even agnostics, for that matter? Can they achieve eternal salvation?

The Second Vatican Council pictured all mankind as forming one community with common questions about life and God.[119] It acknowledged the spiritual and moral values of Judaism, Buddhism, Hinduism, and Islam. These non-Christians, the Council said, "are related to the People of God [the Church] in various ways,"[120] and are included in God's plan of salvation [839-842, 847, 1257, 1260].[121] The same is true of those who practice the most primitive forms of religions [843]:

"Nor is God remote from those who in shadows and images seek the unknown God, since he gives to all men life and breath and all things (cf. Acts 17:25-28), and since the Saviour wills all men to be saved (cf. 1 Timothy 2:4). Those who, through no fault of their own, do not know the Gospel of Christ or his Church, but who

Biblical Salvation Is Completely Secure

Though Catholics can obtain justification in an instant through baptism, they can lose it just as quickly through mortal sin. In the same day a Catholic can wake up justified, lose the grace of justification through mortal sin, and be justified again through the sacrament of penance. For some Catholics this cycle is repeated hundreds of times during a lifetime, yet only the state of the soul at the moment of death ultimately matters.

Biblical salvation, on the other hand, is secure, for it does not depend upon man but upon God. The Lord Jesus promises, "I give eternal life to them, and they shall never perish" (John 10:28). The Holy Spirit takes up residence within each Christian as the guarantor of that

nevertheless seek God with a sincere heart, and, moved by grace, try in their actions to do his will as they know it through the dictates of their conscience—those too may achieve eternal salvation. Nor shall divine providence deny the assistance necessary for salvation to those who, without any fault of theirs, have not yet arrived at an explicit knowledge of God, and who, not without grace, strive to lead a good life."

—Second Vatican Council[122]

Vatican II's unprecedented open-mindedness toward non-Christians surprised Catholics in 1965. At that time the laity were more accustomed to hearing appeals for money for the propagation of the faith to the "heathen" and relief for the "pagan babies." Since then Catholics have had to shift their worldview. They must now acknowledge other religions as valid instruments of salvation, though certainly inferior to the fullness of religion found in the Roman Catholic Church [837, 845-846, 848].

promise (Ephesians 1:13,14). And the Father places each believer in the palm of His hand for safekeeping (John 10:29).

Unlike Roman Catholic salvation, in which no certain link exists between initial justification through baptism and the attainment of eternal life, biblical justification and eternal salvation are inseparable. Biblical justification promises salvation from eternal punishment: "Much more then, having now been justified by His blood, we shall be saved from the wrath of God through Him" (Romans 5:9). If a person is justified, his entry into eternal glory is also secure: "Whom He predestined, these He also called; and whom He called, these He also justified; and whom He justified, these He also glorified" (Romans 8:30). Biblical justification is an irreversible declaration of God. Scripture asks: "Who will bring a charge against God's elect? God is the one who justifies; who is the one who condemns? ... Who shall separate us from the love of Christ?" (Romans 8:33-35).

Roman Catholicism, on the other hand, teaches that one's life on earth is a probational time of testing. The outcome is uncertain. Only the one who perseveres in cooperation with grace to the very end shall be saved [161-162, 837, 1026]:

> If they fail to respond in thought, word and deed to that grace, not only shall they not be saved, but they shall be the more severely judged.
>
> —Second Vatican Council[123]

Since Roman Catholic salvation depends upon the individual's conduct, no one, not even the Pope, can know for certain what his eternal destiny will be [1036, 2005]:

> In addition, no one, so long as he remains in this present life, ought so to presume about the hidden mystery of divine predestination as to hold for certain that he is unquestionably of the number of the predestined, as if it were true that one justified is either no longer capable of sin or, if he sins, may promise himself sure repentance. For, apart from a special revelation, it is impossible to know whom God has chosen for himself.
>
> —Council of Trent[124]

The Bible, on the other hand, teaches that "the gifts and calling of God are irrevocable" (Romans 11:29). Eternal life is so certain that the Bible speaks of it as the present possession of every genuine believer:

> And the witness is this, that God has given us eternal life, and this life is in His Son. He who has the Son has the life; he who does not have the Son

of God does not have the life. These things I have
written to you who believe in the name of the Son
of God, in order that you may know that you have
eternal life.

—1 John 5:11-13

Here the Scriptures state that a person who truly
believes in Christ can *know* that he has eternal life. For a
Christian to have confidence of his standing before God,
therefore, is not presumption but biblically based faith.

Payment for Sin Is Through the Cross Alone

The Scriptures teach that Jesus "released us from
our sins by His blood" (Revelation 1:5). They make no
mention of acts of penance, indulgences, or a place such
as purgatory through which the penalty of sin can be
satisfied.

What About 2 Maccabees 12:39-46?

The Roman Catholic Church claims that purgatory
has a sound biblical basis. Its primary evidence is from
the book of Second Maccabees, part of the Apocrypha
[958, 1032]. The passage in which the Church finds purgatory concerns an event that occurred about 160 B.C.,
during a war between Judas Maccabaeus, a Jewish general, and Gorgias, governor of Idumea. Following a
bloody battle, the Jews observed the Sabbath and then
went out to bury their dead:

> On the following day, since the task had now
> become urgent, Judas and his men went to
> gather up the bodies of the slain and bury them
> with their kinsmen in their ancestral tombs. But
> under the tunic of each of the dead they found
> amulets sacred to the idols of Jamnia, which the
> law forbids the Jews to wear. So it was clear to all
> that this was why these men had been slain.
>
> They all therefore praised the ways of the
> Lord, the just judge who brings to light the

things that are hidden. Turning to supplication, they prayed that the sinful deed might be fully blotted out. The noble Judas warned the soldiers to keep themselves free from sin, for they had seen with their own eyes what had happened because of the sin of those who had fallen.

He then took up a collection among all his soldiers, amounting to two thousand silver drachmas, which he sent to Jerusalem to provide for an expiatory sacrifice. In doing this he acted in a very excellent and noble way, inasmuch as he had the resurrection of the dead in view; for if he were not expecting the fallen to rise again, it would have been useless and foolish to pray for them in death. But if he did this with a view to the splendid reward that awaits those who had gone to rest in godliness, it was a holy and pious thought. Thus he made atonement for the dead that they might be freed from this sin.

—2 Maccabees 12:39-46 NAB

Catholic scholars say that since the slain "had gone to rest in godliness" (2 Maccabees 12:45 NAB), they were not in hell. Yet, since they needed to be freed from sin through atonement, they did not go directly to heaven either. Therefore the souls of the slain must have been in some third location. The Church calls that third place purgatory.

Catholic scholars also point out that the author of Second Maccabees comments that "it was a holy and pious thought" (2 Maccabees 12:45 NAB) for Judas "to provide for an expiatory sacrifice" (2 Maccabees 12:43 NAB) and "to pray for them in death" (2 Maccabees 12:44 NAB). Thereby he "made atonement for the dead that they might be freed from this sin" (2 Maccabees 12:46 NAB).

Though some may consider praying for the dead in purgatory to be a pious thought, it is nonetheless not a biblical one. Second Maccabees 12 does not provide a Scriptural basis for either purgatory or praying for the dead.

Notice first that the passage makes no direct reference to purgatory. As the Church's primary proof for the doctrine of purgatory, 2 Maccabees 12 is surprisingly obscure.

Second, the passage is internally inconsistent. It says that the slain "had gone to rest in godliness" (2 Maccabees 12:45 NAB). Yet the dead warriors were idolaters who had been judged by God for their sin. They died in their guilt.

Third, there is nothing in the law of Moses that would indicate that offerings for the dead were ever an authentic part of the Jewish faith. Second Maccabees 12, therefore, proves nothing more than that the unknown writer of the book believed that sacrifices could atone for the sins of the dead. It does not even prove that Judas Maccabaeus himself believed such a thing. The writer is clearly presenting his own interpretation of Judas' actions and motivations. In the light of Leviticus 4:1-6:7 it seems more likely that Judas Maccabaeus sent the money to Jerusalem to provide for a sin or trespass offering. His purpose would have been to atone for the defilement that the sin of the idolaters had brought upon the camp, in which case the offering was for the living, not the dead.

Finally, a practice recorded in Second Maccabees cannot be admitted as biblical evidence. Second Maccabees is part of the Apocrypha. It is not a genuine part of the Bible (see Appendix C for a discussion of the Roman Catholic Bible and the Apocrypha). The anonymous author of Second Maccabees does not claim to speak for God. He does not even present his book as an original work. He states that it is the abridgement of another man's writings: "All this, which Jason of Cyrene set forth in detail in five volumes, we will try to condense into a single book" (2 Maccabees 2:23 NAB).

What About Matthew 12:32?

Roman Catholic arguments for a biblical basis for purgatory from the New Testament are also weak. Catholic scholars, for example, point to Jesus' words in the Gospel of Matthew [1031]:

> And whoever shall speak a word against the
> Son of Man, it shall be forgiven him; but whoever
> shall speak against the Holy Spirit, it shall not be
> forgiven him, either in this age or in the age to
> come.
>
> —Matthew 12:32

Catholic scholars argue that when Jesus warns here
that speaking against the Holy Spirit *cannot* be forgiven
in the age to come, He implies that some sins *can* be
forgiven in the future life. If they can be forgiven after
death, there must be a place of postdeath atonement,
namely, purgatory.

This conclusion both distorts and goes beyond what
Jesus said. Christ taught that blasphemy against the
Spirit can *never* be forgiven. The converse of a statement
is neither necessarily implied nor necessarily true.

What About 1 Corinthians 3:10-15?

The Roman Catholic Church also points to 1 Corinthians 3 in support of purgatory [1031]:

> According to the grace of God which was
> given to me, as a wise master builder I laid a
> foundation, and another is building upon it. But
> let each man be careful how he builds upon it.
> For no man can lay a foundation other than the
> one which is laid, which is Jesus Christ. Now if
> any man builds upon the foundation with gold,
> silver, precious stones, wood, hay, straw, each
> man's work will become evident; for the day will
> show it, because it is to be revealed with fire; and
> the fire itself will test the quality of each man's
> work. If any man's work which he has built upon
> it remains, he shall receive a reward. If any man's
> work is burned up, he shall suffer loss; but he
> himself shall be saved, yet so as through fire.
>
> —1 Corinthians 3:10-15

To turn this passage into a description of purgatory
is to ignore its context. In the first four chapters of

1 Corinthians Paul is addressing a problem in the church at Corinth. Glory-seeking false teachers were destroying the unity of the church with their worldly wisdom (1 Corinthians 1:10-3:4). In the passage quoted above, Paul is warning these troublemakers that one day they will have to give an account to God for their actions.

Paul illustrates his point by comparing ministry in the church at Corinth to the construction of a building. Paul laid the building's foundation when he planted the church there during his second missionary journey (Acts 18:1-17). The workers constructing the building's walls are those presently ministering in the Corinthian church. If these workers serve well, it is as if they were building with bricks of gold, silver, and precious stones. If they serve poorly—such as those who were causing the division—it is as if they were building with wood, hay, and straw.

In the future, Christ will evaluate the ministry of each servant. Paul compares this judgment to the imaginary building he has just described as being set ablaze. If a man's work remains, having been built with durable materials, he will receive a reward. If a man's work burns up, having been built with inferior materials, he will suffer the loss of the reward that might have been his.

The Roman Catholic interpretation completely misses the point. Paul is using an analogy. He is not talking about a real fire. He is not talking about men and women burning. Paul is speaking of an imaginary building that represents a person's ministry, not the individual himself. Figuratively speaking, it is a person's *work* that will burn, not the person himself. The focus of the illustration is the potential loss of reward for poor service, not the atonement of sin or the cleansing of souls.

Purgatory:
An Essential Roman Catholic Doctrine

Though there is no biblical basis for purgatory, there is a strong philosophical need for it in Roman Catholic theology. The Church views salvation as the objective adornment or beautification of the soul. It is a process which starts at baptism, through which sanctifying grace is initially infused. This makes the soul holy and inherently pleasing to God. Other sacraments and good works further justify the soul and make it increasingly attractive to God. The goal is to transform the essential character of the soul into something which is in itself objectively good. It is therefore only reasonable to require the complete cleansing of every vestige of sin before the soul can come into the presence of God. Purgatory, therefore, is the logical extension of the Church's process of salvation.

Purgatory is also an integral element of the Roman Catholic penitential system. According to the Church, every sin credits temporal punishment to the sinner's account. Acts of penance, suffering, and indulgences debit this account. Since sinners may not make full satisfaction for sin in this life, purgatory in the afterlife is necessary to balance the ledger.

Finally, the Church uses purgatory to motivate Catholics to live righteously. If there were no purgatory, the reasoning goes, people would go on sinning without fear.

Biblical salvation, on the other hand, has no need of a place such as purgatory. Biblical salvation does not rely on the works and sufferings of sinners, but solely upon Christ. The Lord Jesus "made purification of sins" (Hebrews 1:3) on the cross. His blood can cleanse the vilest sinner (Hebrews 9:14). There is no temporal punishment remaining for which the believer must atone; Jesus paid it all: "He Himself is the propitiation for our sins" (1 John 2:2).

Biblical salvation has no need for a place such as purgatory where the soul supposedly becomes objectively beautiful to God. Rather, it is rooted in God's imputation of His own perfect righteousness (2 Corinthians 5:21). Biblical salvation brings a "righteousness that is by faith from first to last" (Romans 1:17 NIV). The sinner places his trust in Christ for justification. He walks by faith, and through the enablement of the Spirit he lives righteously. Nevertheless, he has no hope of ever being personally and objectively good enough *in himself* to stand in the presence of God. *He trusts in Christ alone for salvation* (Philippians 3:7-9).

Rather than focusing on the good works and suffering of the individual, biblical salvation emphasizes the perfect work of Christ. He is sufficient to make sinners "stand in the presence of His glory blameless with great joy" (Jude 24). God no longer looks at the person as a defiled sinner, but sees him only *in Christ* (Ephesians 1:1-14), "holy and blameless before Him" (Ephesians 1:4).

Finally, biblical salvation involves a new birth that results in a new creation (John 3:7; Ephesians 2:15). A born-again Christian wants to obey God. He is motivated by the love of Christ, not the fear of painful retribution (2 Corinthians 5:14; Romans 8:15).

Do Catholics Still Believe in Purgatory?

Many modern Catholics think of purgatory as a relic from the Dark Ages, which they would just as soon forget. Some Catholics even believe that purgatory is no longer a Roman Catholic doctrine.

Despite popular opinion, however, purgatory is still an official dogma of the Roman Catholic Church and an essential part of the Roman Catholic plan of salvation. The Church affirmed the existence of purgatory at each of the last three ecumenical councils: Trent,[125] Vatican I,[126] and Vatican II.[127] The latter council described purgatory as a place where the souls of the dead make expiation "in the next life through fire and torments or purifying punishments."[128] According to Vatican II, "in purgatory the souls of those 'who died in the charity of God and truly repentant, but who had not made satisfaction with adequate penance for their sins and omissions,'[129] are cleansed after death with punishments designed to purge away their debt."[130] The *Catechism of the Catholic Church* describes purgatory as place of "cleansing fire."[1031]

Belief in the existence of purgatory is also expressed at every Mass. During the Liturgy of the Eucharist, prayers are offered for the dead. Usually the Mass itself is also offered for someone suffering in purgatory. The person's name is announced or published in the Sunday bulletin. Each year, in fact, on the anniversary of the death of the last Pope, the present Pope offers Mass for the souls of his two predecessors, who are presumably still suffering in purgatory.[131]

A Biblical Verdict

In the previous five chapters we have seen how the Roman Catholic way of salvation differs from that taught in Scripture. Here we must ask: How serious are these errors?

An answer to this question can be found in Paul's letter to the Galatians. Paul was the first apostle to preach the gospel and form churches in the region of Galatia, part of modern Turkey. Shortly after he left the region, a group of Jewish teachers arrived. They presented themselves as followers of Christ who held to the same faith as the Galatians. Apparently they believed that Jesus was the anointed one of God, who had died, had risen, and was coming again. There is no reason to think that these teachers would not have affirmed the doctrines contained in the Apostles' Creed and the Nicene Creed, had those creeds been in existence in the first century. To the Galatians, these men appeared perfectly orthodox.

These new teachers, however, were critical of Paul. They considered Paul's understanding of justification to be somewhat deficient. Specifically, these Jewish teachers taught that, in addition to believing in Jesus, it was necessary for Christians to obey certain aspects of the law (Galatians 4:21). Gentile believers should be circumcised (Galatians 5:2-4). All believers should keep the Sabbath and the Jewish feasts (Galatians 4:9,10). Such good works, they said, were necessary for justification (Galatians 5:4).

When Paul learned what was going on in Galatia, he penned the sternest letter of the New Testament as inspired by the Holy Spirit. In its opening lines he accused the false teachers of seeking to "distort the gospel of Christ" (Galatians 1:7).

The word translated "distort" means *to pervert* or *to transform the character of one thing into something of exactly the opposite nature*. It is used in Acts 2:20, "The sun shall be turned into darkness," and in James 4:9, "Let your laughter be turned into mourning, and your joy to gloom." Both of these examples describe the transformation of one thing into something else of the opposite character.

That is exactly what the false teachers were doing with the gospel of Jesus Christ. By requiring obedience to the law in order to obtain and maintain justification, they had nullified the grace of God (Galatians 2:21). They had changed the gospel of faith into a gospel of works, the gospel of grace into a gospel of merit.

Paul told the Galatians that in following these false teachers they were "deserting" Christ (Galatians 1:6). They were changing their loyalties from dependence upon Christ "for a different gospel, which is really not another" gospel (Galatians 1:6,7).

The Greek words that Paul uses here tell us that the new gospel in Galatia was not another gospel *of the same sort* but another gospel *of a different sort*. It was not another kind of Christianity with a different emphasis or expression. It was not Christianity at all!

Paul's accusations must have shocked the Galatians. They thought of themselves as devout Christians. Though they had begun to consider obedience to certain aspects of the law as necessary for justification, they had not, at least in their minds, given up their faith in Christ. Justification, as they were now seeing it, was by faith plus works. As far as they were concerned, they were doing more, not less.

Paul warned the Galatians that if they made their standing before God dependent upon what Christ had done plus what they were doing they would be condemned, for with the law comes a curse: "Cursed is everyone who does not abide by all things written in the book of the Law, to perform them" (Galatians 3:10). In other words, those asking God to judge them, even in part, based upon their personal behavior had better realize that the law condemns those who fail to keep it perfectly.

Paul told the Galatians that if they received circumcision, an expression of their intention to live under the law, Christ would "be of no benefit" to them (Galatians 5:2). They would be "under obligation to keep the whole Law" (Galatians 5:3). They would be "severed from Christ" and "fallen from grace" (Galatians 5:4).

Once again, it is important to recognize that the Galatian heresy was not one of direct rejection either of Christ or of the necessity of faith, grace, and salvation. The error was one of requiring, in addition to faith, obedience to certain aspects of the law for justification. It was one of approaching God based upon faith *plus* works.

The problem with this formula for justification is that it is an indirect rejection of the terms of God's offer of salvation. Christ taught, "I have not come to call the righteous but sinners to repentance" (Luke 5:32). When we approach God through our own performance, even in part, we are telling God that we are not that bad, that there is something morally redeeming about ourselves—that, at least in part, we *deserve* eternal life.

God's offer of salvation does not extend to people with such attitudes (John 9:39-41; Luke 5:31). He is willing to forgive only those who come to Him empty-handed, acknowledging the full extent of their guilt. It is for this reason that biblical salvation is by faith, "not as a result of works, that no one should boast" (Ephesians 2:9).

The Roman Catholic Church, even as the false teachers of Galatia, holds that justification is by faith plus works. Even as the false teachers of Galatia required *circumcision* for justification, so the Church requires infants to be *baptized* for justification. Even as observance of the Sabbath and Jewish feasts became mandatory practices in Galatia, so attendance at Sunday Mass is mandatory in Roman Catholicism [2180-2181]. Even as the false teachers required obedience to the law of Moses for salvation, so the Church requires obedience to the Ten Commandments, the moral summary of the law, as necessary for salvation [2052, 2068, 2075].

Roman Catholicism has further distorted the gospel by redefining the biblical meaning of justification, salvation, faith, grace, and even sin. Concepts foreign to the Bible have been added to the gospel: sanctifying grace, seven sacraments, venial sin, temporal punishment, purgatory, acts of penance, indulgences, etc. The Church has set up extensive requirements for adults seeking justification and made salvation into a merit system of sacraments and good works. Even grace and eternal life have become merited rewards.

The Roman Catholic plan of salvation contradicts biblical truth in 24 major areas (listed below). Those who follow it will not escape the consequences of which Paul warned the Galatians. Neither can the leaders and teachers of the Roman Catholic Church escape their guilt in leading millions of people astray. Paul warned:

> But even though we or an angel from heaven should preach to you a gospel contrary to that which we have preached to you, let him be accursed. As we have said before, so I say again now, if any man is preaching to you a gospel contrary to that which you received, let him be accursed.
>
> —Galatians 1:8,9

Salvation: Error Versus Truth

The Catholic Church Teaches	The Bible Teaches
1. Justification is a transformation of the soul in which original sin is removed and sanctifying grace infused [1987-1995].	Justification is an act of God in which He declares a sinner to be righteous in His sight, having forgiven his sins and imputed to him God's own righteousness (Romans 3:21-4:8).
2. Initial justification is by means of baptism [1262-1274].	Justification is by faith alone (Romans 3:28).
3. Adults must prepare for justification through faith and good works [1247-1249].	God justifies ungodly sinners who believe (Romans 4:5). Good works are the *result* of salvation, not the cause (Ephesians 2:8-10).
4. The justified are in themselves beautiful and holy in God's sight [1992, 1999-2000, 2024].	The justified are *in Christ* holy and blameless before God (Ephesians 1:1-14).
5. Justification is furthered by sacraments and good works [1212, 1392, 2010].	Justification is the imputation of the perfect righteousness of God (2 Corinthians 5:21). In Christ the believer has been made complete (Colossians 2:10).
6. Justification is lost through mortal sin [1033, 1855, 1874].	Justification cannot be lost. Those whom God justifies will be saved from the wrath of God (Romans 5:8,9).

7. Catholics guilty of mortal sin are justified again through the sacrament of penance [980, 1446].

There is no second justification. Those whom God justifies He also will glorify (Romans 8:30).

8. Salvation from the eternal consequences of sin is a lifelong process [161-162, 1254-1255].

Salvation from the eternal consequences of sin is an instantaneous and secure act of God coinciding with justification (Romans 5:9).

9. Salvation is attained by cooperating with grace through faith, good works, and participation in the sacraments [183, 1129, 1815, 2002].

Salvation is attained by grace through faith apart from works (Ephesians 2:8,9). Good works are the result, not the cause, of salvation (Ephesians 2:10).

10. Faith is belief in God and the firm acceptance of all that the Church proposes for belief [181-182, 1814].

Saving faith is the entrusting of oneself to Christ as Lord and Savior (Romans 10:8-17).

11. Sanctifying grace is a quality of the soul, a supernatural disposition that perfects the soul [1999-2000].

Grace is the undeserved favor of God (Ephesians 1:7,8).

12. The sacraments are necessary channels for the continual infusion of grace. They bestow grace in virtue of the rite performed [1127-1129].

The child of God is the constant object of the Father's grace (Romans 5:1,2).

13. Grace is merited by good works [2010, 2027].

Grace is a free gift (Romans 11:6).

14. Venial sins do not incur eternal punishment [1855, 1863].

Every sin is punishable by eternal death (Romans 6:23).

15. Serious sins must be confessed to a priest [1456-1457].	Sin is to be confessed directly to God (Ezra 10:11).
16. The priest forgives sin as a judge [1442, 1461].	No one can forgive sin but God alone (Mark 2:7).
17. When the guilt of sin is forgiven, temporal punishment remains [1472-1473].	When God forgives sin, He completely forgives (Colossians 2:13; Isaiah 43:25).
18. Acts of penance make satisfaction for the temporal punishment of sin [1434, 1459-1460].	Jesus made perfect satisfaction for all sins (1 John 2:1,2).
19. Indulgences dispensed by the Church for acts of piety release sinners from temporal punishment [1471-1473].	Jesus releases believers from their sins by His blood (Revelation 1:5).
20. Purgatory is necessary to atone for sin and cleanse the soul [1030-1031].	Purgatory does not exist. Jesus made purification for sins on the cross (Hebrews 1:3).
21. Poor souls suffering in purgatory can be helped by those alive on earth offering up prayers, good works, and the sacrifice of the Mass [1032, 1371, 1479].	Those who sleep in Christ need no help. To be absent from the body is to be at home with the Lord (2 Corinthians 5:8).
22. No one can know if he will attain to eternal life [1036, 2005].	The believer can know that he has eternal life by the Word of God (1 John 5:13).
23. Eternal life is a merited reward [1821, 2010].	Eternal life is the free gift of God (Romans 6:23).

24. The Roman Catholic Church is necessary for salvation [846].

There is salvation in no one but the Lord Jesus Christ, "for there is no other name under heaven that has been given among men by which we must be saved" (Acts 4:12).

❖ PART TWO ❖

THE MASS

Why do Catholics go to Mass? Do they actually worship the Eucharist? Is the Sacrifice of the Mass a real sacrifice?

Part Two will answer these and other important questions concerning the sacrament and the sacrifice of the Eucharist, commonly referred to as the Mass.

The Eucharist has two purposes:

> ... one, that it might be the heavenly food of our souls, enabling us to support and preserve spiritual life; and the other, that the Church might have a perpetual Sacrifice....
>
> —*The Roman Catechism*[132]

These two functions will serve as the framework for this examination of the Mass:

❖ The Eucharist is the body of Christ—the heavenly food of the soul (Chapter 6, *The Body of Christ*).

❖ The Eucharist is the immaculate victim—the perpetual sacrifice of the Church (Chapter 7, *The Blood of Christ*).

In this section you will also join Mrs. Joseph Lorente as she and her family participate in a memorial Mass for her husband's soul.

❖6

THE BODY OF CHRIST

Sunday Mass,
First Anniversary of Joseph's Death

Father Mario Sanchez stood silently at the altar rail as he watched five members of the Lorente family coming down the center aisle, Mrs. Margaret Lorente and her four children. In their hands they carried gifts of bread and wine. In their hearts they carried a deep sense of loss, for today was the first anniversary of the death of Joseph Lorente, their beloved husband and father. At Mrs. Lorente's request, Father Sanchez had agreed to offer this morning's sacrifice of the Mass for Joseph's soul.

As Father Sanchez received the gifts, he felt the family's grief cast its shadow over him. How well he remembered the night of Joseph's death and the funeral that had followed. As he returned to the altar, the priest was hopeful that today's Mass would console the family and speed Joseph's release from purgatory.

Taking the bread, Father Sanchez elevated it above the altar and began the Liturgy of the Eucharist, praying:[133]

> Blessed are You, Lord, God of all creation.
> Through Your goodness we have this bread to
> offer, which earth has given and human hands
> have made. It will become for us the bread of life.

Pouring a small amount of water into a gold goblet, called a *chalice* (already containing wine), Father Sanchez quietly prayed:

> By the mystery of this water and wine may we come to share in the divinity of Christ, who humbled himself to share in our humanity.

Elevating the chalice, he continued:

> Blessed are You, Lord, God of all creation. Through Your goodness we have this wine to offer, fruit of the vine and work of human hands. It will become our spiritual drink.

Father Sanchez then addressed the congregation: "Pray, brethren, that our sacrifice may be acceptable to God, the almighty Father."

To this the people responded, "May the Lord accept the sacrifice at your hands for the praise and glory of His name, for our good, and the good of all His Church."

Extending his hands, the priest blessed the congregation, "The Lord be with you."

"And also with you," they answered.

"Lift up your hearts."

"We lift them up to the Lord."

"Let us give thanks to the Lord our God."

"It is right to give Him thanks and praise."

With increasing solemnity, the climax of the Mass approached. Extending his hands over the bread and wine, Father Sanchez asked God to perform a miraculous transformation:

> Bless and approve our offering; make it acceptable to You, an offering in spirit and in truth. Let it become for us the body and blood of Jesus Christ, Your Son, our Lord.

The priest then began a reenactment of the Last Supper. He picked up a single bread wafer and raised it above the altar. Speaking of Christ, Father Sanchez said:

> The day before He suffered, He took bread into his sacred hands, and looking up to heaven, to You, His almighty Father, He gave You thanks and praise. He broke the bread, gave it to His disciples, and said: "Take this, all of you, and eat it: this is my body which will be given up for you."

With those words, according to the Roman Catholic Church, the bread in Father Sanchez's hands became the body of Jesus Christ. As an expression of this belief, the priest lowered the wafer and bowed before it in adoration.

Reaching for the chalice, Father Sanchez raised it above the altar and continued his narration of Christ's actions at the Last Supper:

> When supper was ended, He took the cup. Again He gave you thanks and praise, gave the cup to His disciples, and said: "Take this, all of you, and drink from it: this is the cup of my blood, the blood of the new and everlasting covenant. It will be shed for you and for all men so that sins may be forgiven. Do this in memory of me."

Again Father Sanchez bowed in silent worship.

The First Mass
[610-611, 1323, 1337-1340]

Roman Catholicism teaches that Christ instituted the Mass at the Last Supper on the night of His betrayal [1323]. When the Lord pronounced over the bread, "This is My body" (Matthew 26:26), and over the wine, "This is My blood" (Matthew 26:28), He changed them [621]. The bread became His body. The wine became His blood [1339]. Christ then offered them as a sacrifice to the Father, and gave them to His disciples to eat and drink [610-611]. This, says the Church, was the first Eucharist.

At the Last Supper, Christ also told His disciples, "Do this in remembrance of Me" (Luke 22:19). The Church teaches that by those words the Lord ordained His disciples as priests and commissioned them to offer the Mass [611, 1337]. They were to celebrate the Eucharist frequently, even daily if possible. Offering the Mass and forgiving sins were to be the two principal functions of their priesthood [1461, 1566].

The Consecration of the Mass
[1333, 1352-1353, 1357-1358, 1373-1377]

The climax of the Mass occurs during the *consecration*, part of the Liturgy of the Eucharist. This is when the priest, repeating the words that Christ spoke at the Last Supper, is believed to change the bread and wine into Christ's body and blood by the power of the Holy Spirit [1105-1106, 1353]:

> ...in the sacrament of the Eucharist Christ is present, in a manner altogether unique, God and man, whole and entire, substantially and continuously.
> —Second Vatican Council[134]

Here the Church describes five characteristics of Christ's presence in the Eucharist:

Unique

In the Eucharist, Christ exists "in a manner altogether unique,"[135] for there is no parallel in nature with what happens upon the altar [1085, 1374].

God and Man

The bread and wine become "God and man,"[136] for the Eucharist is believed to be the incarnate Christ,

"...the true body of Christ the Lord, the same that was born of the Virgin..."[137] [1106, 1374].

Whole and Entire

The bread and wine each contain Christ "whole and entire"[138] [1374]. According to the Church, this means that even the smallest crumb of bread contains Christ's entire body and blood. The same is true of every drop of the wine [1377].[139]

Substantial

Roman Catholicism teaches that only the inner essence, called the *substance*, of the bread and wine change [1374, 1376]. Their outer appearances remain that of ordinary bread and wine.

Continuous

The Church teaches that Christ exists "continuously"[140] in the Eucharist as long as the bread and wine remain incorrupted [1377]. For this reason, great care must be taken to protect consecrated bread and wine from loss or defilement. After communion the priest locks any remaining consecrated wafers in a small immovable safe called a *tabernacle* [1183, 1379]. This is usually a gold-plated structure located on one of the church's altars. A lamp is kept burning in the sanctuary whenever Christ is Eucharistically present in the tabernacle. Catholics entering the church or crossing in front of the tabernacle are to acknowledge the Eucharist by genuflecting, briefly kneeling on the right knee, as a sign of respect [1378]. Some Catholics also make the sign of the cross when driving past a Catholic Church for the same reason.

The Sacrament of the Eucharist
[1322-1419]

According to the Roman Catholic Church, the Mass, even as the Last Supper, is a "sacred meal."[141] In it the Catholic community witnesses to its unity and enjoys communion with God [1118, 1396]. It is an opportunity to remember Christ's works, to proclaim His death, and to express gratitude to God. Consequently, the Church refers to the consecrated bread and wine as the *Eucharist*, from the Greek word for *thanksgiving* [1328, 1358-1361].

The Church teaches that the Eucharist is a means of grace, a sacrament of the Church [1210-1212]. Through it the faithful obtain sanctifying grace and are further justified:

> What material food produces in our bodily life, Holy Communion wonderfully achieves in our spiritual life. Communion with the flesh of the risen Christ, a flesh "given life and giving life through the Holy Spirit," preserves, increases, and renews the life of grace received at Baptism.
>
> —*Catechism of the Catholic Church*[1392]

Through the Eucharist, Catholics also receive actual grace that enables them to keep the commandments and do good works. The Eucharist, says the Church, is "an antidote to free us from daily faults and preserve us from mortal sins," and is "a pledge of our future glory and unending happiness"[142] [1395, 1402-1405, 1436].

According to the Church, the Eucharist is the *Most Blessed Sacrament*, for it is Christ Himself [1330]. It spiritually nourishes the soul and makes the Catholic more like Christ, for "partaking of the Body and Blood of Christ has no less an effect than to change us into what we have received."[143]

A properly prepared Catholic obtains the benefits of the Eucharist by attending Mass and participating with devotion [1385-1388, 1415]. Those receiving holy communion obtain a fuller blessing and enjoy "an intimate union with Christ Jesus"[1391] [1396, 1416].

Since Roman Catholicism holds that the Eucharist helps one attain to eternal salvation, the Church encourages the faithful to receive it daily [1389]. For this same reason, Church law requires Catholics to attend Mass each Sunday and on certain feast days of the Church [1389, 2042, 2181].[144] Catholics must also receive holy communion at least once each year during the Easter season [1417, 2042].[145] It is considered a mortal sin to deliberately disobey these commandments of the Church [2181].

No one, however, may partake of the Eucharist who does not believe in the *real presence* of Christ, that is to say, "a *substantial* presence by which Christ, God and man, makes himself wholly and entirely present"[146] in the consecrated bread and wine [1355, 1374, 1396, 1400-1401]. To guard against sacrilege, as the priest distributes holy communion to each person, he holds the consecrated wafer in front of the communicant, saying, "The body of Christ." Before the person can receive the host, he or she must respond, "Amen," meaning, "Yes, it is true!"[1396]

The Worship of the Eucharist
[1378-1381, 1418]

The Roman Catholic Church teaches that the faithful are to "hold the Eucharist in highest honor...worshiping it with supreme adoration"[147] with "the same worship of latria or adoration that we offer to God"[148] [1178, 1183, 1378, 1418, 2691].

> There should be no doubt in anyone's mind "that all the faithful ought to show to this most holy sacrament the worship which is due to the true God, as has always been the custom of the Catholic Church. Nor is it to be adored any the less because it was instituted by Christ to be eaten."
>
> —Second Vatican Council[149]

Neighborhood churches promote worship of the Eucharist through annual feasts involving the *Exposition of the Blessed Sacrament*. Typically, a large host, a consecrated bread wafer, is placed in a glass receptacle. This is then mounted in the center of an ornate gold vessel called a *monstrance*, which resembles a sunburst, and placed on an altar for the faithful to adore. In predominantly Catholic countries, a priest may also carry the monstrance through the streets of the parish in solemn procession [1378].

The Church also promotes worship of the Eucharist through special orders of men and women dedicated to the continuous adoration of consecrated bread and wine. These include the Nuns of the Perpetual Adoration of the Blessed Sacrament, the Sisters Adorers of the Precious Blood, and the Congregation of the Blessed Sacrament. Saint Pierre Julien Eymard (1811-1868), the founder of the last order listed, described the society's primary purpose as the worship of the Blessed Sacrament:

> ... to adore continuously Our Lord Jesus Christ on His throne of grace and of love; to render Him uninterrupted thanksgiving for the ineffable gift of the Eucharist; to become in union with Him, a victim of propitiation for the many crimes committed throughout the world; to carry out before the Blessed Sacrament a perpetual mission of prayer and supplication.... Such is the life of a religious of the Blessed Sacrament.
>
> —*Saint Peter Julian Eymard*[150]

The following prayer composed by Cardinal Carberry, former archbishop of Saint Louis, is representative of Roman Catholic worship before the Eucharist:

> Jesus, my God, I adore You, here present in the Blessed Sacrament of the altar, where You wait day and night to be our comfort while we await Your unveiled presence in heaven. Jesus, my God, I adore You in all places where the Blessed Sacrament is reserved and where sins are committed against this Sacrament of Love. Jesus, my God, I adore You for all time, past, present and future, for every soul that ever was, is or shall be created. Jesus, my God....
>
> —*Reflections and Prayers*[151]

A BIBLICAL RESPONSE

In Chapter 3, *Increasing and Preserving Justification*, we examined the errors associated with the sacrament of the Eucharist as a means of sanctifying grace. Here we will consider the Eucharist as the body of Christ. Two sections of Scripture used by the Roman Catholic Church to explain the Mass will be our focus: the accounts of the Last Supper (Matthew 26:20-30; Mark 14:17-26; Luke 22:14-38) and Jesus' discourse in John 6. It will be shown that:

- At the Last Supper, Christ spoke of the bread and wine as the symbols, not the substance, of His body and blood.
- In John 6, Christ taught that eternal life is through believing in Him, not through eating His flesh.

The Bread and Wine Are Symbols

There are several problems with the Roman Catholic interpretation that at the Last Supper the bread and wine became the actual "...body and blood of our lord Jesus Christ together with the soul and divinity, and therefore the whole Christ"[152] [1374]. The first is that there is not even the slightest indication that either the bread or the wine changed at the Last Supper. The same is true at the Mass today. The bread and wine before and after the consecration look exactly alike. Furthermore, they smell, taste, and feel the same. In fact, all empirical evidence supports the interpretation that they do not change at all.

The Church maintains that though the bread and wine do not *appear* to change, they change nonetheless. It uses a theory called *transubstantiation* to explain why this alleged miracle cannot be seen [1376, 1413].

The philosophical basis for the theory comes from the writings of Aristotle. He taught that all matter consists of two parts: *accidents* and *substance*. Aristotle defined accidents as the outward appearance of an object, and substance as its inner essence, the core of its reality.

The theory of transubstantiation says that at the consecration of the Mass, the substance of the bread and of the wine change while their accidents remain the same [1373-1377, 1413].[153] The words of consecration, says the Church, "... accomplish three wondrous and admirable effects:"[154]

- The inner essences of the bread and wine cease to exist.

- The outward appearances of the bread and wine remain, though they are no longer connected to any inward reality of their own.

- The inner essence of Christ's true body and blood comes to exist under the appearances of bread and wine.

The Roman Catholic Church is undisturbed by all arguments against transubstantiation drawn from observation or common sense. This change, says the Church, is a supernatural phenomenon, part of the "mystery of the Eucharist."[155] It "defies the powers of conception"[156] [1381]. The Church asserts that the fact that "... such a change takes place must be recognized by faith; how it takes place we must not curiously inquire."[157] The faithful are expected to accept this explanation regardless of how "repugnant it may appear to the senses."[158]

But faith must rest upon divine revelation, and the alleged miraculous change explained by transubstantiation is not in the Bible. Neither is there a biblical precedent for a miracle in which God expects the faithful to believe that something supernatural has occurred when in fact all outward evidence indicates that nothing at all has occurred. God has never dealt with people in that way.

A second problem with the Roman Catholic interpretation of Christ's words at the Last Supper is that it requires the eating of human flesh. The Church teaches that the Eucharist is "...the true body of Christ the Lord, the same that was born of the Virgin...."[159] This is what the disciples supposedly ate at the Last Supper!

One would think that such an absurdity would be enough to throw out the Roman Catholic interpretation as untenable. To the contrary, the Church presses its point, saying that the Lord likewise instructed His disciples to drink His blood!

For a Jew, drinking human blood would have been more than just repulsive; it would have been unlawful. The law of Moses strictly forbade Jews from drinking blood (Leviticus 17:10-14). We can be sure that if the disciples had thought that Jesus was asking them to violate this command, heated discussion and loud protests would have resulted. Yet there is no hint of such controversy in any of the accounts of the Last Supper.

Furthermore, had the disciples drunk Christ's blood at the Last Supper, Peter could not have claimed months later: "...I have never eaten anything unholy and unclean" (Acts 10:14). Additionally, the council at Jerusalem could not have instructed Gentile Christians to "abstain... from blood" (Acts 15:29) if Christians routinely drank Christ's blood at the Lord's Supper.

There is no reason to believe that the disciples thought for one moment that the bread and wine changed into Christ's body and blood. Nowhere do we read of their carefully protecting every crumb of consecrated bread or falling to their knees and worshiping the bread and wine. To the contrary, immediately after the Lord is said to have changed the wine into His blood, the Lord Himself referred to it again as wine:

> But I say to you, I will not drink of this fruit of the vine from now on until that day when I drink it new with you in My Father's kingdom.
>
> —Matthew 26:29

Another point to consider is that when Christ said with reference to the bread "This is My body" (Matthew

26:26), He was physically present with His disciples. Surely they would not have thought that Jesus' body was both at the table and on the table—and later under the table as crumbs were scattered!

But that is the Roman Catholic interpretation. That and much more, for, according to the Church, Christ is bodily present today in thousands of churches worldwide in every consecrated crumb of bread and drop of wine! The Bible, on the other hand, never ascribes more than one location to Christ's body at any given time.

Someone might object, "But isn't Christ God? And isn't God everywhere?" Yes, but this refers to His *spiritual* presence. The Lord Jesus is *spiritually* omnipresent, but He has only one *bodily* presence. According to the Bible, He is now *bodily* seated "at the right hand of the Majesty on high" (Hebrews 1:3).

All the problems listed above are resolved when Jesus' words at the Last Supper are understood in their *figurative* sense. That is, Jesus used bread and wine at the Last Supper as *symbols* of His body and blood.

The figurative interpretation is reasonable. The disciples are not required to drink blood and eat human flesh. Christ's body remains in one location. And there is no need to invent complicated theories to explain away the obvious: The bread and wine remain bread and wine.

The disciples were accustomed to the Lord using figurative language in His teaching. On different occasions, Christ referred to His body as a temple (John 2:19), new life as living water (John 4:10), His disciples as salt (Matthew 5:13), and the Pharisees' teaching as leaven (Matthew 16:6). The Gospel of John records seven figurative statements that Jesus made about Himself. Each uses the same verb that is translated "is" in Jesus' words "This is My body" (Luke 22:19). Jesus said:

- "I am the bread of life" (John 6:48).
- "I am the light of the world" (John 8:12).
- "I am the door" (John 10:9).
- "I am the good shepherd" (John 10:11).

- "I am the resurrection and the life" (John 11:25).
- "I am the way, and the truth, and the life" (John 14:6).
- "I am the true vine" (John 15:1).

All of these statements are meant to be understood in their figurative sense. The last two were even spoken at the Last Supper. A study of Christ's teaching that night reveals several figures of speech. For example, Jesus referred to the new covenant figuratively, saying, "This cup is the new covenant in My blood" (1 Corinthians 11:25). The cup was obviously not the covenant itself but the *symbol* of the covenant. Additionally, following the Last Supper, Jesus told His disciples:

> These things I have spoken to you in figurative language; an hour is coming when I will speak no more to you in figurative language, but will tell you plainly of the Father.
>
> —John 16:25

Defenders of the Roman Catholic interpretation say that the figurative interpretation makes no sense; it renders the bread and wine meaningless, mere symbols. From a Roman Catholic perspective, they may be right. For if the purpose of the Mass is to produce heavenly food to nourish the soul, there will indeed need to be a miraculous change. Moreover, if the Church intends to continue the sacrifice of the cross at the Mass (as we shall see in the next chapter), ordinary bread and wine will clearly be of little use.

However, if the goal is to obey the Lord's command, "Do this in remembrance of Me" (Luke 22:19), ordinary bread and wine are sufficient. The bread represents Christ's body, broken for us on the cross. The wine represents His blood, poured out for our sins. Partaking of each is a public declaration of faith in His finished work of salvation. It is saying, "I have a share in Christ's body and blood. He gave His life for me" (see 1 Corinthians 10:16). When believers partake of one loaf together, they are also witnessing to their unity in Christ as His body (1 Corinthians 10:17). Participating in a careless manner—as was happening in Corinth—is a serious matter, not because of what the bread and wine phsically are, but because of what they *represent* (1 Corinthians 11:18-27).

The figurative interpretation is consistent with Jesus' teaching on the nature of worship. He taught that "God is spirit, and those who worship Him must worship in spirit and truth" (John 4:24). Since spiritual communion is the goal, Christ's bodily presence is unnecessary. Ordinary bread and wine can serve as adequate reminders for Christians as they gather to "proclaim the Lord's death until He comes" (1 Corinthians 11:26). Then they will not need symbols, for they shall have Him!

Eternal Life Is Through Faith in Christ Alone

The Roman Catholic Church bases its explanation of the Last Supper largely upon the sixth chapter of the Gospel of John [1336, 1338, 1406]. This passage records a discussion between Jesus and a group of Jews, most of whom were unbelieving. It occurred in the synagogue of Capernaum at Passover time, one year before the Last Supper.

According to Roman Catholicism, on that occasion Jesus promised to give the Church a heavenly food:

> I am the living bread that came down out of heaven; if anyone eats of this bread, he shall live forever; and the bread also which I shall give for the life of the world is My flesh.
>
> —John 6:51

The bread that Christ would give, says the Church, would be the Eucharist, His actual body and blood. That is what Christ meant, says the Church, when He said: "For My flesh is true food, and My blood is true drink" (John 6:55). As such, the Eucharist would be a source of spiritual life [1509]:

> Truly, truly, I say to you, unless you eat the
> flesh of the Son of Man and drink His blood, you
> have no life in yourselves. He who eats My flesh
> and drinks My blood has eternal life, and I will
> raise him up on the last day.
>
> —John 6:53,54

Here, according to the Church, Christ teaches that
when the faithful receive holy communion during the
Mass, they are nourished with heavenly food for the soul,
"the bread that gives eternal life"[1509] [1383-1384]. They
"... eat the flesh of Christ and drink the blood of Christ,
and thus receive grace, which is the beginning of eternal
life, and the 'medicine of immortality.'..."[160] That is
how the Roman Catholic Church explains John 6. However, if one looks at the context of the passage, a different
interpretation emerges.

John 6 begins with the miraculous feeding of 5000
people at the Sea of Galilee (John 6:1-14). The next day a
group of Jews who had witnessed the miracle of the
loaves and fish came to Capernaum looking for Jesus
(John 6:22-25).

Jesus told these Jews that they were seeking Him for
the wrong reason: "Truly, truly, I say to you, you seek Me
not because you saw signs but because you ate of the
loaves and were filled" (John 6:26). He had something to
offer them that was far greater than a free meal: "Do not
work for the food which perishes, but for the food which
endures to eternal life, which the Son of Man shall give to
you, for on Him the Father, even God, has set His seal"
(John 6:27).

Here Jesus introduced a metaphor into the discussion. Since the Jews appeared to want nothing more than
another free meal, Jesus described His offer in terms of
food: not ordinary nourishment, but "food which endures to eternal life" (John 6:27).

The Jews assumed that they would need to do some
great virtuous act to earn this enduring food. They asked
Jesus, "What shall we do that we may work the works of
God?" (John 6:28).

Jesus answered, "This is the work of God, that you believe in Him whom He has sent" (John 6:29). What they needed to do was to place their trust in Jesus as the One sent from God, the Messiah.

The Jews replied with a challenge: "What then do You do for a sign, that we may see, and believe You? What work do You perform?" (John 6:30).

This response makes two things clear: First, the Jews understood that Jesus was calling them to believe in Him. Second, they were not accepting Jesus' claim to be the Messiah. Although the previous day they had witnessed a remarkable miracle, they wanted more proof, another sign. They even went so far as to suggest that Jesus bring manna down from heaven as Moses had done (John 6:31).

Once again Jesus tied His response into their reference to bread, manna from heaven. The Jews knew that the manna had been essential to the physical survival of the nation in the wilderness. Since Jesus was trying to get them to understand that He was essential to their spiritual survival, He answered, "I am the bread of life; he who comes to Me shall not hunger, and he who believes in Me shall never thirst" (John 6:35). In other words, those who put their trust in Him would be spiritually satisfied forever.

As the discussion intensified, Jesus restated His claim and pressed His analogy harder: "I am the living bread that came down out of heaven; if anyone eats of this bread, he shall live forever; and the bread also which I shall give for the life of the world is My flesh" (John 6:51).

Here Jesus foretells His death on the cross, not the sacrament of the Eucharist. He is predicting the giving of His life on the cross.

When Jesus promised, "If anyone eats of this bread, he shall live forever" (John 6:51), He was not speaking of literal bread, but was teaching that He Himself was the source of eternal life for all those who believe. He states this truth in plain language: "Truly, truly, I say to you, he who believes has eternal life" (John 6:47). He states this truth in figurative language: "I am the bread of life" (John 6:48).

This plain and figurative expression of the same truth can also be seen in the parallel construction of John 6:40 and John 6:54 as demonstrated in the table below:

Stated in Plain Language *John 6:40*	Stated in Figurative Language *John 6:54*
...everyone who	He who
beholds the Son	eats My flesh
and	and
believes in Him,	drinks My blood
may have eternal life;	has eternal life,
and	and
I Myself will raise him up	I will raise him up
on the last day.	on the last day.

Roman Catholic scholars reject the figurative interpretation. They point out that the Jews understood Jesus to be asking them to eat His actual flesh. That is why they grumbled and left. Since Jesus did not correct them on this crucial point, Catholic scholars argue, it is clear that the Jews had properly understood the Lord [1336].

There is some merit to this argument. Some of the Jews did in fact think that Jesus was asking them to eat His physical flesh (John 6:52). But this does not prove that they understood Jesus correctly. People often misunderstood the Lord, usually because they failed to discern when He was speaking figuratively (for example,

John 2:19-21 and 4:10,11). Sometimes Jesus purposely used figurative language to veil truth from hard-hearted and unbelieving listeners (Matthew 13:10-16).

Nevertheless, the claim that Jesus made no attempt to correct the Jews' misunderstanding in John 6 is incorrect. In response to the crowd's grumbling, Jesus said, "It is the Spirit who gives life; the flesh profits nothing; the words that I have spoken to you are spirit and are life" (John 6:63). Eternal life was to be obtained by believing Jesus' *words*. Eating His flesh would be profitless.

As Jesus' Jewish opponents departed in unbelief, He turned to the Twelve to test their faith, asking, "You do not want to go away also, do you?" (John 6:67).

Peter answered, "Lord, to whom shall we go? You have words of eternal life. And we have believed and have come to know that You are the Holy One of God" (John 6:68,69). At least Peter understood that eternal life was through *believing in Christ*, not eating His flesh.

Though Jesus refers to bread in John 6, we should not read the Last Supper into the passage. The contexts of John 6 and the Last Supper are completely different.

In John 6, Jesus is speaking to unbelieving Jews. The subject is eternal life through faith in Him. Jesus uses bread to represent Himself as the One sent from the Father (John 6:29), as the source of life (John 6:35), and as the Savior of the world (John 6:51). The Lord's purpose is to illustrate the need for sinners to place their trust in Him for eternal life.

At the Last Supper, Jesus is speaking to His disciples. He uses bread to represent His body. His purpose is to institute a memorial meal by which they would remember Him. He wants His disciples to proclaim His death in this manner until He returns.

John 6 and the Last Supper are two different events. Using the former to explain the latter distorts the meaning of both. But this is exactly what the Roman Catholic Church has done. Compounding the error, the Church refuses to admit a figurative interpretation of either passage.

A Counterfeit Christ

If Christ taught that the bread and wine *represent* His body and blood, but the Roman Catholic Church teaches that they *become* His body and blood, what difference does it make? If Catholics sincerely believe that Christ is present in the Eucharist, what harm is done?

Much in every way. Each week millions of Catholics line up before altars expecting to receive Christ. They come hoping to obtain heavenly food that will nourish their souls and serve as an antidote against sin [1395, 1405]. The Church promises them that in the Eucharist they will find "the source and summit of the whole Christian life,"[161] "the source of salvation,"[162] "Christ himself"[163] [1324-1327].

But what do Catholics actually receive? Nothing but a thin wafer of unleavened bread—a wafer that does not bring them any closer to eternal salvation. In fact the Mass actually hinders Catholics seeking salvation. Going to Mass is just one more thing that the Church gives the people *to do* in order that they might be saved; one more thing that takes the place of a personal relationship with Christ; one more thing that makes them dependent upon the Church for salvation.

Moreover, the liturgy of the Mass requires Catholics to in effect practice idolatry, to worship the Eucharist "with supreme adoration"[164] [1378-1381]. But what are Catholics actually worshiping? A piece of bread! A cup of wine!

But God forbids the worship of any object, even those which are meant to represent Him:

> You shall not make for yourself an idol, or any likeness of what is in heaven above or on the earth beneath or in the water under the earth. You shall not worship them or serve them....
>
> —Exodus 20:4,5

We can be sure that God will never contradict Himself by entering into material objects such as bread and wine and then ordering people to worship them:

I am the Lord, that is My name;

I will not give My glory to another,

Nor My praise to graven images.

—Isaiah 42:8

❖7

THE BLOOD OF CHRIST

Sunday Morning Mass,
First Anniversary of Joseph's Death

"Let us proclaim the mystery of the faith!"[165] Father Sanchez announced with a strong voice.

As directed by the liturgy, priest and people responded together: "Christ has died. Christ is risen. Christ will come again."

Extending his hands over the consecrated bread and wine before him on the altar, Father Sanchez lifted his eyes to heaven and solemnly commemorated the Lord's death:

> Father, we celebrate the memory of Christ, Your Son. We, Your people and Your ministers, recall His passion, His resurrection from the dead, and His ascension into glory.

The priest then offered to God the Father the sacrifice of His Son:

> From the many gifts You have given us, we offer to You, God of glory and majesty, this holy and perfect sacrifice: the bread of life and the cup of eternal salvation.

With hands still outstretched, he continued:

Look with favor on these offerings and accept them as once You accepted the gifts of Your servant Abel, the sacrifice of Abraham, our father in faith, and the bread and wine offered by Your priest Melchisedech.

Then joining his hands, Father Sanchez bowed low and prayed:

Almighty God, we pray that Your angel may take this sacrifice to Your altar in heaven. Then, as we receive from this altar the sacred body and blood of Your Son, let us be filled with every grace and blessing.

The offering of Christ completed, Father Sanchez prepared to apply the fruits of the sacrifice to Joseph Lorente and the other souls in purgatory. Standing erect, the priest petitioned God:

Remember, Lord, those who have died and gone before us marked with the sign of faith, especially Joseph Lorente. May he, and all those who sleep in Christ, find in Your presence light, happiness, and peace.

After leading the congregation in the Lord's Prayer, Father Sanchez took a large consecrated bread wafer and carefully broke it into three pieces. He dropped the smallest part into the chalice, the cup containing the consecrated wine, quietly saying:

May this mingling of the body and blood of our Lord Jesus Christ bring eternal life to us who receive it. Lord Jesus Christ, with faith in Your love and mercy I eat Your body and drink Your blood. Let it not bring me condemnation, but health in mind and body.

Then aloud the priest proclaimed, "This is the Lamb of God who takes away the sins of the world." As he spoke, he elevated the host before the congregation, adding, "Happy are those who are called to His supper."

The people joined the priest in praying: "Lord, I am not worthy to receive You, but only say the word and I shall be healed."

Again in a soft voice, Father Sanchez addressed God: "May the body of Christ bring me to everlasting life." With those words he ate the remaining pieces of the broken wafer. Then, taking the chalice in his hands, he prayed, "May the blood of Christ bring me to everlasting life," and drank the cup's contents.

Father Sanchez, having received the Eucharist himself, prepared to distribute holy communion to the people. Those in the congregation wishing to receive the Eucharist quietly began forming two lines in front of the altar. Father Sanchez came and stood facing the head of the line. There he raised a consecrated host before each person, saying, "The body of Christ."

Each person responded, "Amen," an affirmation of belief in the real Eucharistic presence of Christ, and received the host on the tongue or in the hand.

When communion was completed, Father Sanchez returned to the altar and began a cleansing ritual. First he collected any crumbs that had fallen from the host and dropped them into the chalice. Next, pouring water into the chalice, he rinsed his fingers of all particles that had adhered to them. He then drank the contents of the cup and dried it with a white linen cloth. In everything Father Sanchez exercised extreme care lest even a fragment of consecrated matter be lost and desecrated. He then locked the remaining consecrated hosts in the church's tabernacle.

"Let us pray," Father Sanchez continued. "Lord, may we who receive this sacrament of salvation be led to the glory of heaven by the prayers of the Virgin Mary. We ask this in the name of Jesus the Lord."[166] Extending his hands toward the congregation, he added, "The Lord be with you."

"And also with you," responded the people.

"May almighty God bless you, the Father, and the Son, and the Holy Spirit," said Father Sanchez, making the sign of the cross.

"Amen."

"The Mass is ended; go in peace."

"Thanks be to God," responded the people.

Father Sanchez bowed, kissed the altar, and exited the sanctuary through a side door. As he did, the congregation began quietly filing out the back doors of the church.

Soon the building was emptied of all but two individuals: Mrs. Lorente praying the Rosary for her husband's soul, and Christ locked within the tabernacle. A red lamp burned in the sanctuary, a silent witness to His bodily presence.

The Continuation of the Cross
[1323, 1330, 1362-1372]

Roman Catholicism teaches that at the Last Supper, after consecrating the bread and wine, Jesus "offered his body and blood to God the Father."[167] Christ then gave His body and blood to the apostles to eat, instructing them, "Do this in remembrance of Me" (Luke 22:19). By those words, according to the Church, Christ ordained His apostles "priests of the new covenant,"[168] and "commanded them and their successors in the priesthood"[169] to continue the offering of the Eucharist [1337]. In this way, Christ—

> ...instituted a new passover, namely the offering of himself by the church through its priests under visible signs, in memory of his own passage from this world to the Father....
>
> —Council of Trent[170]

According to the Roman Catholic Church, the Mass is "a true and proper sacrifice,"[171] not merely a symbolic rite, but the actual "sacrifice of the Eucharist"[172] [1367]. In the offering of the Mass, there is a real victim: the Lord Jesus under the appearance of bread and wine. For this reason the Church refers to consecrated bread wafers as *hosts*, from the Latin word for *victim*. The offering is also real. The priest "...offers the immaculate Victim to God the Father, in the Holy Spirit."[173]

> The sacrificial character of the Eucharist is manifested in the very words of institution: "This is my body which is given for you" and "This cup which is poured out for you is the New Covenant in my blood" (Luke 22:19,20). In the Eucharist Christ gives us the very body which he gave up for us on the cross, the very blood which he "poured out for many for the forgiveness of sins" (Matthew 26:28).
>
> —*Catechism of the Catholic Church*[1365]

Sacrifice is the primary purpose of the Mass. Pope John Paul II wrote: "The Eucharist is above all else a sacrifice. It is the sacrifice of the Redemption and also the sacrifice of the New Covenant."[174]

The Church teaches that the sacrifice of the cross and the Sacrifice of the Mass are "one and the same sacrifice,"[175] for in each, Christ is the offerer and the offering [1367, 1407-1410]. On the cross Christ offered Himself directly to the Father. At the Mass Christ offers Himself to the Father through the hands of the priest [1088]. Nevertheless, Christ is still the principal offerer, for the Church considers the priest to be "another Christ"[176] [1348, 1566]:

> The priest no longer exists as an individual person. He has turned into a sacramental sign, the representative of Christ, present upon the altar and offering himself in sacrifice. Christ is the real priest; it is he who consecrates bread into his body and wine into his blood and offers both as a sacrificial gift to the heavenly Father.
>
> —*Dogmatic Theology for the Laity*[177]

According to the Church, Christ instituted the Mass in order to "perpetuate the sacrifice of the Cross throughout the ages until he should come again"[178] [1323, 1382]. Each Mass would be the "sacramental renewal"[179] of the cross with a threefold purpose [1366]:

> ...in order to leave to his beloved spouse the church a visible sacrifice (as human nature requires), by which that bloody sacrifice carried out on the cross should be represented, its memory persist until the end of time, and its saving power be applied to the forgiveness of the sins which we daily commit....
>
> —Council of Trent[180]

Here the Church describes three relationships between the Mass and the cross. To understand the sacrificial nature of the Mass, it is necessary to examine each of these relationships separately.

Each Mass Presents Again the Sacrifice of the Cross
[1330, 1354, 1357]

In explaining the Last Supper, Roman Catholicism emphasizes that Christ consecrated the bread and wine *separately*. First He changed the bread; then He changed the wine. The priest observes this same order at the Mass:

> For the blood, separately consecrated, serves to place before the eyes of all, in a more forcible manner, the Passion of our Lord, His death, and the nature of His sufferings.
>
> —*The Roman Catechism*[181]

For the same reason, the bread and wine *remain separate* at the Mass:

> ...the eucharistic species under which He is present symbolize the actual separation of His body and blood. Thus the commemorative representation of His death, which actually took

place on Calvary, is repeated in every sacrifice of
the altar, seeing that Jesus Christ is symbolically
shown by separate symbols to be in a state of
victimhood.

—*Mediator Dei*[182]

Consequently, coinciding with the consecration of
the bread and wine is the *immolation* of Christ:

For in the sacrifice of the Mass Our Lord is
immolated when "he begins to be present sacramentally as the spiritual food of the faithful
under the appearances of bread and wine."

—Second Vatican Council[183]

Immolation is the sacrificial killing of a victim. The
Church says, however, that at the Mass Christ does not
suffer, pour out His blood, or die. Rather, Christ experiences an "unbloody immolation"[184] by which He becomes
sacramentally present under the appearances of bread
and wine, a "most holy victim"[185] [1085, 1353, 1362, 1364, 1367,
1383, 1409, 1545].

Roman Catholicism teaches that once Christ is present in a state of victimhood upon the altar, He then
offers Himself to God the Father by the hands of the
priest and in union with the Church [1354, 1357]:

The celebration of the Eucharist is the action
of Christ Himself and the Church; in it Christ the
Lord, by the ministry of a priest, offers Himself,
substantially present under the forms of bread
and wine, to God the Father....

—The Code of Canon Law[186]

This re-presentation of Christ to the Father occurs
at the Mass when the priest prays:

Father...we offer to you, God of glory and
majesty, this holy and perfect sacrifice: the bread
of life and the cup of eternal salvation. Look with

favor on these offerings and accept them....
Almighty God, we pray that your angel may take
this sacrifice to your altar in heaven. Then, as we
receive from this altar the sacred body and blood
of your Son, let us be filled with every grace and
blessing.

—The Memorial Prayer[187]

The Church, therefore, considers the Mass to be a
true sacrifice [1365]:

The august sacrifice of the altar, then, is no
mere empty commemoration of the passion and
death of Jesus Christ, but a true and proper act of
sacrifice, whereby the High Priest by an unbloody
immolation offers Himself a most acceptable victim to the Eternal Father, as He did upon the
cross.

—*Mediator Dei*[188]

To help the faithful remember the connection
between the sacrifice of the cross and the Sacrifice of the
Mass, the Church requires that at every Mass "a cross,
easily visible to the people, should be on the altar or
somewhere not far from it."[189]

Each Mass Is a Memorial of the Sacrifice of the Cross [610-611, 1356-1358, 1362-1372]

According to the Church, each Mass—

... reminds us that there is no salvation except
in the cross of our Lord Jesus Christ and that
God Himself wishes that there should be a continuation of this sacrifice....

—*Mediator Dei*[190]

The Mass "celebrates the memorial of Christ, calling to mind especially his blessed passion, his glorious
resurrection and his ascent to heaven."[191] This is expressed in several ways at the Mass. One example is the

Memorial Acclamation: "Christ has died. Christ is risen. Christ will come again."[192]

Each Mass Applies the Saving Power of the Sacrifice of the Cross [1366, 1407, 1416, 1566]

Roman Catholicism teaches that Christ instituted the Eucharist—

> ...that the Church might have a perpetual Sacrifice, by which our sins might be expiated, and our heavenly Father, oftentimes grievously offended by our crimes, might be turned away from wrath to mercy, from the severity of just chastisement to clemency.
>
> —*The Roman Catechism*[193]

According to Roman Catholic belief, every time a priest offers the Mass, the wrath of God against sin is soothed. The Mass, even as the cross itself, is a propitiatory or appeasing sacrifice:

> In this divine sacrifice which is performed in the mass, the very same Christ is contained and offered in bloodless manner who made a bloody sacrifice of himself once for all on the cross. Hence the holy council teaches that this is a truly propitiatory sacrifice, and brings it about that if we approach God with sincere hearts and upright faith, and with awe and reverence, *we receive mercy and find grace to help in time of need* (Hebrews 4:16). For the Lord is appeased by this offering, he gives the gracious gift of repentance, he absolves even enormous offenses and sins.
>
> —Council of Trent[194]

Appeasement is the Godward effect of the Sacrifice of the Mass. The manward effect is expiation, the freeing of the sinner from the punishment of sin [1371, 1394, 1416]:

> The body of Christ we receive in Holy Communion "is given up for us," and the blood we

drink "shed for the many for the forgiveness of sins." For this reason the Eucharist cannot unite us to Christ without at the same time cleansing us from past sins....

—*Catechism of the Catholic Church*[1393]

The Sacrifice of the Mass benefits both the living and the dead [1371, 1414, 1689]:

Therefore it is quite properly offered according to apostolic tradition not only for the sins, penalties, satisfactions and other needs of the faithful who are living, but also for those who have died in Christ but are not yet fully cleansed.

—Council of Trent[195]

In the words of the new *Catechism*:

As sacrifice, the Eucharist is also offered in reparation for the sins of the living and the dead and to obtain spiritual or temporal benefits from God.

—*Catechism of the Catholic Church*[1414]

The Church teaches that the benefits of the sacrifice of the cross "are received in the fullest measure"[196] through the sacrifice of the Mass:

Hence this usual prayer of the Church: *As often as the commemoration of this victim is celebrated, so often is the work of our salvation being done*; that is to say, through this unbloody Sacrifice flow to us the most plenteous fruits of that bloody victim.

—*The Roman Catechism*[197]

The belief that the Sacrifice of the Mass applies the power of the cross is expressed in the Liturgy of the Eucharist. The priest asks God: "Look with favor on your Church's offering, and see the Victim whose death has reconciled us to yourself."[198] He then adds, "Lord, may this sacrifice, which has made our peace with you, advance the peace and salvation of all the world."[199]

A BIBLICAL RESPONSE

The concept of an ongoing sacrifice for sins is foreign to biblical Christianity. The Scriptures teach that "there is no longer any offering for sin" (Hebrews 10:18). Christ has reconciled us to God "having made peace through the blood of His cross" (Colossians 1:20). Contrary to Roman Catholic doctrine, the Bible teaches that:

- Christ asked to be *remembered,* not sacrificed.
- Christ's work of *redemption* is finished, not continuing.
- Christ made *every* believer a priest, not a select few.

Christ Asked to Be Remembered, Not Sacrificed

At the Last Supper the Lord Jesus instructed His disciples, "Do this in remembrance of Me" (Luke 22:19). The word translated "remembrance" means a *calling to mind.* The Lord wanted His disciples to call to mind His work of salvation on the cross. With bread and wine before them, symbols of His body and blood, they were to "proclaim the Lord's death until He comes" (1 Corinthians 11:26). The meeting that Christians would come to call the "breaking of bread" (Acts 2:42) and the "Lord's Supper" (1 Corinthians 11:20) would be a memorial of His death.

The Scriptures, however, never refer to the Last Supper (the Passover meal eaten on the night of Christ's betrayal) or to the Lord's Supper (the remembrance meal celebrated by Christians) as a sacrifice. Nevertheless, Roman Catholic theologians consider both the Last Supper and the Lord's Supper to be real sacrifices. We will consider six arguments that they put forth from Scripture for the Church's position:

- Foretold by Malachi
  Malachi prophesied that there would be sacrifice in every place (Malachi 1:11).

- Foretold by Jesus
  Jesus prophesied that there would be sacrifice in every place (John 4:21).

- Order of Melchizedek
  Jesus offered bread and wine as a priest according to the order of Melchizedek (Psalm 110:4).

- The Present Tense
  Jesus spoke of His sacrifice in the present tense at the Last Supper (Luke 22:19,20).

- Sacrifice of the New Covenant
  Christ our Passover is the sacrifice of the New Covenant (1 Corinthians 5:7).

- Sacrifice of the Altar
  Paul spoke of the Lord's Supper as a sacrifice of the altar (1 Corinthians 10:21).

Foretold by Malachi

The Roman Catholic Church says that Malachi prophesied that one day all nations would offer sacrifices. The Catholic Bible reads:

> From the rising of the sun, even to its setting, my name is great among the nations;
>
> And everywhere they bring sacrifice to my name, and a pure offering....
>
> —Malachi 1:11 NAB

The Roman Catholic Church teaches that the Eucharist is the fulfillment of Malachi's prophecy [1350, 2643]. The Mass—

> ...is none other than that clean oblation that can be soiled by no unworthiness or evil on the part of those offering, which the Lord foretold

through Malachy as being offered in purity in every place to his name, which would be great among the nations.

—Council of Trent[200]

The Roman Catholic translation and interpretation of Malachi 1:11 are both questionable. The verse does not use the common Hebrew word for sacrifice. In fact, the Hebrew word translated "sacrifice" in the Catholic Bible occurs only in Malachi 1:11 in the entire Scriptures. As with many rare words, its translation is uncertain. It is known that the word is derived from a root meaning "to cause to rise up in smoke."[201] The translators of leading non-Catholic Bibles understand the word to refer to *incense*: "...in every place incense is going to be offered...." (Malachi 1:11). The Septuagint, an ancient Greek translation of the Hebrew Scriptures, also renders the word "incense."

Additionally, the "pure offering" referred to by Malachi does not necessarily refer to a sacrifice for sin. Elsewhere in the Old Testament, the word translated "offering" refers to the grain offering, a voluntary act of gratitude, not an atoning sacrifice for sin (Leviticus 6:14-23).

Finally, Malachi speaks of a time when the Lord's "name will be great among the nations" (Malachi 1:11). That is certainly not the case at present. Today the name of Christ is the object of scorn and ridicule. The context of Malachi's prophesy makes it clear that he is referring to events still in the future that will follow the second coming of Christ.

Incidentally, the Church's description above of the Mass as "that clean oblation that can be soiled by no unworthiness or evil on the part of those offering"[202] expresses another erroneous Roman Catholic belief. The Church teaches that the sacrifice of the Mass is holy and acceptable to God regardless of the spiritual condition of the priest who offers it [1128].[203] In other words, if a properly ordained priest offers the Mass, the sacrifice is holy to the Lord even if the priest offering it is personally practicing the vilest of sins. The Bible, on the other hand, teaches that "the sacrifice of the wicked is an abomination to the Lord..." (Proverbs 15:8).

Foretold by Jesus

Roman Catholic scholars claim that Jesus foretold the coming of the Sacrifice of the Mass while speaking to a woman of Samaria:

> The woman said to Him, "...Our fathers worshiped in this mountain [Mount Gerizim], and you people say that in Jerusalem is the place where men ought to worship." Jesus said to her, "Woman, believe Me, an hour is coming when neither in this mountain nor in Jerusalem shall you worship the Father."
>
> —John 4:19-21

Catholic author Father Matthias Premm comments:

> Thus, not only in Jerusalem or on Mt. Gerizim, but all over the earth ("From the rising of the sun to its setting," says Malachias) there will be sacrifice.
>
> —*Dogmatic Theology for the Laity*[204]

Jesus, however, did not say there would be *sacrifice* throughout the world; He said there would be *worship* (John 4:21). In the verses that follow He describes that worship as being "in spirit and truth" (John 4:23). He makes no mention of atoning sacrifices.

Order of Melchizedek

During the Mass the priest asks God to look with favor on the consecrated bread and wine and accept them even as He did "the bread and wine offered by your priest Melchisedech."[205] The Church teaches that in Genesis 14:18 Melchizedek offered bread and wine to God. This offering, says the Church, prefigured the offering of Christ's body and blood under the appearances of bread and wine at the Last Supper [1333, 1350, 1544]. For this reason, says the Church, Christ is called in Scripture "a priest forever according to the order of Melchizedek" (Psalm 110:4).

Scripture, however, never says that Melchizedek *offered* bread and wine. The passage to which the Church is referring, Genesis 14:13-24, is an account of the victorious return of Abraham and his troops from a great battle. As they approached Jerusalem, Melchizedek came out to greet Abraham:

> And Melchizedek king of Salem brought out bread and wine; now he was a priest of God Most High. And he blessed him and said,
>
> "Blessed be Abram of God Most High,
> Possessor of heaven and earth;
> And blessed be God Most High,
> Who has delivered your enemies into your hand."
>
> —Genesis 14:18-20

The most natural interpretation of this event is that Melchizedek came out to praise God and bless Abraham for the victory. The bread and wine were nourishment for Abraham's weary troops. There is no mention of any sacrifice.

Why then is the Lord Jesus called "a priest forever according to the order of Melchizedek" (Psalm 110:4)? The biblical reason is that both Christ and Melchizedek are presented in Scripture as being immortal.

From a Jewish point of view, Melchizedek is like a man who was never born and never died. In Genesis 14 he comes on the scene without a proper Jewish introduction. There is no mention of his family lineage or even his father's or mother's name. It is as if he had always lived. Melchizedek interacts with Abraham and then departs. Since we never learn of his death, it appears as if he never dies. Scripture says of Melchizedek:

> Without father, without mother, without ge-
> nealogy, having neither beginning of days nor
> end of life, but made like the Son of God, he
> abides a priest perpetually.
>
> —Hebrews 7:3

An immortal life is the scriptural connection between Jesus and Melchizedek. Both are priests having
"neither beginning of days nor end of life" (Hebrews
7:3). Jesus is therefore called "a priest forever according
to the order of Melchizedek" (Psalm 110:4; Hebrews 5:6;
7:17). Neither Jesus nor Melchizedek are said to have
sacrificially offered bread and wine.

The Present Tense

Roman Catholic scholars say that at the Last Supper
Christ made it clear by the words of institution that He
was offering a sacrifice that very night [1365]. The Lord
did not simply say, "This is My body" (Matthew 26:26)
and "This is My blood" (Matthew 26:28), but added the
words "which is given for you" (Luke 22:19) and "which is
poured out for you" (Luke 22:20). Father A. Tanquerey
explains how these phrases support the Roman Catholic
position:

> But these words of themselves mean that the
> body and blood of Christ was offered as a true
> sacrifice.... The same words signify *the actual
> oblation at the Supper* itself. In the Greek the
> present tense is employed: *is given, is handed over,
> is poured forth;* the blood of Christ is said to be
> poured forth *in the chalice,* that is, as it is in the
> chalice, not as it will be on the cross.
>
> *A Manual of Dogmatic Theology*[206]

In other words, Catholic scholars are arguing that
since Christ spoke of His sacrifice at the Last Supper in

the *present* tense, then a sacrifice was occurring at that very instant. The Last Supper, therefore, was a true sacrifice. And since the Last Supper was the first Mass, the Mass today is also a sacrifice.

This interpretation ignores the fact that the phrases "which is given" (Luke 22:19) and "which is poured out" (Luke 22:20) are translations of Greek participles. A participle in the present tense does not necessarily refer to an event in present time: "The time relations of the participle do not belong to its tense, but to the sense of the context."[207]

In context, Jesus is speaking of His death the next day. He uses the present participle to vividly communicate the certainty of that yet *future* event. Greek allows for this futuristic meaning of the present tense.[208] Even the translators of the Catholic *New American Bible* recognize that though Jesus used the present tense at the Last Supper, He was speaking of a future event:

> Then, taking bread and giving thanks, he broke it and gave it to them, saying: "This is my body *to be given* for you. Do this as a remembrance of me." He did the same with the cup after eating, saying as he did so: "This cup is the new covenant in my blood, which *will be shed* for you."
>
> —Luke 22:19,20 NAB, emphasis added

Jesus did not pour out His blood at the Last Supper, but on the cross. It is ridiculous to speak of His blood being "poured forth in the chalice"[209] for the forgiveness of sins.

Sacrifice of the New Covenant

The Last Supper was held on the Feast of the Passover, or Pasch. In accordance with the law of Moses, Christ and His disciples observed the occasion by slaying, roasting, and eating a lamb (Exodus 12). The Roman Catholic Church says that Christ, having celebrated the old Passover, then "...instituted a new passover, namely the offering of himself by the church through its priest under visible signs..."[210] [1339-1340]. The Church claims that this new Passover sacrifice furthers our redemption [1068, 1364, 1405]:

> As often as the sacrifice of the cross by which "Christ our Pasch is sacrificed" (1 Corinthians 5:7) is celebrated on the altar, the work of our redemption is carried out.
>
> —Second Vatican Council[211]

Once again the Church goes beyond what Scripture teaches. Nowhere does the Bible state that the sacrifice of the new covenant is the Last Supper, the Lord's Supper, or the Mass. The only atoning sacrifice of the new covenant is the cross, the finished redemptive work of Christ. That is why when Paul wrote that "Christ our Passover also has been sacrificed" (1 Corinthians 5:7), he put the verb in a form expressing the action as an event in past time.[212] Christ is not *being* sacrificed; He *has been* sacrificed on the cross.

Sacrifice of the Altar

Paul wrote to the Corinthians:

> You cannot drink the cup of the Lord and the cup of demons; you cannot partake of the table of the Lord and the table of demons.
>
> —1 Corinthians 10:21

The Roman Catholic Church claims that this verse shows that Paul understood the Lord's Supper to be a sacrifice.

> And the apostle Paul indicates the same clearly enough in writing to the Corinthians, when he says that those contaminated by sharing in the table of demons cannot be sharers in the table of the Lord, by "table" meaning "altar" in both places.
>
> —Council of Trent[213]

The Church wishes to substitute the word "table" here with the word "altar," because altars are for sacrifices, while tables are for meals. This change would strengthen the Church's claim that the first Christians understood the Lord's Supper to be a sacrifice. Such a substitution, however, cannot be justified.

Moreover, in 1 Corinthians 10:21, Paul used the word "table" with good reason. Partaking in "the table of demons" (1 Corinthians 10:21) is a reference to a practice within Hellenistic religion in which devotees would partake in cultic meals: "The participant believed that he was sitting at . . . the god's table and that through the meal he entered into fellowship with the deity."[214] Paul was warning the Corinthian Christians that they could not participate in these pagan cultic meals and "partake of the table of the Lord" (1 Corinthians 10:21). He spoke of the "table of the Lord" (1 Corinthians 10:21) because the early Christians understood the Lord's Supper to be a fellowship meal in remembrance of Christ, not a sacrifice.

Christ's Work of Redemption Is Completely Finished

Just before the Lord Jesus gave up His spirit upon the cross, He cried out, "It is finished!" (John 19:30). His sacrificial work of redemption was done.

The Greek verb in John 19:30 is in the *perfect tense*. "It implies a process, but views that process as having reached its consummation and existing in a finished state."[215] In other words, the saving work of Christ was completed on the cross and continues in a state of completion. The verse can be translated: "It has been finished and stands complete" (John 19:30).[216]

Roman Catholicism misrepresents the *finished* work of Christ on the cross by saying that the sacrifice of the cross is *continued* in the Mass. The Church claims that " . . . God Himself wishes that there should be a continuation of the sacrifice. . . ."[217] And so Christ " . . . has offered and continues to offer Himself as a victim for our sins...."[218] According to Roman Catholic theology, at over 120 million Masses each year four things occur.[219]

An Immolation

As we have seen, the Church teaches that at each Mass, through the words and actions of the priest, Christ is immolated—made present in His victimhood upon the altar under the appearance of bread and wine. This, says the Church, is "no mere empty commemoration of the passion and death of Jesus Christ, but a true and proper act of sacrifice...an unbloody immolation...a most acceptable victim...."[220] This doctrine terribly misrepresents the present resurrected and glorified state of the Lord Jesus Christ. The Scriptures teach that "Christ, having been raised from the dead, is never to die again; death no longer is master over Him" (Romans 6:9). Christ manifests Himself as "the living One; and I was dead, and behold, I am alive forevermore...." (Revelation 1:18). He then adds, "...and I have the keys of death and of Hades" (Revelation 1:18). Shall the living One who holds all power over death be continually presented in His death? And that by those for whom He died? Clearly not. Furthermore, the Bible makes no mention of an unbloody immolation. Scripture teaches that "without shedding of blood there is no forgiveness" (Hebrews 9:22). If there is no blood, there is no propitiation, "for it is the blood by reason of the life that makes atonement" (Leviticus 17:11).

A Re-Presentation

The Church teaches that at each Mass, Christ "...offers Himself a most acceptable victim to the Eternal Father, as He did upon the cross."[221] In the *Eucharistic Prayer* the priest petitions God, "Look with favor on your Church's offering, and see the Victim whose death has reconciled us to yourself."[222] The Church explains that the priest is praying that "...the Body and Blood of

Christ may be the acceptable sacrifice which brings salvation to the whole world."[223]

This re-presentation of Christ in His victimhood, allegedly occurring millions of times each year at the Mass, misrepresents the *accepted* work of Christ. The Bible teaches that Christ presented the sacrifice of His life to the Father only once. Upon His death the Lord Jesus passed "through the greater and more perfect tabernacle" (Hebrews 9:11). His purpose was "to appear in the presence of God for us" (Hebrews 9:24). Jesus entered the heavenly throne room of God "not through the blood of goats and calves, but through His own blood" (Hebrews 9:12). His purpose was "to make propitiation for the sins of the people" (Hebrews 2:17). He "entered the holy place once for all, having obtained eternal redemption" (Hebrews 9:12).

The Father accepted the perfect sacrifice of Christ without reservation. "Worthy is the Lamb that was slain!" (Revelation 5:12) shall be the praise of myriads of angels in heaven for all eternity.

On earth the Father signaled His acceptance of Christ's work by dramatically removing one of the principal symbols of the separation that sin had caused between God and man. In the Jewish temple, as instructed by God in the Old Testament, a thick curtain formed a wall between the area in which the Aaronic priesthood could minister and the Holy of Holies, where God dwelt. The Scriptures record that as Christ yielded up His spirit, "Behold, the veil of the temple was torn in two from top to bottom" (Matthew 27:51). This removal of the barrier between God and man signaled that Christ's work of redemption had been accepted.

The greatest manifestation of the Father's acceptance of Christ's sacrifice came three days later. The Bible says that Jesus "was raised because of our justification" (Romans 4:25). Christ's offering for sin had been accepted (1 Corinthians 15:17,20).

The Scriptures further teach, speaking of Christ: "When He had made purification of sins, He sat down at the right hand of the Majesty on high" (Hebrews 1:3). He sat down because His work was finished. There He remains until a future day: "He, having offered one sacrifice for sins for all time, sat down at the right hand of God, waiting from that time onward until His enemies be made a footstool for His feet" (Hebrews 10:12,13).

The Roman Catholic Mass distorts these truths by in effect calling Christ off His throne tens of thousands of times each day to reenter the Holy Place and re-present Himself in His victimhood to the Father. There Christ supposedly stands while a priest on earth petitions God: "Look with favor on these offerings and accept them...."[224] This constant re-presentation is a denial of the finished and accepted work of Christ.

An Appeasement

Roman Catholicism teaches that the Sacrifice of the Mass is a "truly propitiatory sacrifice"[225] of "infinite value":[226]

> ...it is quite properly offered according to apostolic tradition not only for the sins, penalties, satisfactions and other needs of the faithful who are living, but also for those who have died in Christ but are not yet fully cleansed.
>
> —Council of Trent[227]

Through each Mass, says the Roman Catholic Church, God's anger against sin is pacified [1371, 1414]:

> ...this is a truly propitiatory sacrifice.... For the Lord is appeased by this offering, he gives the gracious gift of repentance, he absolves even enormous offenses and sins.
>
> —Council of Trent[228]

To the contrary, the Lord is offended by the offering of the Sacrifice of the Mass. God has already told us that

He is fully satisfied with the once-for-all offering of Christ on the cross: "In Him we have redemption through His blood, the forgiveness of our trespasses, according to the riches of His grace" (Ephesians 1:7). The "Holy Spirit also bears witness to us...saying...their sins and their lawless deeds I will remember no more" (Hebrews 10:15,17). The conclusion naturally follows: "Now where there is forgiveness of these things, there is no longer any offering for sin" (Hebrews 10:18). For this reason Scripture repeatedly calls the cross the "once-for-all" offering of Christ (Hebrews 7:27; 9:12,26,28; 10:10; Romans 6:10; 1 Peter 3:18). To continue to try to appease God with an ongoing sacrifice is an act of unbelief.

An Application

Finally, Roman Catholicism teaches that at each Mass the blessings of Calvary are meted out to Catholics:

> The august sacrifice of the altar is, as it were, the supreme instrument whereby the merits won by the divine Redeemer upon the cross are distributed to the faithful....
> —*Mediator Dei*[229]

Since the merits of the cross are primarily available through the Mass, the Church urges priests to celebrate the Eucharist, "the sacrament of redemption,"[1846] frequently, daily if possible. Priests are to do this with the salvation of the world in view:

> We recommend that they celebrate Mass daily in a worthy and devout fashion, so that they themselves and the rest of the faithful may enjoy the benefits that flow in such abundance from the Sacrifice of the Cross. In doing so, they will also be making a great contribution toward the salvation of mankind.
> —*Mysterium Fidei*[230]

The Mystical Mystery of the Mass

If you are finding the Mass difficult to understand, take comfort in knowing that you are not alone. According to the Church, it is an "awesome mystery."[231] Even most Catholics don't understand it.

This, of course, makes explaining what is wrong with the Mass to a Catholic all the more difficult. Before trying to do so, you may need to review with your Catholic friend what the Church actually teaches. A simple catechism, obtainable at any Catholic bookstore, would be a useful aid.

Since the Mass is a mystery, speaking with informed Catholics can be even more frustrating. If, however, you avoid using certain terms, you may be able to get somewhere. Here are a few tips.

When speaking about Christ as the Eucharist, you can say that He is *truly*, *really*, *wholly*, and *continuously* present. But if you say that He is *physically* present, your Catholic friend may conclude, "You just don't understand." A knowledgeable Catholic would inform you that to say that Christ is physically present would be to imply that He is *locally* present, which He is not.[232] The Church says He is *substantially* present. That is why though Christ is present, He doesn't appear to be present. He is there in a *unique* way. So unique, says the Church, that there is no parallel in nature. This, of course, makes it difficult for anyone to understand the Eucharist (or criticize it, for that matter).

Additionally, don't say that Christ is *resacrificed* at the Mass or that the Mass is a *repetition* of the cross. You

And again [1405]:

> In the mystery of the eucharistic sacrifice, in which priests fulfil their principal function, the work of our redemption is continually carried out.
> —Second Vatican Council[234]

Pope Pius XII wrote that Christ—

> ...daily offers Himself upon our altars for

can say that the Mass is a *repetition* of the Last Supper, but not of the cross. The Church says that the Mass *renews* and *re-presents* the cross. It doesn't *repeat* it, for, says the Church, the Mass *is* the cross. Only the *manner* in which it is offered is different (and the time, we might add, by about 2000 years!). Furthermore, though each individual offering of the Mass is said to appease God, the Church emphatically insists that it is not *another* sacrifice. Every Mass, says the Church, is the once-for-all offering of the cross. Christ's Paschal mystery is "the unique event of history which does not pass away," but "transcends all times while being made present in them all."[1085]

One more thing: Never say that Christ *dies* at the Mass. According to the Church, Christ doesn't die; He is *immolated*. At the consecration, Christ is presented *in His death*, or *in a state of victimhood*, but He doesn't die to get there. How this is possible is not explained, but somehow Christ doesn't die at the Mass. Christ does not suffer or die at the Mass for it is an *unbloody* sacrifice. Though the Church teaches that the priest changes the wine into Christ's *blood* and offers it to the Father, the Mass is still somehow an *unbloody* sacrifice!

Watch your terms, and you will avoid being classified as one more uncomprehending faultfinder. And if you honestly don't understand, just remember that even the best of Roman Catholic scholars acknowledge that the Mass is a "mystical reality,"[233] whose meaning is apparent neither to the senses nor to the intellect.

our redemption, that we may be rescued from eternal damnation and admitted into the company of the elect.

—*Mediator Dei*[235]

This relationship between the work of redemption and the Mass is also expressed in the Liturgy of the Eucharist. The priest prays over the gifts:

> May we celebrate these sacred rites worthily,
> O Lord, for each offering of this memorial sacri-
> fice carries on the work of our redemption.
>
> —*Roman Missal*[236]

All of this stands in contradiction to the Bible. Scripture teaches that God freely and immediately bestows upon each true believer "every spiritual blessing in the heavenly places" (Ephesians 1:3). These He lavishes upon His children in Christ (Ephesians 1:7,8). Nowhere does God require a Christian to participate in an ongoing sacrifice to obtain his or her blessings in Christ. The Roman Catholic Church's teaching that the Sacrifice of the Mass is "the supreme instrument whereby the merits won by the divine Redeemer upon the cross are distributed to the faithful"[237] is just one more way in which the Church makes people dependent upon it for the blessings of God.

Christ Made Every Believer a Priest

Since Christians have no need of an ongoing sacrifice for sin, they have no need of a sacrificing priesthood such as found in Roman Catholicism. In fact, they have no need of another man to function as their priest at all, for, according to the Bible, every believer is a priest unto God. In Revelation 1:6, John writes that Christ has made all Christians to be a kingdom of priests (see also Revelation 5:10; 20:6). Peter writes that every true believer is a member of a "royal priesthood" (1 Peter 2:9). All believers are "being built up as a spiritual house for a holy priesthood, to offer up spiritual sacrifices" (1 Peter 2:5). These sacrifices are a yielded life (Romans 12:1), financial support of Christian ministry (Philippians 4:18), and "praise to God" (Hebrews 13:15), but not an ongoing sacrifice for sin.

The Roman Catholic Church recognizes that the Bible speaks of a *general* or *common* priesthood of the faithful [941, 1141, 1546, 1591].[238] The Church teaches that Catholics enter into it through baptism [784, 1268]. This common priesthood qualifies a person to do such things as participate in the Eucharist, read the Word of God in the liturgical assembly, receive the sacraments, pray, and perform good works [901-903, 1657].

In addition to the general priesthood, the Church teaches that there is the *ministerial* or *hierarchical* priesthood [1142, 1547, 1592].[239] This priesthood is open only to men [1577, 1598]. Normally in the Latin Church, candidates must be unmarried and committed to living a celibate life [1599]. The ministerial priesthood is entered into through the laying on of hands by a bishop in the sacrament of ordination, or *Holy Orders* [1573, 1597]. In this way, men "...are signed with a special character and so are configured to Christ the priest in such a way that they are able to act in the person of Christ the head"[240] [1548]. Through ordination they receive the "...power to consecrate and offer the true body and blood of the Lord, and to forgive or retain sins..."[241] [1411, 1461, 1566]. Their appointment to the ministerial priesthood is permanent: "...once a man is ordained a priest, his priesthood, like Christ's 'in the line of Melchizedek,' is forever (Hebrews 5, 6, 7)"[242] [1582]. This priesthood, claims the Church, was established by the Lord at the Last Supper when He said, "Do this in remembrance of Me" (Luke 22:19) [611, 1337].

The Roman Catholic Church cannot establish any of these assertions from Scripture. The New Testament makes no distinction between a *common* and a *hierarchical* priesthood. The claim that Roman Catholic priests share in the priesthood of Melchizedek is unjustified. The priesthood of Melchizedek, as we have seen, is based upon the "power of an indestructible life" (Hebrews 7:16). In that Roman Catholic priests grow old and die even as the rest of us, they fail to qualify. Finally, the Church's primary proof-text for the ordained priesthood, "Do this in remembrance of Me" (Luke 22:19), says nothing about ordination or the priesthood.

Determined to find biblical support, some Roman Catholic scholars argue that the New Testament office of *elder* and the Roman Catholic *priesthood* are one and the same. This view has even found its way into some Roman Catholic translations of the Bible. For example:

> And when they had ordained to them priests in every church...they commended them to the Lord....
> —Acts 14:22 Douay Rheims

> For this cause I left thee in Crete, that thou shouldest...ordain priests in every city, as I also appointed thee:
> —Titus 1:5 Douay Rheims

> Is any man sick among you? Let him bring in the priests of the church....
> —James 5:14 Douay Rheims

In each of these verses the word translated "priests" is the plural form of the Greek word *presbuteros*, meaning *older man* or *elder*. The Scriptures teach that the apostles "appointed elders...in every church" (Acts 14:23), not priests. Titus was to "appoint elders in every city" (Titus 1:5), not priests. And sick Christians were to "call for the elders of the church" (James 5:14), not the local priest. The New Testament word for priest is *hiereus*. It is not found in any of the three passages quoted above from the Catholic Douay Rheims Bible.[243]

A Biblical Verdict

The desire for an ongoing sacrifice can be traced back to New Testament times. Most of the first Christians were Jews who had been accustomed to having a daily sacrificial offering and everything that went with it: the altar, the temple, rituals, feast days, a sacrificing priesthood, and a high priest. New believers found it extremely difficult to leave Judaism. When they did, their families and friends ostracized them and persecuted them as apostates.

Not all of the first Jewish converts who left Judaism and joined the Christian community were steadfast in their decision. Some began to consider going back to Judaism. Back to the law. Back to the temple. Back to the sacrificial offerings.

The New Testament letter to the Hebrews was written to help these weak and wavering Jewish Christians (Hebrews 12:12). The book reminds the readers that Christians have need of no further sacrifice: "We have been sanctified through the offering of the body of Jesus Christ once for all" (Hebrews 10:10). It encourages doubting Christians to "hold fast the confession of our hope without wavering, for He who promised is faithful" (Hebrews 10:23). It exhorts them not to "throw away" their confidence (Hebrews 10:35), to have "endurance" (Hebrews 10:36), and to "live by faith" (Hebrews 10:38). The writer expresses confidence that these Christians will "have faith to the preserving of the soul" (Hebrews 10:39). He describes that faith as "...the assurance of things hoped for, the conviction of things not seen" (Hebrews 11:1).

The book of Hebrews also issues a solemn warning: "Take care, brethren, lest there should be in any one of you an evil, unbelieving heart, in falling away from the living God" (Hebrews 3:12). The writer warns the readers not to "shrink back to destruction" (Hebrews 10:39), for going back to Judaism and the sacrifices of the temple would be an act of unbelief. It would be a rejection of Christ and His finished work of salvation on the cross.

Some had already gone back (Hebrews 6:4-6). As they saw it, one sacrifice for all time was just not enough. Gathering around mere bread and wine to remember Christ seemed meaningless. Christianity appeared to offer them nothing but *unseen* promises: a heavenly calling (Hebrews 3:1), a heavenly tabernacle (Hebrews 9:23,24), a heavenly high priest (Hebrews 8:1,2), and a heavenly country (Hebrews 11:16). They needed a religion they could *see*: a visible temple, a visible priesthood, and a visible sacrifice. And so they went back to Judaism, which they thought had so much to offer them.

Roman Catholicism holds a similar attraction today for those who are religiously minded, but have not found rest in the finished work of Christ. It offers them a religion that they can *see*. The Church describes itself as "a visible organization"[244] and a "visible society"[245] with a "visible social structure"[246] [771]. At its head is the Pope, the "visible head of the whole church."[247] Each sacrament is a "visible form of invisible grace."[248] These are administered by a "visible and external priesthood,"[249] whose primary duties are to forgive sins and offer the Mass, "a visible sacrifice (as human nature requires)"[250] [1366].

The Mass: Error Versus Truth

The Catholic Church Teaches	The Bible Teaches
1. The Last Supper was a real sacrifice in which Christ's blood was poured out for our sins in the cup [610-611, 621, 1339].	The Last Supper was a Passover meal. Christ's blood was poured out for our sins at the cross (1 Peter 2:24).
2. The bread and wine become the real body and blood of Christ [1373-1377].	The bread and wine are symbols of the body and blood of Christ (1 Corinthians 11:23-25).
3. Christ's body and blood exist wholly and entirely in every fragment of consecrated bread and wine in every Roman Catholic church around the world [1374, 1377].	Christ is bodily present in heaven (Hebrews 10:12,13).
4. The consecrated bread and wine are heavenly food which help one to attain to eternal life [1392, 1405, 1419].	The bread and wine are symbols which help one to remember Christ (Luke 22:19).
5. God desires that consecrated bread and wine be worshiped as divine [1378-1381].	God forbids the worship of any object, even those intended to represent Him (Exodus 20:4,5; Isaiah 42:8).
6. Christ has ordained certain men to a ministerial priesthood to perpetuate the sacrifice of the cross [1142, 1547, 1577].	Christ has ordained every believer to a holy and royal priesthood to offer spiritual sacrifices, the praise of their lips, and lives yielded to God (1 Peter 2:5-10; Hebrews 13:15; Romans 12:1).

7. The Sacrifice of the Mass is the sacrifice of the cross [1085, 1365-1367]. Only the manner in which it is offered is different [1367].

The sacrifice of the cross was a historical event. It occurred once, approximately 2000 years ago, outside Jerusalem (Mark 15:21-41).

8. The sacrifice of the cross is perpetuated in the Sacrifice of the Mass [1323, 1382].

The sacrifice of the cross is finished (John 19:30).

9. The Mass makes present Christ in His death and victimhood [1353, 1362, 1364, 1367, 1409].

Christ should not be presented in His death and victimhood, for He has risen and is "alive forevermore" (Revelation 1:17,18; Romans 6:9,10).

10. At each Mass the priest re-presents to the Father the sacrifice of Christ [1354, 1357].

Christ presented the sacrifice of Himself to the Father "once at the consummation of the ages" (Hebrews 9:24-28).

11. The Mass is an unbloody sacrifice which atones for the sins of the living and the dead [1367, 1371, 1414].

Without the shedding of blood there is no forgiveness of sins (Leviticus 17:11; Hebrews 9:22).

12. Each sacrifice of the Mass appeases God's wrath against sin [1371, 1414].

The once-for-all sacrifice of the cross fully appeased God's wrath against sin (Hebrews 10:12-18).

13. The faithful receive the benefits of the cross in fullest measure through the sacrifice of the Mass [1366, 1407].

Believers receive the benefits of the cross in fullest measure in Christ through faith (Ephesians 1:3-14).

14. The sacrificial work of redemption is continually carried out through the sacrifice of the Mass [1364, 1405, 1846].

The sacrificial work of redemption was finished when Christ gave His life for us on the cross (Ephesians 1:7; Hebrews 1:3).

15. The Church is to continue the sacrifice of Christ for the salvation of the world [1323, 1382, 1405, 1407].

The church is to proclaim the Lord's death for the salvation of the world (1 Corinthians 11:26).

❖ PART THREE ❖

MARY

Why do Roman Catholics pray to Mary? Why do some Catholics appear to be more devoted to Mary than to Christ? What are the doctrines of Mary's Immaculate Conception and Assumption into Heaven? Do Catholics actually worship Mary?

Part Three will examine the "pre-eminent"[251] and "unique"[252] role of Mary in Roman Catholicism. She, says the Church, "surpasses all creatures, both in heaven and on earth,"[253] and occupies a position second only to Christ's. Roman Catholicism teaches that Mary rightly deserves this honor, for:

❖ Mary is the sinless, ever virgin, Mother of God (Chapter 8, *The Mother of God*).

❖ Mary, having participated in the redemption, now sits at the right hand of Christ as the mediatress of all grace (Chapter 9, *The Queen of Heaven and Earth*).

In Part Three, you will also learn of Pope John Paul II's personal devotion to Mary, and why he credits Mary with having saved his life.

❖8

THE MOTHER OF GOD

Saint Peter's Square, Rome, May 13, 1981

Monsignor Stanislaus, Pope John Paul II's Polish secretary, tensed as the large white touring car in which they were riding turned into Saint Peter's Square. In front of him stood the Pope waving from the open-roofed vehicle to the enormous crowd filling the piazza. Though in office for only 2½ years, John Paul had already won the hearts of millions.

Nevertheless, Stanislaus, seated in the rear of the vehicle, feared that the Pope was too vulnerable in such a large crowd. Just three days earlier, Monsignor Andrew Mary Deskur, a Vatican prelate, had spoken of a premonition that he had experienced. While standing before an image of the Virgin of Czestochowa, Patron of Poland, Deskur had been overcome by fear for the Pope's life. After a moment of silent concentration, he looked upon the image of the Virgin and calmly said, "His Lady will protect him."[254]

The incident was in Stanislaus's thoughts as the vehicle traversed the outer perimeter of the square. He nervously checked the placement of the Vatican plainclothes security force surrounding the car. Several were former *carabinieri*, the Italian paramilitary police force. *They look tough*, thought the secretary to himself, *but what can they do in a crowd such as this?*

Apparently little, for none of the guards even noticed the young Turk with the icy stare waiting on the northern side of Bernini's colonnade. A 23-year-old with angular features and dressed in a sport coat and white open-neck shirt, the man looked normal enough. The 9-millimeter Browning automatic pistol he clutched in his coat pocket, however, said otherwise.

His name was Mehmet Ali Agca, a convicted murderer, a psychopath with terrorist training. Turkish police had orders to shoot him on sight. That afternoon, however, Agca had plans of his own. As soon as he got his first glimpse of the approaching Pontiff, he carefully disengaged the gun's safety mechanism. He alone heard the muffled click over the noise of the crowd.

A moment later the Pope's car pulled into full view. John Paul's unusual charisma surprised Agca. So did the crowd's enthusiasm for the smiling Pontiff. Agca had never seen such devotion to a man. The young Turk's confidence was rattled, and in that moment of indecision the Pope's vehicle glided past and out of danger.

Agca cursed his own stupidity. The Pope had been so close he could have touched him! He should have fired!

Agca's rage mounted until he suddenly realized that everyone had become still. No one was leaving the square. The Pope's vehicle was making a second loop!

Monsignor Stanislaus began to relax in the rear of the vehicle as he watched the Pope interact with the crowd. Pilgrims from around the world were cheerfully reaching for the Pontiff's hand and handing their young children to him to embrace and to kiss.

It was a joyful day, especially for the Pope, for it was a feast day in honor of Mary, to whom John Paul was deeply devoted. When ordained Auxiliary Bishop of Krakow in 1958, he had chosen as his episcopal coat of arms a cross with the initial "M" in honor of Mary at the foot of it. He adopted as his motto *Totus Tuus*, meaning, with reference to Mary: "Totally yours."[255] It was an expression of his complete consecration to the Blessed

Virgin. The Pope's relationship to Mary made her feast days special occasions for the entire Vatican staff. Today was a particularly important one: the anniversary of the first appearance of Our Lady of Fatima.

The Pope was smiling as he returned a young girl holding a balloon to her mother over the left side of the vehicle. He then moved to the opposite side of the car to greet pilgrims there. As he did, he came almost face-to-face with Agca.

The assassin knew he had his prey. With a smug grin he congratulated his own cleverness. Then in a move practiced a thousand times, he raised his weapon above the crowd, leveled the muzzle, and mercilessly began to fire.

The first bullet broke the index finger of John Paul's left hand and continued on a deadly path through his abdomen. Another bullet passed to the Pope's right, searing his elbow. As the assault continued, two American women in the crowd were struck.

Stunned by the deafening blasts, Monsignor Stanislaus didn't know what to think. A spent bullet lay between him and John Paul, but there was no sign of blood on the Pope's white robes. Only when John Paul began to totter did Stanislaus realize that his good friend had been shot. He quickly rose to catch the falling Pontiff.

"Where are you hit?" asked Stanislaus.

"The stomach," the Pope answered calmly.

Stanislaus was mystified. "Are you in pain?"

"Yes," answered the Pope as he closed his eyes and began to pray.

As the vehicle rushed to a waiting ambulance, Stanislaus could hear the Pontiff repeatedly pleading, "Mary, my mother! Mary, my mother!"[256]

The prayer was still on John Paul's lips when he finally passed out at the Gemelli Hospital 15 minutes later. Internal bleeding had dropped his blood pressure to a life threatening level. As surgeons raced to save his life, Monsignor Stanislaus realized that the responsibility of caring for the Pontiff's soul had fallen on him. With the sign of the cross, Stanislaus began to administer the last sacrament.

News of the event shocked the world. Rome came to a standstill and the crowd in Saint Peter's Square began to grow. Polish pilgrims placed a picture of their country's patron, Our Lady of Czestochowa, on the throne where the Pope would normally have been sitting. On the back of the picture someone had previously written: *May Our Lady protect the Holy Father from evil.* People gathered around the picture as Vatican loudspeakers began to broadcast the Rosary.

At 8:00 P.M. that night the crowd was still praying in the square when news came of John Paul's condition. Though still in surgery, he was stable. Confident that God had heard Mary's pleas for the Pope's life, the crowd began to disperse.

Mary in the Modern Church

Pope John Paul II's devotion to Mary is representative of a growing worldwide movement among Roman Catholics. It began in 1830 with what has become the first of a series of alleged appearances of Mary in various parts of the world, most notably Europe. Best known among these apparitions are: Paris, France (1830); La Salette, France (1846); Lourdes, France (1858); Knock, Ireland (1879); Fatima, Portugal (1917); Beauraing, Belgium (1932); and Banneux, Belgium (1933). The Roman Catholic Church has officially recognized all of these appearances as authentic revelations [67].

Through these apparitions, Mary has called Catholics to repentance, to perform acts of penance, and to pray the Rosary for the conversion of sinners and for peace in the world. She has also asked Catholics to give themselves to greater devotion to herself under the titles of her Immaculate Heart and her Immaculate Conception.

Religious practices have also developed as a result of these appearances, such as the wearing of the miraculous medal and scapular medal, both of which bear images of Mary. In an earlier appearance to Pope John XXII (1316-1334), Mary is said to have instructed Catholics to wear the scapular—two squares of cloth, often bearing images, connected by string and hung around the neck. Mary promised Pope John that Catholics who died wearing the scapular would be delivered from purgatory on the first Saturday after their death.[257]

The sites of Mary's appearances have become important centers of Roman Catholic devotion. Each year 5.5 million Roman Catholic pilgrims visit Lourdes. Almost as many flock to Fatima and the site of Mary's earlier appearance in Guadalupe, Mexico (1531).

In central Europe the primary focus of Marian devotion has become the Shrine of Our Lady of Czestochowa, a wooden icon of a Black Madonna dating from the fourteenth century. The growing popularity of Our Lady of Czestochowa is primarily the result of Pope John Paul II's own devotion to her and his visits to the shrine. Five million Roman Catholics annually visit the Polish city near Krakow.

As devotion to Mary has grown, so have claims of further appearances. Best-known among recent apparitions are those presently occurring in Medjugorje, Bosnia-Herzegovina. Six young peasants say that the Virgin has appeared there to one or more of them almost daily since 1981. Though the Church has not officially recognized their claims, over 10 million Catholics have traveled to Medjugorje since the appearances began.

Pope John Paul II is only one of several recent popes who have promoted the modern Marian movement. They have published numerous encyclicals lauding Mary's virtues, perpetual virginity, and intercessory role as the Mother of God. Two documents are especially significant: Pope Pius IX's *Ineffabilis Deus*, defining Mary's Immaculate Conception (1854), and Pope Pius XII's *Munificentissimus Deus*, defining the Assumption of Mary (1950).

The Immaculate Conception [411, 490-493, 508]

The exalted position of Mary in Roman Catholicism stems from the Church's understanding of her role in salvation. It began, says the Church, in eternity past [488]:

> From the very beginning, and before time began, the eternal Father chose and prepared for his only-begotten Son a Mother in whom the Son of God would become incarnate and from whom, in the blessed fullness of time, he would be born into this world. Above all creatures did God so love her that truly in her was the Father well pleased with singular delight.
>
> —*Ineffabilis Deus*[258]

The Church teaches that for Mary to be "a fit habitation for Christ,"[259] God decided to preserve her from the defilement of Adam's sin. In 1854 the Church formally defined this doctrine, known as Mary's Immaculate Conception [491]:

> We declare, pronounce, and define that the doctrine which holds that the most Blessed Virgin Mary, in the first instant of her conception, by a singular grace and privilege granted by Almighty God, in view of the merits of Jesus Christ, the Savior of the human race, was preserved free from all stain of original sin, is a doctrine revealed by God and therefore to be believed firmly and constantly by all the faithful.
>
> —*Ineffabilis Deus*[260]

Note that the Immaculate Conception refers to *Mary's conception*, not to Christ's conception or to the virgin birth. She, says the Church, was created without a sin nature and was "ever absolutely free of all stain of sin, all fair and perfect,"[261] remaining "free of every personal sin her whole life long."[493] Her holy innocence and sanctity are so excellent that "...one cannot even imagine anything greater, and which, outside of God, no mind can succeed in comprehending fully."[262]

The Virgin Mother of God [484-489, 495-511]

In accordance with the Scriptures, the Roman Catholic Church teaches that when the angel Gabriel appeared to Mary announcing God's plan for her to bear the "Son of the Most High" (Luke 1:32), Mary responded, "Behold, the bondslave of the Lord; be it done to me according to your word" (Luke 1:38).

According to the Bible, a miraculous conception followed in which Mary, though a virgin, "was found to be with child by the Holy Spirit" (Matthew 1:18). At the completion of this pregnancy, Mary gave birth to a Son and named Him Jesus.

The Roman Catholic Church teaches that the birth of Jesus was as miraculous as His conception, for, according to the Church, Mary experienced no pain in giving birth to the child: "To Eve it was said: *In sorrow shalt thou bring forth children* (Genesis 3:16). Mary was exempt from this law...."[263] Additionally, claims the Church, God preserved Mary's "virginal integrity inviolate"[264] [499]. That is, Christ was—

> ...born of His Mother without any diminution of her maternal virginity...just as the rays of the sun penetrate without breaking or injuring in the least the solid substance of glass, so after a like but more exalted manner did Jesus Christ come forth from His mother's womb without injury to her maternal virginity.
>
> —*The Roman Catechism*[265]

Furthermore, although she was wed to Joseph, the Church teaches that, following the birth of Jesus, Mary remained an "immaculate and perpetual"[266] virgin, abstaining from all sexual relations with her husband. The Church calls Mary "the Blessed Mary, ever Virgin,"[267] the "Virgin of virgins,"[268] and the "all-holy ever-virgin Mother of God."[721]

The Assumption of Mary
[966, 974]

In view of Mary's sinless perfection, Roman Catholicism teaches that Mary's body did not undergo decay at the end of her life. God miraculously took her up to heaven. This doctrine, known as the Assumption of Mary, was defined by the Church in 1950:

> ...we pronounce, declare, and define it to be a divinely revealed dogma: that the Immaculate Mother of God, the ever Virgin Mary, having completed the course of her earthly life, was assumed body and soul into heavenly glory.
>
> —*Munificentissimus Deus*[269]

A BIBLICAL RESPONSE

The biblical portrayal of Mary differs significantly from that of Roman Catholicism. The Old Testament mentions Mary only in passing in a few prophetic passages.[270] For example, Isaiah writes, "Behold, a virgin will be with child and bear a son, and she will call His name Immanuel" (Isaiah 7:14). Micah speaks of the time when a Jewish woman would experience labor and give birth to the Messiah in Bethlehem (Micah 5:2,3).

In the New Testament, Mary, as would be expected, plays a significant role in Christ's birth, infancy, and flight into Egypt (Matthew 1,2; Luke 1:26–2:40). The Bible next mentions her together with Joseph when they took Jesus to Jerusalem when he was 12 years old (Luke 2:41-52). Each of these accounts presents Mary as a woman who was a faithful, humble servant of God (Luke 1:38,46-55).

The next New Testament reference to Mary is when Jesus began His public ministry at age 30. There we find Mary with Him at the wedding feast in Cana (John 2:1-11). After informing Jesus that the wine had run out, Mary told the servants of the household, "Whatever He says to you, do it" (John 2:5). These are her last recorded words in the Scriptures. They stand as excellent advice for anyone seeking to please God.

Mary then traveled with Jesus to Capernaum, where they stayed "a few days" (John 2:12). In that there is no further mention of her being with Jesus as He continued His itinerant ministry, she apparently then returned to Nazareth.

In the remainder of the historical accounts of the New Testament, there are only three other references to Mary. The first occurs about halfway through Jesus' ministry (Mark 3:20,21, 31-35). Mary and her other sons came to Capernaum looking for Jesus "to take custody of Him; for they were saying, 'He has lost His senses'" (Mark 3:21). This event casts doubt on how well even Mary herself understood the Lord's identity and mission.

Scripture mentions Mary next at the Lord's crucifixion. There John describes her as "standing by the cross" (John 19:25). At that most difficult time, her love and loyalty for her Son were clearly shown.

The last reference to Mary in the historical narratives of the New Testament occurs following the Lord's ascension into heaven. The apostles, having returned to Jerusalem, gathered in the upper room. There they prayed "along with the women, and Mary the mother of Jesus" (Acts 1:14).

Mary in the New Testament[271]

These are the references to Mary in the New Testament:

- Birth and infancy of Christ
  Matthew 1,2; Luke 1:26-2:40

- Jesus left in Jerusalem at age 12
  Luke 2:41-51

- Marriage feast at Cana
  John 2:1-11

- Short visit to Capernaum
  John 2:12

- Mary and Jesus' brothers come to
     Capernaum
  Matthew 12:46-50; Mark 3:20-35; Luke 8:19-21

- Doubters question Jesus' origin
  Matthew 13:55,56; Mark 6:3,4; John 6:42
- Crucifixion of Jesus
  John 19:25-27
- Prayer after the ascension of Christ
  Acts 1:14
- References by Paul
  Romans 1:3; Galatians 4:4

In the epistles Paul refers to Mary twice without naming her. In Romans he refers to God's Son, "who was born of a descendant of David according to the flesh" (Romans 1:3). In Galatians Paul writes, "But when the fulness of the time came, God sent forth His Son, born of a woman, born under the Law" (Galatians 4:4).

Scripture says nothing about the latter years of Mary's life, her death, or her burial. There is no description of her character, virtue, or physical appearance. Neither are there any biblical examples of anyone praying to her or venerating her.

Many Catholics upon reading the Bible for the first time are surprised by how little is said about Mary. Even more significant is the fact that the Bible contradicts much of what the Church teaches about Mary:

- Mary was the mother of Jesus but not the mother of God.
- Mary was a virgin but not a perpetual virgin.
- Mary was a sinner, not a sinless saint.

Mary Was the Mother of Jesus

Though there is no biblical precedent for it, Roman Catholicism honors Mary as the *Mother of God* [963, 971, 2677]. Since Jesus is God, and Mary is the mother of Jesus, then Mary must be the Mother of God, so the argument goes [495, 509].

The Bible, on the other hand, never calls Mary the Mother of God for a very simple reason: God has no mother. As someone has rightly said, just as Christ's human nature had no father, so His divine nature had no mother. The Bible, therefore, rightly calls Mary the "mother of Jesus" (John 2:1; Acts 1:14), but never the Mother of God.

Roman Catholic scholars counter by saying that Tradition firmly establishes the use of the title. The Council of Ephesus (431), they remind us, formally sanctioned the practice of referring to Mary as the Mother of God [466, 495].[272]

The Council of Ephesus, however, was far from a meeting of spiritual Christians prayerfully seeking the mind of God. Coemperors Theodosius II and Valentinian III summoned the Council of Ephesus in 431 at the request of Nestorius (died c. 451), patriarch of Constantinople. Nestorius was seeking an opportunity to defend himself. A regional council held in Rome the year before had condemned him for his criticism of the use of the Greek word *theotokos*, meaning *God-bearer*, to describe Mary. Nestorius was a strong opponent of Arianism and its teaching that Christ was a created being. Nestorius feared that calling Mary the *God-bearer* implied the same heresy, namely, that Mary had generated a member of the Trinity.

Strong rivalries and church politics dominated the Council of Ephesus. Historians have described the Council as one of the most repulsive contests in church history. Before all the bishops even arrived in Ephesus and with Nestorius absent, his opponents accused him of splitting Christ into two distinct persons. Though it is not clear that Nestorius actually held that belief, the Council declared him a heretic and the 34 bishops who supported him apostates. The Council went on to affirm the use of the title *theotokos*, God-bearer, with relation to Mary, though taking care to steer away from any implication that Christ was a created being [466].

It is this term, *theotokos*, that is translated today by the Roman Catholic Church in its most glorious sense as *Mother of God*. However, in view of the hyperexalted position that Mary has come to occupy in Roman Catholicism, the lack of a biblical precedent for the title, and the historical context of the Council of Ephesus, Christians would be wise to avoid using the title and instead use actual biblical terms.

Mary Was Not a Perpetual Virgin

Scripture teaches that Mary, though a virgin, came to be with child by the power of the Holy Spirit (Luke 1:26-35). The Bible says nothing about God preserving Mary's "virginal integrity inviolate"[273] during the birth process, or that Mary refrained from sexual contact with her husband after the birth of Christ.

The Roman Catholic Church bases its belief in the perpetual virginity of Mary upon Tradition and upon philosophical considerations. Thomas Aquinas provided four reasons why the doctrine is fitting:[274]

- Since Christ is the only begotten Son of the Father, it was "becoming"[275] that Christ should also be the only begotten Son of His mother.
- Intercourse with Joseph would have "desecrated"[276] the virginal womb of Mary. This would have been an insult to the Holy Spirit, whose shrine was her womb.
- It would have been below "the dignity and holiness"[277] of Mary to forfeit her miraculous virginity by carnal intercourse with Joseph. Such an act would also show that she was ungrateful or not content with being the mother of Jesus.
- It would have been "extreme presumption"[278] for Joseph to have attempted "to violate"[279] Mary, whom he knew had conceived by the power of the Holy Spirit.

Aquinas concluded, "We must therefore simply assert that the Mother of God, as she was a virgin in conceiving Him and a virgin in giving Him birth, so did she remain a virgin ever afterwards."[280]

Though much could be said about Aquinas's understanding of marital intercourse, the fact that the Church feels free to dogmatically assert a doctrine that has no biblical basis is more pertinent to our topic. It is especially significant since the Scriptures, rather than supporting the doctrine of Mary's perpetual virginity, lead us to believe the direct opposite.

There are several biblical references to events involving the Lord Jesus' half-brothers and half-sisters. The first event occurs following the wedding feast at Cana. The Bible says that Jesus traveled to Capernaum with "His mother, and His brothers, and His disciples" (John 2:12). Later we read that Christ's "mother and brothers" came looking for Him in Capernaum (Matthew 12:46; see also Mark 3:31 and Luke 8:19). A short time afterward, Christ's opponents are quoted as asking, "Is not this the carpenter's son? Is not His mother called Mary, and His brothers, James and Joseph and Simon and Judas? And His sisters, are they not all with us?" (Matthew 13:55,56; see also Mark 6:3,4). In the last year of His life we find Christ's brothers taunting Him (John 7:2-10). John comments, "For not even His brothers were believing in Him" (John 7:5).

Sometime later the Lord's brothers apparently repented and came to faith in Him. Luke writes that following the ascension the apostles gathered for prayer "along with the women, and Mary the mother of Jesus, and with His brothers" (Acts 1:14). Much later Paul writes that when he visited Jerusalem, he went to see "James, the Lord's brother" (Galatians 1:19), who by then was a leading figure in the church in Jerusalem (Galatians 2:9-12; Acts 15:13-21). In his letter to the Corinthians, Paul also refers to "the brothers of the Lord" (1 Corinthians 9:5).

Roman Catholic scholars brush these Scriptures aside, saying that all of them refer to the Lord's cousins and not His actual half-brothers or half-sisters. They claim that Jews often used terms such as "brothers" to include near kinsmen [500].

Saints

[828, 946-962, 2683-2684]

The Roman Catholic Church has *canonized*, or given the title of *saint*, to many deceased heroes of the faith. Saints, because of their excellent virtue and merit, are believed to be already in heaven. They serve the faithful still on earth as "models and intercessors."[828]

Catholics can ask the saints, even as they do Mary, to intercede with God on their behalf. This is possible because of what the Church calls the *communion of saints* [954-962, 1474-1475]. The Church describes this communion as a mystical relationship and cooperation between all Catholics, whether living on earth, suffering in purgatory, or enjoying the glories of heaven [954, 1689].

The prayers of the saints are said to be "...particularly effective, since they love God so intimately and can point to all the merit and sacrifices of their life on earth"[281] [956]. The Church advises Catholics to approach God through the saints, for: "There are many things which God does not grant without a mediator and intercessor."[282]

Catholics choose which saint to pray to based upon need, occupation, or country. Here are just a few of the saints and their particular areas of patronage:

- St. John of God: heart patients
- St. Blase: throat ailments

How these scholars know that cousins, rather than brothers and sisters, are the ones whom the New Testament is referring to is not clear. It is true that the Greek words for brother, *adelphos*, and sister, *adelphe*, can be understood in a wider sense. But their primary meaning speaks of a relationship of shared parentage. Unless context suggests otherwise, it is the primary meaning of a word that is intended. Had the Holy Spirit wanted Christians to venerate Mary as *ever virgin*, He would not have referred to these relatives of Jesus as His brothers and sisters without further qualification.

Additionally, had the Holy Spirit wished to express

- St. Lucy: eye diseases
- St. Francis de Sales: deaf
- St. Thomas Aquinas: students
- St. Monica: mothers
- St. Matthew: tax collectors
- St. Joseph: carpenters
- St. Nicholas of Myra: bridges
- St. Valentine: greetings
- St. Francis of Assisi: animals
- St. Clare of Assisi: television
- St. Anthony: lost items
- St. Jude: hopeless causes
- St. Boniface: Germany
- St. Patrick: Ireland
- Our Lady of Guadalupe: Mexico
- The Immaculate Conception: Brazil

The Bible, on the other hand, refers to all true believers as saints by virtue of their position in Christ (Ephesians 1:1). They are "sanctified in Christ Jesus, saints by calling" (1 Corinthians 1:2). As for the Roman Catholic practice of the living invoking the spirits of the dead, it has more in common with spiritism and divination, both condemned in Scripture, than with any Christian practice (Deuteronomy 18:10,11).

a less close relationship than brother or sister, two other Greek words were available. Paul employs the word *anepsios*, meaning cousin, to identify Mark as "Barnabas' cousin" (Colossians 4:10). Luke uses *sungenis*, having a more general meaning of *kinsman*, to identify Elizabeth as Mary's "relative" (Luke 1:36).

Furthermore, among the messianic Psalms we find a prophecy of the animosity that the Lord Jesus initially experienced from His brothers. There the Messiah laments, "I have become estranged from my brothers, and an alien to my mother's sons" (Psalm 69:8). The relationship between Jesus' brothers and His mother could not be more explicit.

Finally, Matthew writes that Joseph, after taking Mary to be His wife, "kept her a virgin until she gave birth to a Son" (Matthew 1:25). The implication is plain enough.

Mary Was Not a Sinless Saint

As a descendant of Adam, Mary, like the rest of us, was born a sinner. The Bible says that "just as through one man sin entered into the world, and death through sin, and so death spread to all men, because all sinned" (Romans 5:12).

Nevertheless, the Roman Catholic Church asserts the doctrine of the Immaculate Conception, namely, that Mary "...in the first instant of her conception...was preserved free from all stain of original sin..."[283] [491]. Catholic scholars claim that this belief is taught in Scripture in the *Annunciation*, the angel Gabriel's announcement of Christ's incarnation to Mary: "Hail, full of grace, the Lord is with thee: blessed art thou among women" (Luke 1:28 Douay Rheims) [490-491]. This, says the Church, reveals that Mary "was never subject to the curse"[284] and that she was "immune from all sin, personal or inherited."[285]

The angel, however, never said that Mary was "full of grace" (Luke 1:28 Douay-Rheims). This Roman Catholic translation is based on Latin texts. Translations from the original Greek read "Hail, favored one! The Lord is with you" (Luke 1:28). God *favored* Mary by choosing her to bear His Son, not by preserving her from Adam's sin. God blessed Mary "*among* women" (Luke 1:28 KJV), not *above* women.

The Bible teaches that the only One who has ever lived on this earth without sin was the Lord Jesus Christ (2 Corinthians 5:21; 1 Peter 2:22; 1 John 3:5). Scripture leaves no room for any other exception: "Indeed, there is not a righteous man on earth who continually does good and who never sins" (Ecclesiastes 7:20). The angels above worship the Lord, proclaiming, "Thou alone art holy"

(Revelation 15:4). The Lord Jesus said, "No one is good except God alone" (Luke 18:19). Paul wrote, "...all have sinned and fall short of the glory of God" (Romans 3:23). And again:

> There is none righteous, not even one...
> There is none who does good,
> There is not even one.
> —Romans 3:10,12

Mary, like every other human being, was a sinner who needed to be redeemed. She herself acknowledged this when she prayed, "My soul exalts the Lord, and my spirit has rejoiced in God my Savior" (Luke 1:46,47).

The Church concedes that Mary was redeemed, but only from the *debt* of original sin. It claims that she was not redeemed from the *stain* of sin, for Mary "was preserved free from all stain of original sin"[286] [491-492, 508].

Scripture recognizes no such distinction. The fact that Mary died is proof enough that she was subject to the *full* penalty of sin (Genesis 2:17; 3:19; Romans 6:23).

Again the Church disagrees. It says that Mary did not die because of sin, either personal or inherited.[287] Rather, she died because "God was pleased that Mary should in all things resemble Jesus; and as the Son died, it was becoming that the mother should also die...."[288] Furthermore, claims the Church, God took Mary bodily into heaven. Her body did not decay in the grave under the curse of sin, for she was sinless.

In the document defining the Assumption of Mary, Pope Pius XII cited several Scriptures in an attempt to demonstrate a biblical basis for the doctrine.[289] In doing so he acknowledged that most of the Scriptures referenced had been put forth by theologians and preachers who had "...been rather free in their use of events and expressions taken from Sacred Scripture to explain their belief in the Assumption."[290] The fact of the matter is that none of the Scriptures the Pope cited said anything about Mary's Assumption. Only one, Luke 1:28, even refers to Mary. Nevertheless, the Pope used them anyway.

Another Mary

The Mary of Roman Catholicism is not the Mary of the Bible. Scripture says nothing of a woman conceived without sin, perfectly sinless, ever virgin, and assumed into heaven.

Nevertheless, the Church, with greater regard for Tradition and human reason than for sacred Scripture, has declared the virgin Mary to be the *ever virgin Mary*, the mother of Jesus to be the *Mother of God*, and the favored woman to be *Mary full of grace*. Determined to exalt Mary, the Church has distorted and disregarded the plain teaching of the Bible. In the process, having left the truth and security of Scripture, the Roman Catholic Church has exposed its people to mystical and even bizarre apparitions of a self-promoting spirit who identifies itself as Mary. These appearances have led Catholics away from undistracted devotion to Christ and dependence upon Him alone for salvation. Whether these apparitions are real or imagined, by their fruits they have proven themselves to be not from God.

❖9

THE QUEEN
OF HEAVEN AND EARTH

Fatima, Portugal, May 13, 1982

From the elevated podium in front of the Basilica of Our Lady of Fatima, Pope John Paul II looked out upon an immense crowd. Before him stood over 200,000 Catholics. As he began his address, it was a historic moment both for the Church and for the Pope:

> I come here today because on this very day last year, in Saint Peter's Square in Rome, the attempt on the Pope's life was made, in mysterious coincidence with the anniversary of the first apparition at Fatima, which occurred on May 13, 1917.[291]

John Paul's visit to Fatima was the fulfillment of a tacit promise he had made after the attempt on his life in 1981. Upon regaining consciousness, the Pope said that his first thoughts were of Our Lady of Fatima. Later he decided to visit Fatima on the first anniversary of the assassination attempt. The purpose, as the Pope put it, would be "... to place in the heart of the heavenly Mother my thanks for having saved me from danger. I saw in everything that was happening—I never tire of repeating it—a special motherly protection of our Lady."[292] He was convinced that when Mehmet Ali Agca squeezed the trigger of his weapon one year earlier, a miracle had taken place. "One hand fired," the Pope would say, "and another one guided the bullet."[293] The Pope was certain that the hand that guided belonged to Mary.

Doctors confirmed that John Paul had indeed been fortunate. The bullet that had pierced his abdomen lacerated his colon and intestines. It also severely damaged the sacral vein system, causing profuse internal bleeding. But had the bullet not cleared his aorta by a few millimeters, it would have instantly killed the Pope. The bullet had actually passed straight through his body without damaging any vital organ.

Now, one year later and fully recovered, Pope John Paul II had come to Fatima not only to thank Mary, but to consecrate to her the entire human race:[294]

> We have recourse to your protection, holy Mother of God.... Embrace, with the love of the Mother, and Handmaid, this human world of ours, which we entrust and consecrate to you.... In entrusting to you, O Mother, the world, all individuals and peoples, we also entrust to you the consecration itself, for the world's sake, placing it in your motherly Heart. Oh, Immaculate Heart! Help us to conquer the menace of evil.... Accept, O Mother of Christ, this cry.... Let there be revealed, once more, in the history of the world your infinite power of merciful Love. May it put a stop to evil. May it transform consciences. May your Immaculate Heart reveal for all the light of Hope.[295]

The Co-Redeemer
[494, 963-973]

Though John Paul II's intense devotion to Mary and his consecration of the world to her may seem strange to non-Catholics, it is by no means unusual within Roman Catholicism. Indeed, such devotion is the intended goal of the Church's teaching about Mary. For in Roman

Catholicism, Mary is much more than a model of virtue; she is the co-redeemer of the human race [964, 968, 970].

According to the Roman Catholic Church, when Mary accepted God's invitation for her to bear His Son, she "...was already collaborating with the whole work her Son was to accomplish"[973]:

> The Father of mercies willed that the Incarnation should be preceded by assent on the part of the predestined mother, so that just as a woman had a share in bringing about death, so also a woman should contribute to life.... Rightly, therefore, the Fathers see Mary not merely as passively engaged by God, but as freely cooperating in the work of man's salvation through faith and obedience. For, as St. Irenaeus says, she "being obedient, became the cause of salvation for herself and for the whole human race." Hence not a few of the early Fathers gladly assert with him in their preaching: "the knot of Eve's disobedience was untied by Mary's obedience: what the virgin Eve bound through her disbelief, Mary loosened by her faith." Comparing Mary with Eve, they call her "Mother of the living," and frequently claim: "death through Eve, life through Mary."
>
> —Second Vatican Council[296]

According to the Roman Catholic Church, Mary's participation in the incarnation was only the beginning of her role in salvation. The Church teaches that "it was God's design that the Blessed Virgin Mary, apparently absent from the public life of Jesus, should assist him when he was dying nailed to the Cross."[297] United with Christ, Mary offered Him as a sacrifice to God on the cross:

> She it was who, immune from all sin, personal or inherited, and ever more closely united with her Son, offered him on Golgotha to the Eternal Father together with the holocaust of her maternal rights and motherly love....
>
> —*Mystici Corporis*[298]

Not only did Mary offer her Son to God, but she remained at the cross to suffer with Christ [964]:

> Thus the Blessed Virgin advanced in her pilgrimage of faith, and faithfully persevered in her union with her Son unto the cross, where she stood, in keeping with the divine plan, enduring with her only begotten Son the intensity of his suffering, associated herself with his sacrifice in her mother's heart, and lovingly consenting to the immolation of this victim which was born of her.
>
> —Second Vatican Council[299]

According to the Church, Mary's sufferings were so intense that they brought her to the very threshold of death. She, says the Church, "participated with Jesus Christ in the very painful act of redemption":[300]

> Mary suffered and, as it were, nearly died with her suffering Son; for the salvation of mankind she renounced her mother's rights and, as far as it depended on her, offered her Son to placate divine justice; so we may well say that she with Christ redeemed mankind.
>
> —*Inter Sodalicia*[301]

Thus Mary, in a subordinate role to Christ, had a "part with him in the redemption of the human race."[302] She is therefore called by the Church the "the co-operatrix in man's redemption,"[303] "our coredemptor."[304] For at the cross, Mary triumphed "utterly over the ancient serpent."[305]

Following the death and resurrection of Christ, says the Church, Mary was a major force in the spread of the gospel [965]:

> It is no exaggeration to say that it is due chiefly to her leadership and help that the wisdom and teachings of the Gospel spread so rapidly to all the nations of the world in spite of the most

obstinate difficulties and most cruel persecutions and brought everywhere in their train a new reign of justice and peace.

—*Adiutricem Populi*[306]

Finally, the Roman Catholic Church teaches that when Mary's life on earth was completed, God miraculously took her into heaven. There He crowned her Queen of Heaven and Earth [966]:

> The Blessed Virgin Mary is to be called Queen not only on account of her divine motherhood but also because by the will of God she had a great part in the work of our salvation.... In this work of redemption the blessed Virgin Mary was closely associated with her Christil.... Just as Christ, because he redeemed us, is by a special title our King and Lord, so too is Blessed Mary, our Queen and our Mistress, because of the unique way in which she co-operated in our redemption. She provided her very substance for his body, she offered him willingly for us, and she took a unique part in our salvation by desiring it, praying for it, and so obtaining it....
>
> —*Ad Coeli Reginam*[307]

The Mediatress of All Grace
[968-971, 975, 2673-2682]

Roman Catholicism teaches that Mary, by her participation in our redemption, also earned the privilege of being the one through whom God would dispense all grace to the world:

> When the supreme hour of the Son came, beside the Cross of Jesus there stood Mary His Mother, not merely occupied in contemplating the cruel spectacle, but rejoicing that her Only Son was offered for the salvation of mankind, and so entirely participating in His Passion, that

if it had been possible she would have gladly borne all the torments that her Son bore. And from this community of will and suffering between Christ and Mary she merited to become most worthily the Reparatrix of the lost world and Dispensatrix of all the gifts that Our Saviour purchased for us by His Death and by His Blood.

—*Ad Diem*[308]

According to the Church, Mary is God's unique channel of blessing. Christ "grants all graces to mankind through her,"[309] and "nothing is imparted to us except through Mary."[310] She is "the seat of all divine graces... an almost infinite treasury"[311] to whom the Church exhorts the faithful to flee in time of need:

Let all the children of the Catholic Church, who are so very dear to us, hear these words of ours. With a still more ardent zeal for piety, religion and love, let them continue to venerate, invoke and pray to the most Blessed Virgin Mary, Mother of God, conceived without original sin. Let them fly with utter confidence to this most sweet Mother of mercy and grace in all dangers, difficulties, needs, doubts and fears. Under her guidance, under her patronage, under her kindness and protection, nothing is to be feared; nothing is hopeless. Because, while bearing toward us a truly motherly affection and having in her care the work of our salvation, she is solicitous about the whole human race. And since she has been appointed by God to be the Queen of heaven and earth, and is exalted above all the choirs of angels and saints, and even stands at the right hand of her only-begotten Son, Jesus Christ our Lord, she presents our petitions in a most efficacious manner. What she asks, she obtains. Her pleas can never be unheard.

—*Ineffabilis Deus*[312]

The Church teaches that "... nothing comes to us except through Mary's mediation, for such is God's

Will."[313] Mary is "...the most powerful mediatrix and advocate of the whole world with her Divine Son,"[314] a "glorious intermediary."[315] St. Bernard of Clairvaux's popular Latin axiom, *Ad Jesum per Mariam*, "To Jesus Through Mary," summarizes well the Church's teaching. For her intercession Catholics plead as they pray the *Hail, Holy Queen*, one of the traditional concluding prayers of the Rosary:

> Hail, Holy Queen, Mother of Mercy. Hail, our life, our sweetness, and our hope. To you do we cry, poor banished children of Eve; to you do we send up our sighs, mourning and weeping, in this valley of tears. Turn then, most gracious advocate, your eyes of mercy towards us; and after this our exile, show unto us the blessed fruit of your womb, Jesus. O clement, O loving, O sweet Virgin Mary, pray for us, O holy Mother of God. That we may be made worthy of the promises of Christ.

Veneration of Mary
[971, 2676-2679, 2682]

In view of Mary's role as the Mother of God, her exemplary virtue and holiness, her participation in our redemption, and her appointment as mediatress of grace and Queen of Heaven and Earth, the Roman Catholic Church teaches that Catholics should greatly venerate Mary:

> Mary has by grace been exalted above all angels and men to a place second only to her Son, as the most holy mother of God who was involved in the mysteries of Christ: she is rightly honored by a special cult in the Church.
>
> —Second Vatican Council[316]

This special cult, or form of devotion, is called *hyperdulia*. It is one of the three degrees of honor recognized by the Church:

- *Latria*—This is the highest form of adoration. The Church teaches the faithful to worship God alone in this manner.

- *Hyperdulia*—*Hyperdulia* is one step below *latria* worship. It is the highest degree of veneration that can be given to a created being. The Church teaches that Mary alone deserves this form of honor.

- *Dulia*—This is simple veneration. Catholics are to show this degree of honor to saints and angels.

The most common way in which Catholics venerate Mary is by saying the Rosary [971, 1674, 2708]. Considered by the Church an "epitome of the whole Gospel,"[971] it is a series of prayers counted on a string of beads. These are arranged in groups of ten small beads separated by one large bead. There are five sets of these *decades*. On the large bead, the *Our Father* or *Lord's Prayer* is said. On each of the ten small beads, Catholics pray the *Hail Mary* [2676-2677]:

Hail Mary, full of grace, the Lord is with thee. Blessed art thou among women and blessed is the fruit of thy womb, Jesus. Holy Mary, Mother of God, pray for us sinners now and at the hour of our death. Amen.

The Church offers a partial indulgence, the removal of part of the temporal punishment due to sin, to Catholics who pray the Rosary [1471-1479, 1498]. They can also earn a plenary indulgence, a complete remission of all temporal punishment stored up at that time, by praying the Rosary, receiving the sacraments of confession and Eucharist, and offering prayers for the Pope's intentions [1471].

A BIBLICAL RESPONSE

Though Scripture presents Mary in a favorable light, the unrestrained praise and sentimental effusion so common in Roman Catholicism is not to be found in the Bible. Far less is there any hint that Mary participated in the redemption, and is therefore the Mediatress of all grace. To the contrary, the Bible teaches that:

- There is one redeemer, not two.
- There is one mediator, not two.

There Is Only One Redeemer

Scripture is clear in stating that the Lord alone is our redeemer. To Israel God proclaimed, "I, the Lord, am your Savior and your Redeemer, the Mighty One of Jacob" (Isaiah 49:26). The New Testament Scriptures reveal that it is in God's "beloved Son in whom we have redemption, the forgiveness of sins" (Colossians 1:13,14). God justifies sinners "through the redemption which is in Christ Jesus" (Romans 3:24).

The Church's claim that Mary offered Christ "on Golgotha to the Eternal Father"[317] contradicts Scripture. The Bible says that Christ "offered *Himself* without blemish to God" (Hebrews 9:14, emphasis added).

Similarly, there is no biblical support for the Roman Catholic claim that Mary "with Christ redeemed mankind."[318] The Church says, speaking of Mary:

> In her, the many and intense sufferings were amassed in such an interconnected way that they were not only a proof of her unshakable faith but also a contribution to the Redemption of all.
>
> ...it was on Calvary that Mary's suffering, beside the suffering of Jesus, reached an intensity which can hardly be imagined from a human point of view but which was mysteriously and supernaturally fruitful for the Redemption of the world.
>
> —*Salvifici Doloris*[319]

Here the Church, rather than picturing Mary as a grateful redeemed sinner at the feet of her Savior, portrays her as making "a contribution to the Redemption of all"[320] through her own sufferings. In the words of the Second Vatican Council [968]:

> She conceived, brought forth, and nourished Christ, she presented him to the Father in the temple, shared her Son's sufferings as he died on the cross. Thus, in a wholly singular way she cooperated by her obedience, faith, hope and burning charity in the work of the Savior in restoring supernatural life to souls.
>
> —Second Vatican Council[321]

Genesis 3:15

Some Catholic scholars point to Genesis 3:15 in support of the Church's teaching of Mary as the co-redeemer. In many Roman Catholic versions of the Bible, such as the Douay Rheims (the standard Roman Catholic English Bible until the middle of the twentieth century), God's curse upon Satan reads:

> I will put enmities between thee and the woman, and thy seed and her seed: she shall crush thy head, and thou shalt lie in wait for her heel.
>
> —Genesis 3:15 Douay Rheims

Based on this verse, many statues and paintings of Mary show her crushing a serpent under her foot—a graphic representation of her role as co-redeemer. This imagery is also found in Catholic documents:

> Hence, just as Christ, the Mediator between God and man, assumed human nature, blotted the handwriting of the decree that stood against us, and fastened it triumphantly to the cross, so the most holy Virgin, united with him by a most intimate and indissoluble bond, was, with him and through him, eternally at enmity with the evil serpent, and most completely triumphed over him, and thus crushed his head with her immaculate foot.
>
> —*Ineffabilis Deus*[322]

This imagery, however, is based upon a faulty translation of Genesis 3:15 from the Latin texts of the Vulgate Bible, the official Bible of the Roman Catholic Church since the fourth century. Until recently the Latin Vulgate served as the base text for all Roman Catholic translations, including the English Douay Rheims Bible.

In the Hebrew text, the original language of the Old Testament, the subject of Genesis 3:15 is masculine, not feminine. Therefore, rather than reading "she shall crush thy head" (Genesis 3:15 Douay Rheims), the verse should be translated "He shall bruise you on the head" (Genesis 3:15 NASB). The verse is prophetically speaking of Christ's victory over Satan, not Mary's.

Though recent Roman Catholic translations have corrected the error, Roman Catholic theology remains uncorrected.

Luke 2:34,35

Another passage that the Church uses to support its teaching of the "union of the mother with the Son in the work of salvation"[323] is Luke 2:34,35. Joseph and Mary had taken the infant Jesus to Jerusalem to present Him in the temple. Simeon, a righteous man who was looking for the coming of the Messiah, took the child into his arms and said to Mary:

> Behold, this Child is appointed for the fall and rise of many in Israel, and for a sign to be opposed—and a sword will pierce even your own soul—to the end that thoughts of many hearts may be revealed.
>
> —Luke 2:34,35

According to the Church, the sword here speaks of Mary's participation with Christ in suffering for our redemption [618]. She, wrote Pope John Paul II, made "a contribution to the Redemption of all":[324]

> ...it was on Calvary that Mary's suffering, beside the suffering of Jesus, reached an intensity

which can hardly be imagined from a human point of view but which was mysteriously and supernaturally fruitful for the Redemption of the world.

—*Salvifici Doloris*[325]

The Roman Catholic claim that Mary suffered for the redemption of the world is unjustified for three reasons.

1. *Mary did not suffer for sin.* As Mary watched her Son hanging on the cross, she undoubtedly suffered greatly. However, the same could be said of the others present who loved the Lord and witnessed His sufferings: John, Mary Magdalene, Salome, and Mary the wife of Clopas (John 19:25-27; Mark 15:40). We might describe the nature of this kind of sorrow as the *suffering of compassion.*

It is also likely that Mary, even as Christ, endured the taunts and ridicule of evil men. She did so willingly, knowing that God had called her to serve as the mother of Jesus. Scripture describes this kind of persecution as *suffering for the sake of righteousness* (1 Peter 3:14).

These two kinds of suffering, however, must be distinguished from what Christ experienced on the cross. He *suffered for sin.* Christ, "having become a curse for us" (Galatians 3:13), became the object of God's wrath as the Father "caused the iniquity of us all to fall on Him" (Isaiah 53:6). This kind of suffering the Lord Jesus, "smitten of God, and afflicted" (Isaiah 53:4), suffered in solitary agony:

> Reproach has broken my heart, and I am so sick.
> And I looked for sympathy, but there was none,
> And for comforters, but I found none.
> —Psalm 69:20

Apparently neither Mary nor any of the others at the foot of the cross were even aware that before them the Son of God was suffering for the sins of the world.

2. *Mary did not suffer death for sin.* Despite the intensity of Christ's physical sufferings, the Scriptures consistently link our redemption not to His pain, but to His

death. Paul writes that "we were reconciled to God through the *death* of His Son" (Romans 5:10, emphasis added). The writer of Hebrews reminds us that "a death has taken place for the redemption of the transgressions" (Hebrews 9:15). John tells us that Jesus "released us from our sins by His blood" (Revelation 1:5).

The reason, of course, is that the penalty for our sin is *death* (Genesis 2:17; Romans 6:23). A life, therefore, had to be given to redeem us. That is why Christ came: "to give His life a ransom for many" (Mark 10:45). Christ "died for sins once for all, the just for the unjust, in order that He might bring us to God..." (1 Peter 3:18). Nowhere do the Scriptures teach that we were redeemed by Christ's righteous life, His faithful obedience, or even His sufferings at the hands of cruel men.

Here again the sufferings of Mary fall short of being redemptive.[326] The Church claims that "Mary suffered and, as it were, nearly died with her suffering Son,"[327] that she "in her heart died with him, stabbed by the sword of sorrow."[328] But the fact of the matter is that Mary did not die at Calvary. Christ alone gave His life for our redemption.

3. *Mary was not qualified to redeem mankind.* Even if Mary had died at Calvary, her death would not have redeemed anyone. As we saw in the last chapter, Mary herself was a sinner. As such, she was guilty before God and unfit to redeem anyone. The same is true of every other man or woman. Scripture teaches:

> No man can by any means redeem his brother,
> Or give to God a ransom for him—
> For the redemption of his soul is costly,
> And he should cease trying forever.
> —Psalm 49:7,8

That is why God sent His Son, the Lord Jesus Christ, to redeem us. *He alone was qualified.* Since He was the Son of God, His life was of infinite value and able to redeem all mankind. Having been made "in the likeness of men" (Philippians 2:7), He was capable of both representing humanity before God and physically dying (Hebrews 2:14-17). Since He was without sin, His life was an acceptable sacrifice (1 Peter 1:19; 2:22). Christ *alone*, therefore, deserves the title of Redeemer. "Worthy is the Lamb that was slain" (Revelation 5:12).

There Is Only One Mediator

There is no biblical support for the Roman Catholic claim that Mary serves as a go-between, or mediatress, between God and man. Neither is there a biblical example of a Christian praying to Mary or obtaining a blessing from God through her heavenly intercession.

The Roman Catholic Church disagrees, claiming that there is clear biblical support for Mary's mediation. It points to the wedding feast in Cana. There, says the Church, Mary "...brought about by her intercession the beginning of miracles of Jesus the Messiah (cf. John 2:1-11)."[329] The Church teaches that in the same way today "Mary is all powerful with her divine Son."[330]

A closer look at the wedding feast in Cana, however, reveals a somewhat different emphasis. Mary, realizing that the wine had run out, brought the need to Jesus, saying, "They have no wine" (John 2:3). Jesus replied, "Woman, what do I have to do with you? My hour has not yet come" (John 2:4). The Lord wanted Mary to understand that in His divine mission He was not subject to her requests. He came to do His heavenly Father's will, not His earthly mother's. Having made that clear, the Lord graciously provided wine for the guests with as little fanfare as possible. If the passage has anything to say about intercessory prayer, it teaches that we should take our requests directly to the Lord Jesus even as Mary herself did. He is our only mediator: "For there is one God, and one mediator also between God and men, the man Christ Jesus" (1 Timothy 2:5).

The Second Vatican Council affirmed the unique mediatorship of Christ, saying, "There is but one mediator."[331] It even quoted 1 Timothy 2:5. At the same time, however, the Council reasserted Mary's roles as "Advocate, Helper, Benefactress, and Mediatrix,"[332] the last title being a feminine form of *mediator* [969].

The Council offered three explanations for why Mary's role as mediatress does not infringe upon Christ's role as the sole mediator:

Explanation 1: Mary's Mediation Shows the Power of Christ's Mediation [970]

> Mary's function as mother of men in no way obscures or diminishes this unique mediation of Christ, but rather shows its power.
>
> —Second Vatican Council[333]

This denial, however, rings hollow when Mary's mediation as the mother of men and the Mother of God is fully understood.

According to the Church, Mary became our mother and mediatress at Calvary. As Christ hung upon the cross, His eyes fell upon His mother. Beside her stood the apostle John, to whom the Lord said, "Behold, your mother!" (John 19:27). The Church says that by those words Mary became the "Mother of the human race"[334] and "Mother of the Church."[963]

Roman Catholicism teaches that the faithful, therefore, "...naturally turn to the powerful Mother of God...always the chief and sovereign refuge of Catholics in the trials they underwent."[335] "Trust Mary, implore her aid,"[336] advises the Church, for her ability to influence her Son is incomparable:

> The Catholic Church has always and with justice put all her hope and trust in the Mother of God. She who is associated with him in the work of man's salvation has favor and power with her Son greater than any other human or angelic creature has ever obtained or ever can obtain.
>
> —*Supreme Apostolatus*[337]

Mary, claims the Church, can persuade God to grant requests that He might otherwise turn down:

> All men, moreover, are full of the hope and confidence that prayers which might be received with less favor from the lips of unworthy men, will be accepted by God when they are recommended to him by the Most Holy Mother and will be favorably heard.
>
> —*Octobri Mense*[338]

Mary is presented as a softhearted mother:

> St. Dominic knew well that while on the one hand Mary is all powerful with her divine Son who grants all graces to mankind through her, on the other hand she is by nature so good and so merciful that inclined to aid spontaneously those who suffer, she is absolutely incapable of refusing her help to those who invoke her. The Church is in the habit of greeting the Virgin as the *Mother of Grace* and *Mother of Mercy*, and so she has always shown herself, especially when we have recourse to her by means of the Holy Rosary.
>
> —*Fausto Appetente Die*[339]

God, on the other hand, is portrayed as a somewhat cold and reluctant benefactor who must be approached through Mary:

> We have a confident hope that God will at length let himself be moved and have pity upon the state of his Church, and give ear to the prayers coming to him through her whom he has chosen to be the dispenser of all heavenly graces.
>
> —*Superiore Anno*[340]

Pope Pius XII taught: "While Peter has the keys of heaven, Mary has the key to God's heart...."[341] When she turns that key, the Church guarantees that the lock will open:

> We could not find a more powerful pro-
> tectress or one more irresistible before God. She
> is for us the best of mothers, our safest confidante
> and in fact the very motive of our hope; she
> obtains all she asks for and her prayer is always
> heard.
>
> —*Exultavit Cor Nostrum*[342]

As Christ's Mother, "Mary is all powerful with her divine Son,"[343] for "she is the mighty Mother of God":[344]

> For, while the prayers of those in heaven have
> certainly some claim on the watchful eye of God,
> Mary's prayers place their assurance on the right
> of a mother. For that reason, when she approaches
> the throne of her Divine Son, she begs as advo-
> cate, she prays as handmaid, but she commands
> as mother.
>
> —*Tanto Studio*[345]

Mary's powers in mediation, says the Church, even
extend to salvation. When praying the *Hail Mary*, Catholics ask her, "Pray for us sinners, now and at the hour of
our death" [1014]. The Church comments:

> By asking Mary to pray for us, we acknowledge
> ourselves to be poor sinners and we address our-
> selves to the "Mother of Mercy," the All-Holy
> One. We give ourselves over to her now, in the
> Today of our lives. And our trust broadens fur-
> ther, already at the present moment, to surrender
> "the hour of our death" wholly to her care. May
> she be there as she was at her son's death on the
> cross. May she welcome us as our mother at the
> hour of our passing to lead us to her son, Jesus in
> paradise.
>
> —*Catechism of the Catholic Church*[2677]

All of this is, of course, fallacious. The notion that
Mary would be more receptive to our prayers than our

heavenly Father who gave His only begotten Son for us is contrary to the character of God. Additionally, the proposition that Jesus' mother has authority over Him is a theological impossibility. The eternal God has no mother—far less a "mighty Mother"[346] whom He must obey. Furthermore, Jesus never made Mary the mother of mankind or the mother of the church when He was dying upon the cross. His words are clear enough when we read them in context:

> When Jesus therefore saw His mother, and the disciple whom He loved standing nearby, He said to His mother, "Woman, behold, your son!" Then He said to the disciple, "Behold, your mother!" And from that hour the disciple took her into his own household.
>
> —John 19:26,27

Jesus was arranging for the care of His mother after His death. The passage says nothing about Christ making Mary the mother of mankind or of the church.

Catholics who have surrendered the hour of their death "wholly to her care"[2677] will be tragically disappointed. Apart from the Lord Jesus, "there is no other name under heaven that has been given among men by which we must be saved" (Acts 4:12).

Explanation 2: Mary's Mediation Draws Its Power from Christ's Mediation [970]

The second reason the Council offered to explain how Mary's mediation does not infringe upon Christ's role as the sole mediator has to do with merit. The Council said that Mary's mediation—

> ...flows forth from the superabundance of the merits of Christ, rests on his mediation, depends entirely on it and draws all its power from it.
>
> —Second Vatican Council[347]

Pope Pius X made the same point, but added a significant qualification:

> We are then, it will be seen, very far from attributing to the Mother of God a productive power of grace—a power which belongs to God alone. Yet, since Mary carries it over all in holiness and union with Jesus Christ, and has been associated by Jesus Christ in the work of redemption, she merits for us *de congruo*, in the language of theologians, what Jesus Christ merits for us *de condigno*, and she is the supreme Minister of the distribution of graces.
>
> —*Ad Diem*[348]

In other words, if merit is strictly defined as the right to a reward justly earned, then Christ alone merited grace. But if merit is defined less narrowly—if the reward involves an element of God's generosity—then, as stated above, Mary also merited for us "what Jesus Christ merits for us." Furthermore, her merits along with Christ and the saints form one great reservoir [1476-1477]:

> The "treasury of the Church" is the infinite value, which can never be exhausted, which Christ's merits have before God. They were offered so that the whole of mankind could be set free from sin and attain communion with the Father. In Christ, the Redeemer himself, the satisfactions and merits of his Redemption exist and find their efficacy. This treasury includes as well the prayers and good works of the Blessed Virgin Mary. They are truly immense, unfathomable and even pristine in their value before God.
>
> —Second Vatican Council[349]

Not only are Mary's so-called "unfathomable"[350] merits said to be part of the treasury of the Church, but it is she who has earned the right to dispense all these treasures to the faithful:

And from this community of will and suffering between Christ and Mary she merited to become most worthily the Reparatrix of the lost world and Dispensatrix of all the gifts that Our Saviour purchased for us by His Death and by His Blood.

—*Ad Diem*[351]

In Roman Catholicism, Mary rather than Christ is "the supreme Minister of the distribution of graces."[352]

Explanation 3: Mary's Mediation Promotes Immediate Union with Christ

The final reason that the Second Vatican Council gave to justify Mary's role as co-mediator was that her mediation—

...does not hinder in any way the immediate union of the faithful with Christ but on the contrary fosters it.

—Second Vatican Council[353]

How Mary's mediation fosters *immediate* union with Christ is not clear, for the Church actually discourages Catholics from trying to go directly to Christ. It starts by telling the faithful that the custodian of all heavenly blessing is not Christ, but Mary. She is "... the seat of all divine graces and is adorned with all gifts of the Holy Spirit.... an almost infinite treasury, an inexhaustible abyss...."[354] According to the Church:

God has committed to her the treasury of all good things, in order that everyone may know that through her are obtained every hope, every grace, and all salvation. For this is his will, that we obtain everything through Mary.

—*Ubi Primum*[355]

If Catholics desire to receive anything from God, the Church says they must first speak to Mary. She sits

"... at the right hand of her Son—a refuge so secure and a help so trusty against all dangers that we have nothing to fear or to despair of under her guidance, her patronage, her protection."[356] There she functions as the "Mediatrix to the Mediator."[357] Every request to the throne of God must first pass her scrutiny: "...just as no one can approach the highest Father except through the Son, so no one can approach Christ except through His Mother."[358] Attempting to get to God without first going through Mary is like "trying to fly without wings."[359]

Moreover, all blessing coming down from heaven must first pass through Mary:

> Every grace granted to men has three successive steps: By God it is communicated to Christ, from Christ it passes to the Virgin, and from the Virgin it descends to us.
>
> —*Jucunda Semper*[360]

Christ is the source of blessing, but Mary is the channel: "...every blessing that comes to us from the Almighty God comes to us through the hands of Our Lady."[361] This includes salvation. Mary is said to be the "Mediatrix of our salvation"[362] and the "instrument and guardian of our salvation."[363] Pope Leo XIII prayed:

> O Virgin most holy, none abounds in the knowledge of God except through thee; none, O Mother of God, obtains salvation except through thee, none receives a gift from the throne of mercy except through thee.
>
> —*Adiutricem Populi*[364]

Pope Leo's prayer would be accurate if he had been speaking of the Lord Jesus rather than of Mary. Only through Christ can we know God (John 1:18), obtain salvation (John 14:6), and receive mercy before the throne of grace (Hebrews 4:14-16). It is "through Him we both have our access in one Spirit to the Father" (Ephesians 2:18). This is the biblical formula for approaching

God: through the Son, in the Spirit, to the Father. Christ taught His disciples to pray in the name of the Son directly to the Father (John 16:26,27). Consequently, biblical Christians pray in the name of Jesus, not Mary (John 14:13,14).

The believer approaching the throne of God through Jesus may do so assured of acceptance: "We have confidence to enter the holy place by the blood of Jesus" (Hebrews 10:19). In Christ Jesus "...we have boldness and confident access through faith in Him" (Ephesians 3:12). Scripture exhorts: "Let us therefore draw near with confidence to the throne of grace, that we may receive mercy and may find grace to help in time of need" (Hebrews 4:16).

The Roman Catholic Church's teaching that the faithful must go through Mary to Jesus contradicts these truths. It destroys the close and direct contact between Christ and the redeemed, which is their privilege.

The Bible describes this relationship in terms of a body. Christ is the "head of the body, the church" (Colossians 1:18). All "are members of His body" (Ephesians 5:30). This metaphor speaks of the immediate and unimpeded union of every believer with Christ. It leaves no room for the mediation of Mary as taught by the Roman Catholic Church.

While the Church agrees that the faithful are the body of Christ and that He is their head [787-796], it nevertheless adds that Mary is—

> ...the connecting portion the function of which is to join the body to the head and to transmit to the body the influences and volitions of the head—We mean the neck. Yes, says St. Bernardine of Sienna, "she is the neck of Our Head, by which He communicates to His mystical body all spiritual gifts."
>
> —*Ad Diem*[365]

Mary's function as the neck of the body of Christ is also without biblical support. Between God and men, there is *one* mediator, not two (1 Timothy 2:5). Mary's role as the dispenser of all spiritual gifts is equally unbiblical. Scripture, without any mention of Mary, says that all spiritual blessings come from our heavenly Father:

> Every good thing bestowed and every perfect gift is from above, coming down from the Father of lights, with whom there is no variation or shifting shadow.
>
> —James 1:17

A Biblical Verdict

Though opportunities arose during His earthly ministry to do so, Jesus never taught that Mary was to receive special honor. Once, as the Lord spoke to a multitude, a woman in the crowd shouted out to Him, "Blessed is the womb that bore You, and the breasts at which You nursed!" (Luke 11:27). But Jesus deflected such honor ascribed to Mary, responding instead, "On the contrary, blessed are those who hear the word of God and observe it" (Luke 11:28). Another time it was announced to Jesus, "Behold, Your mother and Your brothers are standing outside seeking to speak to You" (Matthew 12:47). Again Jesus refused to elevate Mary, answering instead:

> "Who is My mother and who are My brothers?" And stretching out His hand toward His disciples, He said, "Behold, My mother and My brothers! For whoever does the will of My Father who is in heaven, he is My brother and sister and mother."
>
> —Matthew 12:48,49

Here the Lord Jesus asserted His independence from mere human relationships. He taught that a personal spiritual relationship with Him stemming from submission to God was of far greater importance than physical kinship based upon ties of the flesh. Paul echoes this theme, saying of the Lord Jesus, "... even though we have known Christ according to the flesh, yet now we know Him thus no longer" (2 Corinthians 5:16).

In contrast to Christ's example, Roman Catholicism takes advantage of every opportunity to exalt Mary. The Church expresses this intention in the Latin axiom *De Maria Nunquam Satis*, "Concerning Mary One Can Never Say Enough."

As we have seen, however, too much has already been said of her. In contradiction to Scripture, the Church has declared Mary to be the Immaculate Conception, the Mother of God, the Perpetual Virgin, the Co-redeemer, the Assumption, the Queen of Heaven and Earth, and the Mediatress of All Grace.

These doctrines have taken glory from God and have resulted in countless Catholics showing greater devotion to Mary than to Christ Himself. One must ask: Has the Roman Catholic Church led its people into idolatry?

To answer this question, we must first consider the biblical meaning of idolatry. In the Ten Commandments, God said:

> I am the Lord your God. ... You shall have no other gods before Me. You shall not make for yourself an idol. ... You shall not worship them or serve them; for I, the Lord your God, am a jealous God....
>
> —Exodus 20:2-5

If these commands are understood to simply forbid the worship of other gods *above* the Lord, then no one could accuse the Roman Catholic Church of promoting idolatry among its people. Roman Catholicism teaches that Mary is a created being. Her role in salvation is secondary to that of Christ. The devotion that the Church's theologians say she deserves is of a lower degree than that which is to be given to God.

But in the Ten Commandments the Lord does not forbid His people from having other gods *above* Him but *before* Him. He commands, "You shall have no other gods before Me" (Exodus 20:3), or literally, "before My face." God reveals Himself in the verses that follow as a "jealous God" (Exodus 20:5). He demands *undivided* loyalty and devotion. His people are to have no other gods "in addition"[366] to Him.

It is here that Roman Catholic devotion to Mary first crosses the line into idolatry. When misguided Catholics kneel before a statue of Mary, kiss her feet, and offer to her heartfelt praise and petition, they give to a creature the devotion which belongs to God alone. It is irrelevant that the Church defines this honor as secondary to that which is to be given to God. God will have no other gods *before* Him, regardless of how inferior. And though the Roman Catholic Mary is not an infinite and eternal being such as the God of the Bible, she is every bit as much a goddess as were the false gods and goddesses of the ancient world. These pagan deities were generally perceived as finite beings with very human characteristics and passions. Mary, as promoted by the Church, far exceeds most of these in her excellency, power, and achievements.

Indeed, Mary as defined by the Roman Catholic Church is virtually indistinguishable from the Son of God Himself in excellency, power, and achievement. They differ only by degree.

The Lord Jesus, according to Scripture, was without sin (1 John 3:5). Mary, according to the Church, was "immaculate in every respect."[367] The Church teaches that when speaking of sin, "the holy Virgin Mary is not even to be mentioned."[368]

Jesus pleased the Father in all that He did (Luke 3:22). As for Mary, according to the Church, "...in her was the Father well pleased with singular delight."[369]

As Jesus suffered and died for our redemption, so Mary "...suffered in the very depths of her soul with his most bitter sufferings and his torments...[and] in her heart died with him, stabbed by the sword of sorrow."[370] Moreover, because of their physical union, the Church says, "The blood of Christ shed for our sake, and those members in which he offers to his Father the wounds he received as the price of our liberty are no other than the flesh and blood of the Virgin...."[371] Thus "...she with Christ redeemed mankind,"[372] and "...has crushed the poisonous head of the serpent."[373]

When Mary's life on earth was completed, the Church says that she, like Christ, died. But even as her Son, Mary did not die because of her own sins. Rather, Mary died that she "...should in all things resemble Jesus; and as the Son died, it was becoming that the mother should also die...."[374]

Then, says the Church, Mary was bodily resurrected even as Christ.[375] She "...suffered temporal death, but still could not be kept down by the bonds of death...."[376] She was therefore "...raised body and soul to heavenly glory and likened to her risen Son in anticipation of the future lot of all the just...."[377]

Once in heaven, the Church says that Mary was "...exalted by the Lord as Queen over all things, that she might be the more fully conformed to her Son, the Lord of lords..."[378] [966]. Now, even as Christ sits at the right hand of God (Hebrews 1:13), "Mary sitteth at the right hand of her Son..."[379] [1053]. Thus began "...her heavenly glorification after the example of her only begotten Son, Jesus Christ...."[380] Her dominion is the same as His; she is "Queen of Heaven and of earth."[381] Her glory can be compared to none but Christ's:

> ...God has lavished upon this loving associate of our Redeemer, privileges which reach such an exalted plane that, except for her, nothing created by God other than the human nature of Jesus Christ has ever reached this level.
>
> —*Munificentissimus Deus*[382]

From this exalted plane, Roman Catholicism teaches that Mary serves as "...Advocate, Helper, Benefactress, and Mediatrix"[383] [969]. In this way she fulfills roles attributed in Scripture to the Father (James 1:17), the

Son (1 John 2:1; 1 Timothy 2:5), and the Holy Spirit (John 14:16).

Paralleling biblical descriptions of the Lord Jesus, the Church calls Mary the "inexpressible gift of the Almighty,"[384] the "Cause of Our Joy,"[385] the "Morning Star,"[386] the "Gate of Heaven,"[387] the "Refuge of Sinners,"[388] and "Our Lady of Perpetual Help."[389] She, with Christ, is said to be ". . . the instrument and guardian of our salvation."[390] The Church promises that "all those who seek Mary's protection will be saved for all eternity."[391]

The Roman Catholic Church makes similar comparisons between God the Father and Mary. As God is our Father, "Mary is our Mother."[392] As Jesus is the only begotten Son of the Father, so Mary remained a virgin that Jesus might be the "only-begotten son of His Mother."[393] The Scriptures describe God as "God Almighty" (Genesis 17:1). The Church describes Mary as the "Virgin Most Powerful."[394] She is ". . . the mighty Mother of God."[395] The power ". . . in her hands is all but unlimited."[396] The Scriptures describe God as the source of all wisdom (James 1:5). The Church describes Mary as the "Seat of Wisdom."[397] The Bible says that God is the God of the living (Mark 12:27). The Church says that Mary is the "Mother of the living."[398] God is the "Father of mercies" (2 Corinthians 1:3). Mary is the "Mother of Mercy."[2677] God dwells in perfect holiness seated on a throne guarded by Seraphim (Isaiah 6:1-3). Mary, according to the Church, is "'the All-Holy' (*Panagia*)"[493]:

> God alone excepted, Mary is more excellent than all, and by nature fair and beautiful, and more holy than the Cherubim and Seraphim. To praise her all the tongues of heaven and earth do not suffice.
>
> —*Ineffabilis Deus*[399]

This is the Mary of Roman Catholicism, a woman whom the Church has exalted above every other created being and has assigned attributes, titles, powers, and prerogatives that in Scripture belong to God alone. To her the Church has erected statues, shrines, churches, cathedrals, and basilicas. To her the Church calls all the faithful to lift their prayers, petitions, and praise.

This is nothing more than pagan goddess worship dressed up in Roman Catholic gowns. It is just as idolatrous as the ancient worship of the Semitic goddess Astarte. Known as Ishtar among the Babylonians, God condemned apostate Judah for worshiping her, even as the Roman Catholic Church does Mary, under the title of "queen of heaven" (Jeremiah 7:18; 44:17-19,25). The veneration shown to Mary in Roman Catholicism is no less offensive to God than the worship that wicked King Manasseh gave to the Tyrian goddess Asherah. He had a carved image of her set up in the house of the Lord (2 Kings 21:7). For this abomination, God brought "calamity on Jerusalem and Judah" (2 Kings 21:12). In the same way, the Roman Catholic Church has formed an idol with its own hands and called it Mary. The image can be found in virtually every Roman Catholic Church. In its doctrine, the Church enthrones Mary in heaven at the right hand of Christ. Can the Roman Catholic Church hope to escape the judgment of God?

Mary: Error Verses Truth

The Catholic Church Teaches	The Bible Teaches
1. Mary was preserved from all stain of original sin from the first instant of her conception (The Doctrine of the Immaculate Conception) [490-492].	Mary, a descendant of Adam, was born in sin (Psalm 51:5; Romans 5:12).
2. Mary, "the All-Holy," lived a perfectly sinless life [411, 493].	Mary was a sinner; God alone is holy (Luke 18:19; Romans 3:23; Revelation 15:4).
3. Mary was a virgin before, during, and after the birth of Christ [496-511].	Mary was a virgin until the birth of Christ (Matthew 1:25). Later she had other children (Matthew 13:55,56; Psalm 69:8).
4. Mary is the Mother of God [963, 971, 2677].	Mary was the earthly mother of Jesus (John 2:1).
5. Mary is the Mother of the Church [963, 975].	Mary is a member of the church (Acts 1:14; 1 Corinthians 12:13,27).
6. Mary is the co-redeemer, for she participated with Christ in the painful act of redemption [618, 964, 968, 970].	Christ alone is the Redeemer, for He alone suffered and died for sin (1 Peter 1:18,19).

7. At the end of her life, Mary was assumed body and soul into heaven (The Doctrine of the Assumption) [966, 974].

Upon her death, Mary's body returned to dust (Genesis 3:19).

8. Mary is the co-Mediator to whom we can entrust all our cares and petitions [968-970, 2677].

Christ Jesus is the one mediator to whom we can entrust all our cares and petitions (1 Timothy 2:5; John 14:13,14; 1 Peter 5:7).

9. We should entrust ourselves to Mary, surrendering "'the hour of our death' wholly to her care" [2677].

We should entrust ourselves to the Lord Jesus, surrendering the hour of our death wholly to His care (Romans 10:13; Acts 4:12).

10. God has exalted Mary in heavenly glory as Queen of Heaven and Earth [966]. She is to be praised with special devotion [971, 2675].

The name of the Lord is to be praised, for He alone is exalted above heaven and earth (Psalm 148:13). God commands, "You shall have no other gods before Me" (Exodus 20:3).

❖ PART FOUR ❖

AUTHORITY

❖ ❖ ❖

How did the Pope become the leader of the Roman Catholic Church? Who determines what Roman Catholics believe? Why is the gospel according to Rome so different from that of Christianity based solely upon the Bible?

Part Four will answer these questions by examining the authority structure of the Roman Catholic Church. It is a system based upon three beliefs:

- ❖ The Catholic bishops, with the Pope as their head, are the apostles' successors (Chapter 10, *The Pope and Bishops*).
- ❖ The Catholic bishops are the authoritative teachers and guardians of the Roman Catholic faith (Chapter 11, *The Magisterium*).
- ❖ The Catholic faith is contained in written Scripture and unwritten Tradition (Chapter 12, *Scripture and Tradition*).

In Part Four you will also get a glimpse at how Roman Catholic authority functions. In Chapter 10 you will go back to the days of the Roman Empire and the rise of papal power. There you will meet Sylvester, Bishop of Rome, and learn of his powerful new ally, Emperor Constantine. In Chapter 11 you will attend the First Vatican Council. At that historic meeting you will listen as the bishops of the Roman Catholic Church debate the doctrine of papal infallibility. Finally, in Chapter 12 you will see how Roman Catholic beliefs develop. There you will look over the shoulder of Pope Pius XII as he signs the document that made the Assumption of Mary a dogma of the Church.

❖10

THE POPE AND BISHOPS

Rome, May 20, 325 A.D.

From his palace balcony, Sylvester, Bishop of Rome, watched with fascination as scores of laborers below him carried stone to an adjacent building site. *Thank God for the Emperor!* Sylvester thought to himself, fully aware that if Emperor Constantine had not stopped the persecution of Christians, he himself might be down there hauling rock. More likely he would be in the penal lead mines of Sardinia. Most likely he would be dead!

Sylvester could trace his good fortune to an event that had occurred 13 years earlier.[400] In 312 A.D. Emperor Constantine, while preparing for battle against his arch-rival, Maxentius, saw a cross in the midday sun inscribed with the words *In This Sign Conquer*. Constantine immediately ordered his soldiers to mark their shields with the sign of Christ and to engage the enemy. The outcome was a remarkable victory that all accredited to the hand of the Christian God. Soon after this Constantine ordered an end to the persecution of Christians throughout the Empire and began to favor Christianity above all other religions.

Thank God for the Emperor! repeated Bishop Sylvester to himself as he retreated to the cool of his palace. Formerly the residence of Fausta, the Emperor's second wife, Constantine had donated it to the Bishop of Rome. There Sylvester reclined on a large couch. It also was a gift from the Emperor. So was the rest of the furniture, and the art, and the servants. In fact, everything in sight was from the Emperor—even the silk brocade robes that the Bishop wore. Everything! And more was on the way.

Constantine, an energetic man, had great plans for the Church. He had already arranged for a fixed portion of the provincial revenues to be deposited directly into Church coffers. He had granted the clergy a special tax exemption. He had made Sunday a public holiday. He had approved plans for magnificent shrines to be built in Bethlehem, the birthplace of Christ, and in Jerusalem at the site of the Holy Sepulcher. Rome was to be adorned with three large basilicas: one for Peter, one for Paul, and one for the Bishop of Rome.

The latter structure, already under construction adjacent to Sylvester's palace, would serve as the bishop's cathedral. The design called for seven golden altars. Workmen were preparing a canopy of solid silver to cover the main altar. Fifty chandeliers would crown the church.

The Emperor had also put at Sylvester's disposal the imperial mail and transportation systems. Worldwide councils would now be possible. In fact, even as Sylvester rested, the opening of the first ecumenical or general council was in progress.[401] The location was Nicaea, 1200 miles away. Constantine had invited 300 bishops to attend—all expenses paid. At that very moment, in fact, the Emperor was giving the bishops their opening instructions.

Vatican City

Imperial favor shaped the destiny of the Bishop of Rome and the Roman Catholic Church more than any other temporal factor. Its effects can still be seen in the Church today.

Most apparent are the physical monuments. The

basilica built next to Sylvester's palace, Saint John Lateran, is still considered the highest-ranking Roman Catholic church. Saint Peter's Basilica, however, has become the center of papal ceremonies. Originally constructed by Constantine in the fourth century, it was rebuilt in the sixteenth century following a design by Michelangelo. The modern structure stands 40 stories high and can hold 50,000 people, as many as a modern sports stadium.

Saint Peter's Basilica is located in Vatican City, an independent state within the city of Rome. About the size of a university campus, it is the world's smallest sovereign nation. Vatican City has its own government, flag, postal system, coins, radio station, and diplomatic corps. It is also the residence of the Pope and the location of the offices of the Roman Curia, the administrative and judicial arm of the Church.

Imperial influence in shaping the Roman Catholic Church can also still be seen in the geographic divisions that the Church borrowed from the political structure of the Empire. Around the world, Roman Catholic neighborhood churches serve districts called *parishes* [2179]. These are grouped into about 2000 regions called *dioceses* or *sees*, from the Latin for *seat*, each of which is governed by a bishop [833, 1560]. The Church has further grouped these dioceses into about 500 jurisdictions called *provinces*. The principal diocese in a province is called an *archdiocese* and is governed by an *archbishop* [887]. Rome is considered to be the principal archdiocese of the Church [834]. It is the *Apostolic See*, for, according to the Church, Peter was Rome's first bishop.

The Roman Catholic People

There are about 945 million Roman Catholics in the world today.[402] They represent 18 percent of the world's population. Roman Catholics are the primary religious group in South America (89 percent) and Central America (87 percent). A large percentage of Europeans (40 percent), Oceanians (27 percent), and North Americans (24 percent) are also Roman Catholics. They can also be found in Africa (14 percent) and Asia (3 percent).

The nations with the largest Catholic populations are Brazil (135.2 million), Mexico (83.8 million), the United States (56.4 million), Italy (55.7 million), the Philippines (52.3 million), France (47.6 million), Spain (37.0 million), Poland (36.6 million), Colombia (31.3 million), and Germany (28.6 million). The Catholics of these ten countries represent nearly 60 percent of the total membership of the Roman Catholic Church.

The Pope and Bishops
[551-553, 857-896, 1555-1561]

The Roman Catholic Church is a hierarchical organization arranged into ranks much like an army [771, 779]. At the top are the Church's *bishops*. They are considered to be "the successors of the apostles"[403] [77, 861-862, 869, 880, 938, 1087, 1562, 1594]:

> ...the bishops have by divine institution taken the place of the apostles as pastors of the Church, in such wise that whoever listens to them is listening to Christ and whoever despises them despises Christ and him who sent Christ.
>
> —Second Vatican Council[404]

Roman Catholicism teaches that the Church's bishops have inherited a threefold power from the apostles [873, 939, 1536, 1558]:

- Teaching power [77, 888-892].
  The bishops have the authority "to teach all peoples."[405] They alone have the right to interpret and teach revelation with authority [85, 100].

- Sanctifying power [893].
  The Church teaches that bishops have the power "to sanctify men in truth and to give

them spiritual nourishment."[406] Only bishops have the authority to ordain priests or other bishops [1559, 1575-1576]. They also oversee the administration of the sacraments [1369].

- Ruling power [883, 894-896].
  The bishops shepherd and govern the Church. They "have supreme and full authority over the universal Church."[407]

Roman Catholicism recognizes the Bishop of Rome as the head of the Church's bishops [880-883]. He is the *Pope*, meaning *father*, for he is the supreme teacher and shepherd of the Church [882, 937].

Papal authority has its roots in a doctrine referred to as *primacy*, from the Latin word meaning *first* [881]. Peter, says the Church, was first among the apostles and the primary ruler of the Church [552, 765, 862]:

> We teach and declare that, according to the gospel evidence, a primacy of jurisdiction over the whole church of God was immediately and directly promised to the blessed apostle Peter and conferred on him by Christ the lord.
>
> —First Vatican Council[408]

According to the Church, sometime after Pentecost Peter moved to Rome and became its first bishop. From there he ruled the universal church as head of the world's bishops. Whoever succeeds Peter as the bishop of Rome, therefore, also succeeds him as Pope [834, 862, 880, 882, 936].

Roman Catholicism teaches that the Pope is the vicar, or representative, of Christ on earth [869, 936]. His other official titles include Successor of Saint Peter, Prince of the Apostles, Supreme Pontiff of the Universal Church, Patriarch of the West, Primate of Italy, Archbishop of the Metropolitan of the Roman Province, and Sovereign of the State of Vatican City.

Serving the Pope as his top advisers and administrators are a select group of men, usually ordained bishops, called *cardinals*. Should the Pope die or resign, it is the duty of the cardinals to elect the next Pope.

Below the Pope and bishops in the hierarchical order are *priests* [1562-1568]. Most priests serve in parish churches, where they are responsible for pastoring and administering the sacraments [1595]. Their chief duties are to offer the Sacrifice of the Mass and to forgive sins through the sacrament of penance [1566, 1411, 1461].

Assisting priests with the sacraments, preaching, and parish administration are *deacons* [1569-1571]. Ordained by a bishop, deacons can perform the sacraments of baptism and marriage but do not have the authority to offer the Sacrifice of the Mass or hear confessions [1256, 1411, 1495, 1570, 1596, 1630].

Unordained men and women also serve the Church in hundreds of religious institutes [914-945]. Men in these organizations are called *brothers* and women are called *sisters* or *nuns*. These men and women minister in a wide variety of areas, including education, health care, social welfare, administration, and missions.

Within the Roman Catholic Church, there are two dominant *rites* or *forms of liturgy* [1200-1209]. The first developed in the Western Roman Empire and is called the *Western, Roman,* or *Latin Rite*. It spread throughout Western Europe and later was brought by Catholic missionaries to the Americas. Practiced today by the vast majority of Catholics, Roman Catholic churches following the Western Rite can be found throughout the world.

About 14 million Catholics follow the *Eastern Rite*.[409] The churches of this rite include the Maronite, Greek Melkite, Rumanian, Ukrainian, and Syro-Malabar (India). They form what is called the *Eastern Catholic Church* or the *Catholic Church of the Eastern Rite*. The principal bishops of this rite are called *patriarchs*. Though the liturgy of the Eastern Catholic Church is different from that of the Western, its doctrine is the same. This includes, of course, submission to the Bishop of Rome as the Supreme Pontiff.

The Roman Catholic Church[410]

Pope	1
Cardinals	148
Patriarchs	10
Archbishops	777
Bishops	3250
Priests	404,031
Deacons	18,408
Brothers	62,184
Sisters	875,332
Laity	943,213,859
Total	944,578,000

A BIBLICAL RESPONSE

The authority of the Roman Catholic hierarchy rests upon three beliefs: Christ made Peter the head of the apostles and the universal church; the apostles appointed bishops as their successors; the Pope, as the Bishop of Rome, is Peter's successor.

None of these claims, however, can be established from Scripture. It will be shown that:

- Peter was not the head of the apostles and the church.
- The bishops are not the apostles' successors.
- The Pope is not Peter's successor.

Peter Was Not the Head of the Apostles and the Church

Though the Roman Catholic Church agrees that Scripture teaches that Christ is the head of the Church (Colossians 1:17,18), it adds that the Pope is the "visible head of the whole church"[411] [669, 882, 936]:

> ...the Roman pontiff is the successor of blessed Peter, the prince of the apostles, true vicar of Christ, head of the whole church and

father and teacher of all christian people. To
him, in blessed Peter, full power has been given
by our lord Jesus Christ to tend, rule and govern
the universal church.

—First Vatican Council[412]

We will examine the four primary arguments that
the Church puts forth from Scripture in support of these
claims:

- Upon this rock
  Jesus said that Peter was the rock upon which
  He would build His Church (Matthew 16:18).

- Keys of the kingdom
  Jesus gave to Peter the keys to the kingdom of
  heaven (Matthew 16:19).

- Shepherd my sheep
  Jesus made Peter the shepherd of the universal
  church (John 21:16).

- Peter led the apostles
  The New Testament has many examples of
  Peter's leadership over the apostles and the
  church.

Upon This Rock

In the Gospel of Matthew we read:

Now when Jesus came into the district of Caesarea Philippi, He began asking His disciples,
saying, "Who do people say that the Son of Man
is?" And they said, "Some say John the Baptist;
and others, Elijah; but still others, Jeremiah, or
one of the prophets." He said to them, "But who
do you say that I am?" And Simon Peter answered
and said, "Thou art the Christ, the Son of the
living God." And Jesus answered and said to him,
"Blessed are you, Simon Barjona, because flesh
and blood did not reveal this to you, but My
Father who is in heaven. And I also say to you
that you are Peter, and upon this rock I will build

My church; and the gates of Hades shall not overpower it."

—Matthew 16:13-18

The Roman Catholic Church interprets Jesus here to say, "You are Peter, and upon you, Peter, I will build My church." Peter would be the rock upon which the Church would be built [552, 586, 881]. He would be the "prince of all the apostles and visible head of the whole church."[413]

There are several problems with this interpretation. The first is that someone reading Matthew's Gospel in Greek, the original language of the New Testament, would not have immediately concluded that Peter was the rock. In the Gospel of Matthew, when Jesus said to Simon, "You are Peter, and upon this rock I will build My church" (Matthew 16:18), His choice of words was significant. Though Peter's name means *rock* (*petros*), Jesus did not say, "You are Peter (*Petros*), and upon this rock (*petros*) I will build my church." What He said was, "You are Peter (*Petros*), and upon this rock (*petra*) I will build My church."

The word Jesus chose to use for rock, *petra*, is a feminine noun that refers to a *mass of rock*. The New Testament uses this word in Matthew 7:24,25 to refer to the bedrock upon which a wise man built his house. *Petra* is also found later in Matthew's Gospel with reference to Jesus' tomb, which workers had carved out of solid rock (Matthew 27:60).

Peter's name, *Petros*, on the other hand, is masculine in gender and refers to a *boulder* or a *detached stone*. Greek literature also uses it of a small stone that might be picked up and thrown.

What Jesus said to Peter could be translated, "You are *Stone*, and upon this *bedrock* I will build My church." His choice of words would indicate that the rock on which the church would be built was something other than Peter.

Anyone reading the Gospel of Matthew in the original Greek language would have noticed the difference.

The reader would have had to pause and decide what was meant by "upon this rock" (Matthew 16:18). The reader would not immediately have equated the rock (*petra*) with Peter (*Petros*), because the words are different.

To determine the best interpretation, the reader would have had to look more closely at the context. This is the second and greatest weakness with the Roman Catholic interpretation: It fails to give proper emphasis to the context.

The context of Matthew 16:13-20 is not about Peter; it is about Jesus. It starts with a question that Jesus raises about His identity: "Who do people say that the Son of Man is?" (Matthew 16:13). It reaches a climax with Peter's declaration: "Thou art the Christ, the Son of the living God" (Matthew 16:16). It concludes with the Lord warning His disciples "that they should tell no one that He was the Christ" (Matthew 16:20).

When Peter correctly answered Jesus' question as to His identity, the Lord remarked, "Blessed are you, Simon Barjona, because flesh and blood did not reveal this to you, but My Father who is in heaven" (Matthew 16:17). Peter's insight into Jesus' true identity was a revelation from God. In this context, Jesus, making a play on words, says, "You are Peter, and upon this rock I will build My church" (Matthew 16:18).

The context argues for interpreting "this rock" as referring back to the revelation and its content. In other words, the Lord Jesus as "the Christ, the Son of the living God" (Matthew 16:16) would be the solid rock upon which the Christian faith would rest. Every doctrine and practice would be founded upon Him. Every true believer would hold to a common conviction: Jesus is "the Christ, the Son of the living God" (Matthew 16:16).[414]

The cultural context of the passage also supports interpreting "this rock" as referring to Jesus in His identity as the Son of God. Matthew wrote his Gospel for a Jewish audience. He expected his readers to be familiar with Old Testament imagery.

How would a Jewish reader interpret "upon this rock"? G. Campbell Morgan answers, "If we trace the figurative use of the word rock through Hebrew Scriptures, we find that it is never used symbolically of man, but always of God."[415] For example:

> There is no one holy like the Lord;
> Indeed, there is no one besides Thee,
> Nor is there any rock like our God.
>
> —1 Samuel 2:2

> For who is God, but the Lord?
> And who is a rock, except our God?
>
> —Psalm 18:31

> Is there any God besides Me,
> Or is there any other Rock?
> I know of none.
>
> —Isaiah 44:8

The wider context of the New Testament also confirms that Jesus, not Peter, is the rock. For example, Peter himself wrote of Christ as a rock (*petra*):

> For this is contained in Scripture: "Behold I lay in Zion a choice stone, a precious corner stone, and he who believes in Him shall not be disappointed." This precious value, then, is for you who believe. But for those who disbelieve, "The stone which the builders rejected, this became the very corner stone," and, "A stone of stumbling and a rock (*petra*) of offense."
>
> —1 Peter 2:6-8

Paul also refers to Christ by the Greek word *petra*. In Romans he wrote of Christ as "a rock (*petra*) of offense" (Romans 9:33) over which the Jews had stumbled. In First Corinthians he wrote of a spiritual rock encountered by Israel in the wilderness. He identified that rock, saying, "...and the rock (*petra*) was Christ" (1 Corinthians 10:4).

Interpreting Christ as the rock upon which the church would be built also harmonizes well with other statements in Scripture. Paul warned, "No man can lay a foundation other than the one which is laid, which is Jesus Christ" (1 Corinthians 3:11). Here he emphasizes that Christ is the *foundation* upon which the church is built. In Ephesians, Paul speaks of the church as "having been built upon the foundation of the apostles and prophets, Christ Jesus Himself being the corner stone" (Ephesians 2:20). Here Paul pictures Christ as the *principal stone* and the apostles and prophets as secondary stones.

Roman Catholic proponents, aware that Matthew's use of the word *petra* in the phrase "upon this rock" does not help their cause, counter by arguing that Jesus taught in Aramaic, not Greek. They claim that when Jesus *spoke* the words recorded in Matthew 16:18, He did not change His words but repeated Peter's Aramaic name *Kepha*. What Christ said, they claim, was: "You are *Kepha*, and upon this *kepha* I will build my Church." And so, they say, it is clear that Peter was to be the foundation upon which the Church would be built.

What is clear is that Rome's interpretation of Matthew 16:18 cannot bear the scrutiny of close examination. Consequently, Roman Catholic defenders must move the discussion off the inspired page and onto the field of speculation.

The inspired New Testament Scriptures were written in Greek, not Aramaic. What Jesus might have said in Aramaic is conjecture. Furthermore, if, as some contend, the Aramaic is clear but the Greek inadequate or confusing, why did not the Holy Spirit simply import the Aramaic words? There are many such examples in the New Testament.[416] There are even nine places where the Scriptures refer to Peter as *Cephas*, the Aramaic form of his name.[417] Or why did not the Holy Spirit just repeat the word *petros*, as Catholic defenders speculate He did in the Aramaic? Then Matthew 16:18 would read, "You are Peter (*Petros*), and upon this rock (*petros*) I will build My church."

But rather than speculate, why not let the passage speak for itself? When the Holy Spirit inspired the Greek text of the New Testament, He made a distinction between Peter (*Petros*) and the rock (*petra*). The reason for the difference is clear from the context.

Keys of the Kingdom

After Jesus told Peter that He would build His church, He said to him:

> I will give you the keys of the kingdom of heaven; and whatever you shall bind on earth shall be bound in heaven, and whatever you shall loose on earth shall be loosed in heaven.
>
> —Matthew 16:19

The Roman Catholic Church teaches that the keys here represent *supreme authority* [553]. Peter was to be the head of the apostles and the Church [552-553, 1444-1445].

Keys can indeed represent authority. However, in that no other Scripture confirms that Peter ever exercised *supreme* authority over the apostles or the church, this interpretation must be rejected.

Additionally, other figurative references in Scripture to keys specify their significance as being the authority *to grant access* or *to deny access*, the power *to open* or *to close* (Isaiah 22:22; Luke 11:52; Revelation 3:7,8; 9:1,2; 20:1-3). There are biblical examples of Peter exercising that kind of authority.

It was through Peter, along with the eleven, that God first offered salvation to the Jewish nation after its rulers had crucified Christ (Acts 2:14-36). It was through Peter, along with Philip and John, that the gospel first came to the Samaritans (Acts 8:4-25). God also used Peter to open the kingdom of heaven to the first Gentile believers (Acts 9:32-10:48). Peter initially and Paul later were the human instruments by which God "opened a door of faith to the Gentiles" (Acts 14:27).

The second part of Matthew 16:19 provides further information about the kind of authority that Peter was to exercise. There it speaks of Peter having the authority to "bind" or to "loose." Christ gave this same authority to all the disciples in Matthew 18:18. The context there is *church discipline.* The Lord told His disciples that if they followed His instructions in disciplining an unrepentant member of the church, God would honor their decision: "Truly I say to you, whatever you shall bind on earth shall be bound in heaven; and whatever you loose on earth shall be loosed in heaven" (Matthew 18:18). In that this is the same promise that Christ gave earlier to Peter, it is reasonable to conclude that the two passages are speaking about the same kind and degree of authority.

Shepherd My Sheep

Christ said to Peter:

> "Simon, son of John, do you love Me?" He said to Him, "Yes, Lord; You know that I love You." He said to him, "Shepherd My sheep."
>
> —John 21:16

The Roman Catholic Church says that in John 21:15-17 Christ declared that Peter was to be the supreme pastor of the universal Church [553, 816, 937]. Catholic scholars say that two words that Jesus uses in this passage, "tend" (John 21:15,17) and "shepherd" (John 21:16), denote—

> ...authority in society. Since this authority is given only to Peter, then Peter holds the true primacy through which he performs the offices of the supreme pastor of Christ's Church.
>
> —*Manual of Dogmatic Theology*[418]

Elsewhere in the Bible, however, the word translated "tend" (John 21:15,17) does not appear to have quite such an expansive and noble meaning as that assigned to it by Catholic scholars. The seven other uses of the word in the New Testament refer to tending or feeding swine!

For example, Luke, speaking of the prodigal son, says that the young man's employer "sent him into his fields to feed swine" (Luke 15:15). It is doubtful that the prodigal understood this directive as the bestowal upon him of a primacy of any kind!

The word translated "shepherd" means *to care for, protect,* and *nurture*. It can mean *to lead, to guide,* and even *to rule*. But nothing in the context of John 21:1-23 would indicate that Jesus was asking Peter to do anything more than to care for His sheep—that is, to show pastoral concern for those who would become Christians.

The Scriptures teach that shepherding is a shared responsibility. Paul instructed elders that in the local church it was their responsibility "to shepherd the church of God" (Acts 20:28). Peter himself taught the same:

> Therefore, I exhort the elders among you, as your fellow elder and witness of the sufferings of Christ, and a partaker also of the glory that is to be revealed, shepherd the flock of God among you, exercising oversight not under compulsion, but voluntarily, according to the will of God; and not for sordid gain, but with eagerness; nor yet as lording it over those allotted to your charge, but proving to be examples to the flock. And when the Chief Shepherd appears, you will receive the unfading crown of glory.
>
> —1 Peter 5:1-4

Here Peter describes shepherding as leadership by example. It is a ministry of the elders of the local church. He describes himself not as the *supreme shepherd* but as "your fellow elder" (1 Peter 5:1). Peter explicitly forbids anyone from "lording" (1 Peter 5:3) authority over other Christians. He identifies the "Chief Shepherd" (1 Peter 5:4) not as himself, but as the Lord Jesus Christ.

Peter Led the Apostles

Roman Catholic scholars claim that Peter's primacy is demonstrated throughout the New Testament:

- Peter played a key role in many events.
- Peter's name is first in lists of the names of the apostles.
- Peter was the spokesman for the apostles.
- Peter was the first witness of the resurrection.
- Peter wrote two New Testament epistles.
- Peter exercised supreme leadership at the Council of Jerusalem.
- Peter was the first to preach to the Jews and to the Gentiles.

Do these points indeed prove that Peter was the supreme head of the apostles and the universal church? We will consider these claims individually and then collectively.

Did Peter play a key role in many events?

There is no dispute as to whether or not Peter played an important role during Jesus' earthly ministry and in the early church. As an apostle, he had authority. As a man of God, he had respect. He was openhearted, full of conviction, and courageous. In many ways he was the dominant figure among the apostles. There is no evidence, however, that Peter ruled the apostles or had *supreme* authority over the early church.

Why does Peter's name appear first in lists of the apostles (Matthew 10:2-4; Mark 3:16-19; Luke 6:14-16)?

Peter's important and often dominant role among the apostles may account for the fact that his name is listed first. The order may indicate nothing more, however, than that Peter was the oldest. Jews were scrupulous about honoring the eldest in such lists.

Though the Gospels list Peter first, when Paul identified those "who were reputed to be pillars" in the church of Jerusalem, he listed Peter second: "James and Cephas and John" (Galatians 2:9). Paul acknowledged these three as being of "high reputation" (Galatians 2:6), but then added, "What they were makes no difference to me; God shows no partiality" (Galatians 2:6). Clearly,

Paul did not think of these three as the hierarchial leaders of the universal church or Peter as its head.

Was Peter the spokesman for the apostles?

It is true that Peter was usually the first to react. As a young man he was outspoken, impetuous, and self-confident (not positive traits by biblical standards). The results were not always predictable. When Jesus told the apostles that He would soon die, Peter took Him aside and rebuked Him, saying, "This shall never happen to You." Jesus replied to Peter, "Get behind Me, Satan! You are a stumbling block to Me; for you are not setting your mind on God's interests, but man's" (Matthew 16:21-23). Not a very good start for the new Pope!

Did the Lord first appear to Peter?

It is not true that Christ appeared first to Peter after the resurrection. That honor went to Mary Magdalene. First the Lord appeared to Mary (Mark 16:9-11; John 20:11-18). Then He appeared to a group of faithful women (Matthew 28:8-10). Then He appeared to Peter, the first man so privileged (1 Corinthians 15:5).

Did Peter write two New Testament books?

Peter did receive the honor of writing two books of the New Testament. This, however, proves nothing about primacy. If it did, Paul, who wrote 13 books, should have been Pope.

Was Peter the supreme leader at the Council of Jerusalem?

At the Council of Jerusalem, the apostles and many elders came together to settle a controversy regarding the relationship of Judaism and Christianity (Acts 15:1-5). Specifically: Did Gentile converts need to be circumcised? There was much debate (Acts 15:7). Peter made an important contribution, but not a decisive one (Acts 15:7-11). It was James who gave the final speech (Acts 15:13-21). Speaking from the Old Testament, the authoritative norm of the early church, James passed judgment on the issue (Acts 15:19-21). The council formed a consensus, and the matter was closed. Peter neither ruled the council nor decided its outcome.

Call No Man Father

Jesus taught:

"Do not be called Rabbi; for One is your Teacher, and you are all brothers. And do not call anyone on earth your father; for One is your Father, He who is in heaven. And do not be called leaders; for One is your Leader, that is, Christ. But the greatest among you shall be your servant" (Matthew 23:8-11).

The Roman Catholic Church has organized and titled its hierarchy with total disregard for these commands. Here are some of the most common titles that the Church uses:

Abbot: A superior of a monastery. From the Aramaic word *abba*, meaning *father.*

In summary, when Peter's life is considered as a whole, it is evident that though Peter was a leader *among* the apostles and the early church, he was not the supreme leader *over* the apostles and the early church. The Lord Jesus was the head of the apostles (John 13:13), and the Lord Jesus, according to the Bible, is the head of the universal church:

> He is also head of the body, the church; and
> He is the beginning, the firstborn from the dead;
> so that He Himself might come to have first place
> in everything.
> —Colossians 1:18

Primacy belongs to Jesus alone!

The Bishops Are Not the Apostles' Successors

The Church claims that by divine right its bishops are the apostles' successors. The four primary arguments from Scripture put forth by Roman Catholic scholars for this claim are:[419]

Doctor: A group of 32 teachers canonized as saints and recognized as trustworthy guides for the faithful. From the Latin word for *teacher.*

Monsignor: A title of honor bestowed on some priests for outstanding service. From the Italian for *my lord.*

Father: A title first given to bishops and later to all priests.

Holy Father: One of the titles of the Pope. In the Scriptures, it is a title reserved for God alone (John 17:11).

Pope: A title first given to all bishops and later reserved for the Bishop of Rome. From the Latin word *papa,* meaning *father.*

- Indefectibility of the Church
  Apostolic succession is necessary that the Church might stand against the forces of Hell (Matthew 16:18).
- End of the age
  Christ promised to be with the apostles "... always, even to the end of the age" (Matthew 28:20).
- Entrust to faithful men
  Paul told Timothy to pass his office on "... to faithful men, who will be able to teach others also" (2 Timothy 2:2).
- Timothy and Titus
  Paul ordained Timothy and Titus as bishops and bestowed on them his apostolic power.

Indefectibility of the Church

Christ promised:

> ... I will build My church; and the gates of Hades shall not overpower it.
>
> —Matthew 16:18

Roman Catholic scholars reason that for the Church to prevail until the end of time, it is necessary that the power of Peter and the other apostles to teach, sanctify, and rule also continue to the end [552]. For this reason, they argue, the apostles must have passed their power on to bishops as their successors.

In making such claims, however, Catholic scholars go beyond what is written in Scripture. In Matthew 16:18 Christ promised that His church would prevail. He said nothing about accomplishing that goal through apostolic succession.

End of the Age

Before Jesus ascended into heaven, He promised His disciples:

> ...lo, I am with you always, even to the end of the age.
> —Matthew 28:20

The Church says that if Jesus was going to be with the apostles to the end of the age, they had to have successors [860]. These, it is claimed, are the bishops of the Roman Catholic Church.

Here again the verse cited says nothing about apostolic succession. In the previous verse Jesus told His apostles to go and "make disciples of all the nations" (Matthew 28:19), not to go and appoint bishops over all dioceses. In Matthew 28:20 Jesus' promise is to personally be with His disciples, the disciples they would produce, and so on until the end of time.

Entrust to Faithful Men

Paul instructed Timothy:

> The things which you have heard from me in the presence of many witnesses, these entrust to faithful men, who will be able to teach others also.
> —2 Timothy 2:2

Roman Catholic scholars say that this verse teaches that just as Paul, by the laying on of hands, had bestowed his apostolic powers upon Timothy, so Timothy was to pass these powers on to others. Timothy was to select faithful men and ordain them as bishops. These bishops were to ordain others, and so on down through the centuries [861-862, 1556].

This extension of 2 Timothy 2:2 is unjustified. Paul, writing from prison, expected to be executed at any time (2 Timothy 4:6). He instructed Timothy, whom He had trained, to select faithful men and hand on to them "the things which you have heard from me" (2 Timothy 2:2). Timothy was to pass on the truths and skills that Paul had taught him. The passage says nothing about Paul passing his powers on to Timothy, or of Timothy passing on these powers and the office of bishop to others.

Timothy and Titus

Roman Catholic scholars claim that Paul ordained Timothy as Bishop of Ephesus and Titus as Bishop of Crete [1590]. This, they say, can be seen in the threefold apostolic powers that both Timothy and Titus exercised [1558]: teaching power (2 Timothy 4:2-5; Titus 2:1), ruling power (1 Timothy 5:19-21; Titus 2:15), and sanctifying power (1 Timothy 5.22; Titus 1:5).

These Scriptures, however, establish nothing more than that Timothy and Titus were involved in active and important ministries in association with Paul. When writing to the Corinthians, Paul told them to receive Timothy not because he was a bishop but because "he is doing the Lord's work, as I also am" (1 Corinthians 16:10). Speaking of Timothy and Apollos, Paul told the Corinthians to "be in subjection to such men and to everyone who helps in the work and labors" (1 Corinthians 16:16). "As for Titus," wrote Paul, "he is my partner and fellow worker among you" (2 Corinthians 8:23). Scripture never identifies Timothy or Titus as bishops. Nowhere do we find them (or anyone else, for that matter), meeting with a college of bishops and ruling the universal church.

The Church cannot even establish from Scripture the degree of power that it says belonged to the apostles and was passed on to bishops. Nowhere does the Bible teach that the apostles ruled the universal church. According to the Scriptures, Christ rules the church (Colossians 1:18). Nowhere does the Bible teach that the apostles had the power to sanctify. According to the Scriptures, sanctification is a work of God, not men (Ephesians 5:26; 1 Thessalonians 5:23; 2 Thessalonians 2:13).

The apostles did have a significant teaching role, especially as witnesses of Christ's resurrection (Acts 1:22). Their teaching, together with the prophets, formed the foundation of the Christian faith (Ephesians 2:20). That foundation, however, has now been laid. Consequently, their unique teaching office cannot be claimed today by others.

The Pope Is Not Peter's Successor

The Roman Catholic Church does not offer even a single scriptural argument to substantiate its claim that the Bishop of Rome is Peter's successor and thereby the Pope. It cannot, for there is none. Instead, it must again resort to human reasoning and conjecture.

The Roman Catholic belief that the Bishop of Rome is Peter's successor rests not on Scripture but on an argument from history [834, 882, 936]. It basically says that the Bishop of Rome is Peter's successor because historically that is what happened.

More specifically, the historic argument says that Christ made Peter the head of the apostles and the Church. In this way the Lord established a "hierarchical and monarchical"[420] society, the Roman Catholic Church. Sometime after Pentecost, the argument goes, the apostles ordained bishops as their successors. These submitted to Peter as their head. When Peter moved to Rome and became its first bishop, he established that city as the apostolic seat of government.

Peter, says the Church, was succeeded by Linus (67-76) as Bishop of Rome and head of the Church. Linus was succeeded by Anacletus (76-88), who was succeeded by Clement (88-97), Evaristus (97-105), Alexander I (105-115), Sixtus I (115-125), and so on down to modern times. The ten most recent popes have been Pius IX (1846-1878), Leo XIII (1878-1903), Pius X (1903-1914), Benedict XV (1914-1922), Pius XI (1922-1939), Pius XII (1939-1958), John XXIII (1958-1963), Paul VI (1963-1978), John Paul I (1978), and John Paul II (1978-present).

Roman Catholic scholars teach that this continuity of succession, together with Tradition and the infallible teaching of the bishops, establishes that it is historically certain that the Roman Pontiff by divine right is Peter's successor.

These claims, however, cannot be established either biblically or historically. Scripture makes no reference to Peter being the Bishop of Rome, ruling the universal church, or having a successor. Neither is there any indication in Scripture that Rome was the governmental center of the early church. In that Peter's apostleship was exercised in a special way to the Jewish nation (Galatians 2:7,8), we would not expect him to be based in Rome. Though Jews lived there, it was not the center of Judaism. In fact, it is known that in about 50 A.D. "... Claudius had commanded all the Jews to leave Rome" (Acts 18:2). Furthermore, from the first 15 chapters of Acts and the book of Galatians we know that Peter's ministry, at least until 49 A.D., was in the Middle East: Jerusalem, Judea, Samaria, Galilee, and Antioch.

If Peter established his ministry in Rome at some later date, one would think that Paul would have mentioned him in his letter to the Romans. Written about 58 a.d., Paul neither addresses the letter to Peter nor makes any mention of him, even though he greets 26 other people in Rome by name (Romans 16:1-16). Neither does Paul refer to Peter in any of his four letters written from a Roman prison about A.D. 61: Ephesians, Philippians, Colossians, Philemon. In his last letter from Rome, written about A.D. 66, Paul writes, "At my first defense no one supported me, but all deserted me; may it not be counted against them" (2 Timothy 4:16). At the time the letter was written, he states, "Only Luke is with me" (2 Timothy 4:11).

Nevertheless, some scholars believe that Peter came to Rome before he was martyred there about 67 A.D. They point to the closing greetings of his first letter as evidence. Peter writes: "She who is in Babylon, chosen together with you, sends you greetings, and so does my son, Mark" (1 Peter 5:13). Some believe that Babylon was a code name for Rome.

As for Peter's alleged successors, the New Testament says nothing. From other historical sources, little is known about them through the first two centuries. Church historian Philip Schaff writes: "The oldest links in the chain of Roman bishops are veiled in impenetrable darkness."[421] Consequently, it is impossible for the Roman Catholic Church to substantiate its claims of papal succession from Peter to the present Pope.

Furthermore, though published lists of popes down through the centuries look impressive, one should be aware that a comparison of the present list with those of earlier years reveals continuing revision, the last being made in 1947 by A. Mercati. Since then other changes have been found necessary. It is not even clear how some of the men listed have any claim at all to being Peter's successor as the Bishop of Rome, in that from 1305 to 1378 seven consecutive popes chose as their residence and seat of government not Rome, but Avignon, France!

Disputes involving the lineage of the popes further obscure the picture. Roman Catholic scholars identify over 30 men as *antipopes*, or false claimants. Most notable among the antipopes are those involved in a 39-year period called the Great Schism. In 1378 the cardinals elected Urban VI as pope. Soon after this they announced that they had made a terrible mistake. Urban, in their opinion, was an apostate, and so they elected a new Pope, Clement VII. Urban countered by appointing a new college of cardinals. After years of dispute, further successors, and great confusion, cardinals from both sides met and elected yet another man as Pope, Alexander V. When even this did not settle the controversy, Emperor

Sigismund called the Council of Constance (1414-1418) to address the problem. When the smoke finally cleared, yet another man, Martin V, was found sitting on the papal throne. Official lists of the lineage of the popes today identify Martin V as the 206th successor in the "unbroken" lineage of the popes.

In a very real sense, it is misleading for the Roman Catholic Church even to list popes during the first five centuries of church history. Church historian Michael Walsh observes:

> Papal authority as it is now exercised, with its accompanying doctrine of papal infallibility, cannot be found in theories about the papal role expressed by early Popes and other Christians during the first 500 years of Christianity.
>
> —*An Illustrated History of the Popes*[422]

The papacy as it is known today took centuries to develop. Its origin can be found in the emergence of bishops in the second century and events which took place in the political structure of the Roman Empire during the fourth and fifth centuries. To pick up the trail of the evolution of the modern papacy, it is necessary to go back to the New Testament church.

Following Pentecost, the apostles spread the gospel throughout much of the Mediterranean world. Guided by the Holy Spirit, they instructed new believers to gather together for instruction, fellowship, the breaking of bread, and prayer (Acts 2:42). In each community of believers, the apostles directed that two groups of servant-leaders be recognized.

The first group was the *diakonoi*, or *deacons*, which means *servants* (1 Timothy 3:8-13). Their role was to provide practical service to the church in areas such as dispensing food to the needy (Acts 6:1-6) and caring for widows (1 Timothy 5:9-16).

The second group was the *presbuteroi* (1 Timothy 3:1-7; Titus 1:5-9). The word literally means the *older men* and is usually translated *elders*. The title stresses the spiritual maturity and experience needed to qualify for the position. The New Testament also refers to elders as the *episkopoi*, meaning the *over-watchers*, *overseers*, or *bishops*. The title emphasizes the role of an elder in watching over and caring for the flock. The New Testament makes it clear that the elders and bishops were one and the same group. A comparison of Acts 20:17 with Acts 20:28 and of Titus 1:5 with Titus 1:7 confirms this point.

During the second and third centuries two significant developments took place. First, over some communities a single bishop emerged as the primary leader. This resulted in a three-tiered hierarchy: a single bishop, a group of elders, and a group of deacons [1554]. Despite the lack of a biblical basis for the change, the pattern quickly spread.

Next a hierarchy developed among the bishops, paralleling the political framework of the Roman Empire. Bishops of urban churches were given greater honor than those of rural churches. Bishops of provincial capitals rose above those of smaller cities. In the East, these bishops were called *metropolitans*, and in the West they were called *archbishops*.

During the fourth century, imperial favor raised the power and prestige of the bishops to even greater heights. Constantine awarded the bishops the status of government officials. Later emperors elevated them to the position of imperial princes. The greatest honor went to the bishops of the four capitals of the Roman Empire: Rome, Constantinople, Alexandria, and Antioch. The bishop of Jerusalem, the site of the first church, was likewise honored. These bishops were called *patriarchs*.

By the fifth century, bishops were the chief teachers and unchallenged leaders of the church. The stage was now set for one patriarch, the Bishop of Rome, to claim jurisdiction over the entire church. This development, however, would take yet more time to evolve. Historian Bruce Shelley comments: "Up to the time of Constantine history offers no conclusive evidence that the bishop of

Rome exercised jurisdiction outside of Rome. Honor, yes; jurisdiction, no."[423]

The ascent leading to the modern papacy can be traced through eight bishops, Sylvester (314-335) being the first. When in 330 Constantine moved his capital east to Byzantium and renamed it Constantinople (modern day Istanbul), a power vacuum was left in the West. This, coupled with the decline of the Roman Empire, proved to be fertile ground for the ambitions of Sylvester and his successors.

Next in the line of notable popes was Leo I (440-461). Not without cause does the Church call him Leo the Great. As the Roman Empire was crumbling, Leo's extraordinary abilities as a leader became evident. When Attila the Hun crossed the Alps in 452, it was Leo who went out to face him and single-handedly persuaded the barbarian to return to his home in peace. When in 455 the Vandals stormed Rome, once again it was Leo who saved the people from massacre and the city from the torch.

Many researchers also credit Leo with being the first bishop to effectively set forth the claim of the Bishop of Rome to primacy as Peter's successor. Leo argued that Scripture proved that Peter was the head of the apostles. He next reasoned that Rome was the *Apostolic See*, for Peter had been the first Bishop of Rome. Using Roman law, Leo then explained how each successive Bishop of Rome was the rightful heir to Peter's primacy.[424]

According to Roman law, Leo may have been right. But biblically, there was no basis for any of his claims. Regardless, the other bishops in the West were in no position to oppose him. Leo enjoyed the full support of Emperor Valentinian III, who issued an imperial edict confirming the primacy of the Bishop of Rome. Bishops in the East, however, were less than compliant. Historian Will Durant comments:

> The bishops of the West generally acknowl-
> edged, those of the East resisted, this supremacy.

> The patriarchs of Constantinople, Antioch, Jerusalem, and Alexandria claimed equal authority with the Roman see; and the furious controversies of the Eastern Church proceeded with scant obeisance to the bishop of Rome.
>
> —*The Story of Civilization*[425]

The dignity and power of the papacy rose yet further during the papacy of Gregory the Great (590-604). Some historians consider him to have been the first actual Pope of the Western Church. Though he harshly criticized John IV, patriarch of Constantinople, for being so arrogant as to claim the title of universal bishop, Gregory himself took every opportunity to extend the power of his own office. By the end of his reign he had set the course for the Church's theology through the Middle Ages, developed a distinctive musical form of liturgy (the Gregorian Chant), inaugurated the conversion of the Anglo-Saxons in the British Isles, and established the Roman Church as the largest landowner in Italy.

Up until this time all bishops had been addressed as *papa* (Latin) or *papas* (Greek), meaning *father*, a title of honor recognizing their spiritual paternity. By the end of the seventh century in the Western Church, however, the title was being reserved for the Bishop of Rome.

Another milestone in the evolution of the papacy was passed on Christmas Day in the year 800. That is when Pope Leo III (795-816) placed a golden crown upon the head of Charlemagne, King of the Franks, and pronounced him Emperor of the restored Christian Empire. How the tables had turned! Durant comments, "... thereafter no man could be an accepted emperor in the West without anointment by a pope."[426] Charlemagne reciprocated by ensuring that Roman liturgy and discipline were observed throughout the Empire.

In the eleventh century the ambitions of the papacy turned to military conquest. In 1095 Pope Urban II took up the sword and called for the first crusade to liberate the Holy Land from Moslems. During the next 200 years popes sent out thousands of crusaders to kill and be killed in eight futile crusades. The damage done by these crusades in alienating millions of people from the gospel of Jesus Christ cannot be measured.

By the reign of Pope Gregory IX (1227-1241), it was the Pope who was being crowned:

> The pope was no longer only consecrated. He was crowned with a tiara, a helmet-shaped head covering used originally by the deified rulers of Persia. The coronation rite, so redolent of imperial prerogatives, was used in the conferral of the papacy from that time until 1978....
>
> —*Catholicism*[427]

The ruling power of the Pope now well-established, Gregory IX turned his attention to strengthening his teaching authority. In 1231 he instituted the Roman Inquisition to purge the Church of heretics. This and the later Spanish Inquisition (1478-1820) resulted in the trial, torture, and imprisonment of thousands of people. Those who refused to recant were executed—usually by burning—by civil authorities acting on behalf of the Church. Pope Boniface VIII (1294-1303) defended this relationship between Church and state by saying that there are—

> ...two swords, namely spiritual and temporal.... each is in the power of the Church, that is, a spiritual [sword] and a material sword. But the latter, indeed, must be exercised for the Church, the former by the Church. The former [by the hand] of the priest, the latter by the hand of kings and soldiers, but at the will and sufferance of the priest. For it is necessary that a sword be under a sword and that temporal authority be subject to spiritual power....
>
> —*Unam Sanctam*[428]

Many of those who perished during the inquisition were Christians trying to practice a simple biblical faith.

The summit of the modern papacy was reached during the reign of Pope Pius IX (1846-1878). It was then that the First Vatican Council (1869-1870) declared that the Pope, in view of his supreme apostolic authority, was infallible, divinely protected from error in his official teaching.

Though in recent years the papacy has toned down its public image considerably, it has not backed away from any of its previous claims. Quite the contrary, the Second Vatican Council reasserted them.[429]

Why Do Catholics Submit?

As we have seen, the attempts of the Roman Catholic hierarchy to establish its authority from Scripture are astonishingly weak. The Church's claim that Christ made Peter the head of the universal church rests almost completely on the Roman Catholic interpretation of Matthew 16:18,19. The assertion that the Roman Catholic bishops are the apostles' successors is based upon the thinnest of implications. The Church does not even offer a biblical case to support its claim that since the Pope is the Bishop of Rome he is also Peter's successor.

These claims form the foundation upon which the authority of the Roman Catholic hierarchy rests. Yet the Church cannot prove any of them from the Bible. So why do Catholics submit to the rule of the Pope and bishops?

Many Catholics mistakenly assume that strong biblical support exists for the Roman hierarchy. "Thou art Peter; and upon this rock I will build my church" (Matthew 16:18 Douay Rheims) is one of the few verses that Catholics can quote. Not many, however, have ever stopped to ask what this verse has to do with the Roman Catholic Pope and bishops.

Other Catholics are satisfied with arguments based upon Tradition and the authoritative teaching of popes and bishops.

Still others have submitted to the Roman hierarchy without ever having asked why. They believe it would be disloyal to God for them to even think of questioning the credentials of the Pope and bishops. Yet Christ commended the Ephesians for essentially doing the same: "... you put to the test those who call themselves apostles, and they are not, and you found them to be false..." (Revelation 2:2).

Finally, many Catholics submit to the Pope and bishops because they are impressed with the size and antiquity of the Roman Catholic Church. "God," they reason, "must be the empowering force behind it. How else," they ask, "could so few men come to rule over so many people and such great wealth?"

But certainly, if it were God's intention that the Roman Catholic Pope and bishops were to rule over the church, God would have made that fact clear in the Scriptures. Since this clearly is not the case, we must conclude that the power of the Pope and bishops does not come from God.

❖11

THE MAGISTERIUM

Rome, July 11, 1870

With the First Vatican Council about to reconvene, bishops from around the world began quietly filing into Saint Peter's Basilica.[430] Already seated, Bishop Vincent Ferrer Gasser, prince of the crownland of Austria, was putting the finishing touches on a speech he was about to deliver to the Council. In it he would explain the merits of a proposal before the council that the Church officially declare that the Pope is infallible, incapable of teaching error. Some bishops had already voiced their opposition.

Bishop Gasser quickly reviewed his speech. He began by silently rehearsing his introduction: "Most eminent presidents, eminent and reverend fathers: I get up to speak today with great sadness and even greater fear . . . lest a great cause be ruined by its advocate. Nevertheless, I proceed, counting on divine grace and your good will."[431]

None of the committee that had drafted the proposal shared Bishop Gasser's fears that their cause might suffer loss in his hands. In their opinion, he was an ideal spokesman: a former professor of dogmatic theology, a respected scholar, a skilled debater.

Bishop Gasser's goal was to demonstrate that papal infallibility was part of the Catholic faith received from

Christ. He would state this objective early in his speech: "Since this infallibility is a revealed truth, it should be proved from the fonts of revelation, that is, from Sacred Scripture and tradition."[432]

With time running out, Gasser scanned the list of authorities he would cite. He would start with Scripture, making reference to the four Gospels and the letters of Paul. Then he would move to the witnesses of sacred Tradition. From among them, he would quote two ancient Church Fathers, Irenaeus and Epiphanius, and three Doctors of the Church: Jerome, Augustine, and Ambrose. Next he would go to the sixteenth century, employing the writings of theologians Cardinal Cajetan and Melchior Cano. He would also remind the bishops of a well-known inscription within Saint Peter's Basilica: "From this place one faith shines on the world." Finally he would quote three ecumenical councils: Constantinople IV, Lyons, and Florence.

As the last bishop took his seat, Gasser carefully reviewed his two main arguments. The first was that Christ gave Peter the ability to teach without error. This, he would argue, occurred when the Lord made Peter the head of the apostles and of the universal church. The second point logically followed: since the Pope is Peter's successor, he is also heir to Peter's gift of infallibility.

The ringing of a bell brought Bishop Gasser's preparation to a close. The First Vatican Council was in session.

Bishop Gasser spoke eloquently and with conviction that day, his speech taking four hours. When he finished, he took his seat, fully aware of the historic significance of the moment.

Bitter controversy followed. The bishops rejected the first draft of the decree in a private vote; 88 bishops stood opposed. The document was sent back to committee for revision.

Five days later, after further debate, the bishops held another vote. This time they approved the decree:

533 in favor, 2 opposed. Henceforth the Roman Catholic Church would dogmatically teach that God had revealed that the Roman Pontiff is immune from even the possibility of teaching error. The decision would be irreversible, irreformable, and binding upon Catholics everywhere. *Roma locuta est; causa finita est*—Rome has spoken; the case is closed.

Teaching Authority
[85-90, 168-171, 888-892, 2032-2040, 2049-2051]

Roman Catholicism teaches that God has appointed bishops as the teachers of the Catholic faith [77, 888-892]:

> In order that the full and living Gospel might always be preserved in the Church the apostles left bishops as their successors. They gave them "their own position of teaching authority."
>
> —Second Vatican Council[433]

The teaching authority of the Church resides in the bishops and is called the *Magisterium*, from the Latin word for *master*. Only the bishops of the Church have the right to judge the true meaning of revelation and to teach it with authority [85, 100, 939]:

> The task of giving an authentic interpretation of the Word of God, whether in its written form or in the form of Tradition, has been entrusted to the living teaching office of the Church alone. Its authority in this matter is exercised in the name of Jesus Christ.
>
> —Second Vatican Council[434]

Catholics, therefore, are to obey the bishops even as they would Christ Himself [87, 862]:

> ...the bishops have by divine institution taken the place of the apostles as pastors of the

Church, in such wise that whoever listens to them is listening to Christ and whoever despises them despises Christ and him who sent Christ (cf. Luke 10:16).

—Second Vatican Council[435]

Consequently [891, 2034, 2037, 2041, 2050]:

...the faithful, for their part, are obliged to submit to their bishops' decision, made in the name of Christ, in matters of faith and morals, and to adhere to it with a ready and respectful allegiance of mind.

—Second Vatican Council[436]

Matters of *faith* here refers to the doctrinal *beliefs* of the Roman Catholic religion, such as the real presence of Christ in the Eucharist and the Immaculate Conception of Mary. Matters of *morals* refers to proper *conduct*, such as loving one's neighbor and obedience to the commandments.

Church doctrine relating to *faith and morals* is to be distinguished from Church *discipline and practice*. The latter involves aspects of the Roman Catholic religion that may be optional, such as praying the Rosary, or that may change, such as abstinence from eating meat on Fridays. Conversely, Roman Catholic teaching as to faith and morals, says the Church, does not change:

...that meaning of the sacred dogmas is ever to be maintained which has once been declared by holy mother church, and there must never be any abandonment of this sense under the pretext or in the name of a more profound understanding.

—First Vatican Council[437]

Roman Catholicism, claims the Church, is always the same: "...the same doctrine, the same sense, and the same understanding"[438] [84]. Hence the Latin axiom *Semper Eadem*, "Always the Same."

Infallibility
[890-891, 2032-2040, 2051]

The Bishops

Roman Catholicism teaches that God supernaturally protects the Magisterium from teaching falsehood. The bishops do not err and cannot err when teaching doctrine related to faith and morals. They are said to possess the gift of *infallibility*.

The bishops are believed to be infallible in their teaching not as individuals but collectively. In other words, those beliefs that they hold in common with each other and in harmony with the Pope represent the authentic and inerrant Catholic faith [890-891, 939]. This principle applies to the bishops' teaching regardless of whether it is expressed by the decree of an ecumenical council or through their everyday ministry [2033-2034, 2049].[439]

The Pope

Roman Catholicism teaches that the gift of infallibility extends to the teaching of the Bishop of Rome in a special way. The First Vatican Council (1869-1870) decreed:

> ... we teach and define as a divinely revealed dogma that when the Roman pontiff speaks *ex cathedra*, that is, when, in the exercise of his office as shepherd and teacher of all Christians, in virtue of his supreme apostolic authority, he defines a doctrine concerning faith or morals to be held by the whole church, he possesses, by the divine assistance promised to him in blessed Peter, that infallibility which the divine Redeemer willed his church to enjoy in defining doctrine concerning faith or morals.
>
> —First Vatican Council[440]

Speaking *ex cathedra* literally means speaking *from the chair* of authority. This means that when the Pope speaks as the supreme teacher of the Church, Roman Catholicism holds that he does not and cannot teach false doctrine. For this reason the dogmatic teaching of the Pope cannot be called into question:

> The Roman Pontiff, head of the college of bishops, enjoys this infallibility in virtue of his office, when, as supreme pastor and teacher of all the faithful... he proclaims in an absolute decision a doctrine pertaining to faith or morals. For that reason his definitions are rightly said to be irreformable by their very nature and not by reason of the assent of the Church, in as much as they were made with the assistance of the Holy Spirit promised to him in the person of blessed Peter himself; and as a consequence they are in no way in need of the approval of others, and do not admit of appeal to any other tribunal.
>
> —Second Vatican Council[441]

However, even when the Pope is not making a dogmatic and thereby infallible pronouncement, Catholics are expected to obey him without question [892, 2037, 2050]:

> This loyal submission of the will and intellect must be given, in a special way, to the authentic teaching authority of the Roman Pontiff, even when he does not speak *ex cathedra* in such wise, indeed, that his supreme teaching authority be acknowledged with respect, and that one sincerely adhere to decisions made by him....
>
> —Second Vatican Council[442]

A BIBLICAL RESPONSE

Despite the bishops' claim to absolute teaching authority over the Church, Catholics today are thinking for themselves as never before. Many are educated, open-minded, and independent. As to faith and morals, the beliefs of some are so diverse that the term *Cafeteria Catholics* has been coined to describe the way they pick and choose what they believe. As one person expressed it, "I'm Catholic by *my* definition, which is the only one that counts."

Regardless, the Vatican has no intention of relinquishing its claim to "supreme teaching authority."[443] Quite the contrary, in recent years the Church's hierarchy has been ever more emphatic that *its* definition of Catholicism is the only one that counts [2039]. And that definition is one that is becoming increasingly conservative and traditional.

The present direction of the Church is largely due to the leadership of John Paul II. During the first 15 years of his pontificate, John Paul appointed over 1600 new bishops, roughly 40 percent of the present total number of bishops and archbishops. An internal Church document describing the guidelines that the Vatican has been using to select candidates for promotion to the office of bishop was recently leaked to the press. Among the criteria were "daily celebration of the Mass," "Marian piety," "convinced and faithful adherence to the teaching and magisterium of the church," "obedience to the Holy Father," "faithfulness to true church tradition," "commitment to Vatican II and the renewal that followed it, according to papal instructions," and support for *Humanae Vitae*, Pope Paul VI's 1968 encyclical prohibiting the use of all artificial means of birth control [2366-2372].[444]

In view of the conservative direction of the Vatican and the absolute claims of the Church's hierarchy to teaching authority, the focus of this book, as stated in the prologue, was chosen to be mainline, traditional Roman Catholicism as taught by the Magisterium. In this chapter we will examine the teaching of the Magisterium regarding its own authority. Here it will be shown that contrary to Roman Catholic doctrine, the Bible teaches that—

- Scripture, not the Magisterium, is the Christian's infallible guide to the interpretation of Scripture.
- The Holy Spirit, not the Magisterium, is the Christian's infallible and authoritative teacher.

Scripture Is the Christian's Only Infallible Guide

The primary argument used by the Roman Catholic Church in presenting its case for the infallible teaching authority of the Magisterium is one of inheritance. It rests upon two premises. First, Christ gave the apostles, with Peter as their head, teaching authority over the Church and the gift of infallibility [890-891]. Second, the apostles gave "their own position of teaching authority"[445] to bishops as their successors [77].

As for the first premise, all can agree with at least this much: The apostles taught with authority. Scripture tells us that the first Christians "were continually devoting themselves to the apostles' teaching" (Acts 2:42). Scripture does not, however, suggest that the apostles were *infallible* except in their inspired writings.

The Roman Catholic Church points to a long list of verses in its attempt to prove apostolic infallibility.[446] Most of these Scriptures, however, are so obliquely related to the subject that without explanation it would be difficult to see any connection whatsoever.

The apostle Paul certainly did not think he was infallible. Neither did he want others to think that he was incapable of error. He told the Galatians:

> But even though we, or an angel from heaven, should preach to you a gospel contrary to that which we have preached to you, let him be accursed.
>
> —Galatians 1:8

He then added, leaving little room for the infallibility of Peter or anyone else:

As we have said before, so I say again now, if
any man is preaching to you a gospel contrary to
that which you received, let him be accursed.

—Galatians 1:9

Paul taught that no one's teaching should be accepted without careful evaluation: "But examine everything carefully; hold fast to that which is good" (1 Thessalonians 5:21). John taught the early Christians to be
suspicious of anyone who claimed to speak for God:

Beloved, do not believe every spirit, but test
the spirits to see whether they are from God;
because many false prophets have gone out into
the world.

—1 John 4:1

The standard of measure for examining teaching in
the early church was not Peter or the apostles, but the
Scriptures. Originally the Old Testament served in this
capacity. Later the inspired writings of the apostles and
their associates took their place alongside the Hebrew
Scriptures.

Even the apostles themselves submitted to the
supreme authority of Scripture. For example, at the
Council of Jerusalem, after much debate, Peter gave his
opinion. James concurred by saying, "And with this the
words of the Prophets agree, just as it is written..." (Acts
15:15). He then quoted Amos 9:11,12. James compared
Peter's counsel with that of Old Testament prophecy,
found agreement, and knew that the consensus that the
apostles and elders had reached was correct. Only then
was James prepared to state his conclusion (Acts 15:19).

Apostolic submission to Scripture can also be seen
in the teaching of Paul. Though he was an apostle and
had received revelation directly from the Lord (Galatians 1:12; Ephesians 3:3), he nevertheless regularly
added the words "as it is written" to his writings. He

The catholic church

There was a time when every Christian was pleased to identify with the catholic church—catholic with a small "c," that is. Following Pentecost, the gospel spread rapidly. Despite seasons of intense and violent persecution, pockets of believers emerged throughout the Roman Empire. These early Christians held to a common faith and enjoyed a God-given affinity wherever they met. Paul's teaching of the church as one body made up of all true believers provided a theological understanding of this new relationship (1 Corinthians 12:12-31).

Early Christians used the term *catholic*, a Greek word meaning *concerning the whole*, to describe this worldwide nature of the church. When early Christians referred to the *catholic faith*, they were speaking of the faith of the whole or universal church. The oldest document containing the term is a letter by Ignatius from the early

---

would then quote a relevant Old Testament text as confirmation that what he was saying was truth from God. In his letter to the Romans, Paul makes 45 such references to Scripture. He knew that the Christians of first-century Rome expected all new teaching to be confirmed through comparison with earlier revelation.

Such was the heritage that the early Christians inherited from their Jewish roots. Paul's experience in the Macedonian city of Berea demonstrates this point. When Paul first preached the gospel to the Jews there, they immediately turned to their infallible guide: the Old Testament Scriptures. Luke writes:

> Now these were more noble-minded than those in Thessalonica, for they received the word with great eagerness, examining the Scriptures daily, to see whether these things were so.
>
> —Acts 17:11

Finding a clear correspondence between Paul's teaching and God's Word, "Many of them therefore

second century. He wrote, "Wherever Jesus Christ is, there is the catholic church."[447] In the first three centuries, "the catholic church" referred to all believers holding to the same faith throughout the world.

With such a noble heritage, it is not surprising that today not only the Roman Catholic Church but most Christian denominations claim to hold to the *catholic* faith—that is, the faith of the whole church in apostolic times. The distinguishing mark of those identified as Roman Catholics is submission to the Pope, the Bishop of Rome, as Christ's representative on earth [834, 837, 936]. Nevertheless, the Church rarely refers to itself as the *Roman* Catholic Church. It prefers to call itself the *Catholic Church* so as not to limit in any way its claim to universal jurisdiction as the one, holy, catholic, and apostolic church [811-812].

believed, along with a number of prominent Greek women and men" (Acts 17:12).

As for the second premise, that the Roman Catholic bishops inherited the apostles' infallible teaching authority, it rests completely on the theory of apostolic succession. As demonstrated in the previous chapter, this theory itself cannot be established from Scripture: Peter was not the head of the apostles and the church; the Roman Catholic bishops are not the apostles' successors; and the Pope is not Peter's successor. The Magisterium, therefore, has no claim to the teaching office of Peter or the apostles whether they were infallible or not.

The Holy Spirit Is the Christian's Only Infallible and Authoritative Teacher

A second argument that Roman Catholic scholars use in presenting the case for the Magisterium is one of "moral necessity."[448] It basically says that a strong and infallible teaching authority is highly desirable in order that the faith might be preserved, defended, and explained

[77, 889]. Without the Magisterium, the argument goes, chaos would reign in a cacophony of opinions. Catholic proponents point to the ever-increasing number of Protestant denominations as all the proof needed to show that a single authoritative teaching body is necessary. One Catholic scholar concludes:

> In all likelihood, therefore, we should believe that Christ, who wanted His Gospel preached to every creature, chose as a religious authority a living and infallible magisterium.
>
> —*A Manual of Dogmatic Theology*[449]

On the surface the concept of a Magisterium may appear attractive. If God had established an authoritative teaching body and promised to supernaturally protect it from all error, the Christian life would in some respects be far simpler. But because Scripture does not teach that God established such a body, inventing one out of "moral necessity" and treating its teaching as infallible can only lead to tragic doctrinal error.

Furthermore, even with its Magisterium, the Roman Catholic Church is hardly an oasis of doctrinal harmony in a theologically troubled world. Indeed, the very purpose of the new *Catechism of the Catholic Church* is to quell ever-increasing dissent within the Church. In a book explaining the need for the *Catechism*, Monsignor Michael J. Wrenn, special consultant for religious education to Cardinal John O'Connor, listed just some of the doctrinal areas in which independent-minded Roman Catholic priests and theologians are challenging the Church's official teaching: the existence of angels, the direct creation of the human soul, the fall of man in Adam, the virgin birth of Christ, the atoning sacrifice of Christ, the perpetuation of the cross in the Mass, the real presence of Christ in the Eucharist, the infallibility of the Magisterium, the hierarchical authority of the Pope and bishops, the efficacy of the sacraments, the Trinity, purgatory, and sexual ethics.[450]

The Magisterium has also failed to produce a common faith among the laity. Many Catholics are opposed to the Church's ban on contraceptives and its exclusion of women from ordination to the priesthood. They sympathize with a growing number of clergy who believe that mandatory priestly celibacy is doing more harm than good. Some Catholics have stopped listening to the Magisterium altogether.

Finally, the Magisterium is not a moral necessity. Christ promised His disciples, "I will not leave you as orphans.... The Helper, the Holy Spirit, whom the Father will send in My name, He will teach you all things, and bring to your remembrance all that I said to you" (John 14:18, 26).

The Holy Spirit, not the Pope and bishops, is the living teaching authority of the church (John 16:13-15). As a counselor and comforter, the Spirit indwells each believer (John 14:16-18; Ephesians 1:13). He guides in conduct (Romans 8:14). He directs in ministry (Acts 8:29).

The Holy Spirit also gives some Christians special ability to teach the Scriptures with clarity and authority (1 Corinthians 12:28). This authority, however, does not reside within these teachers personally, but is derived from the source of their teaching, the inspired Word of God.

Additionally, the Holy Spirit raises up elders to oversee the local church, to pastor the flock, and to protect the believers from wrong doctrine. For this reason elders must "be able both to exhort in sound doctrine and to refute those who contradict" (Titus 1:9).

The Holy Spirit's primary instrument in teaching the church is the Word of God. The Bible is the "sword of the Spirit" (Ephesians 6:17). As believers read and study the Scriptures, the Spirit illuminates their minds, giving them understanding and speaking to them as individuals (1 Corinthians 2:10-16; Hebrews 4:12).

Confident of the Spirit's teaching ministry, biblical Christianity treats the Bible as an open book—a book of the people. Personal study, interpretation, and application are encouraged.

The same was true in the early church. Long before anyone had ever heard of the Magisterium or its claims, Christians were reading and obeying the Scriptures. After all, the Holy Spirit addressed the books of the New Testament to *ordinary people*—not to apostles, not to bishops, not to a Pope, and not to a Magisterium. Not even Paul's letter to the Romans was addressed to the Roman Catholic Church, but "to all who are beloved of God in Rome, called as saints" (Romans 1:7).

Neither did God entrust the Christian faith to the Pope and bishops. Rather, He delivered it "to the saints" (Jude 3). The task of defending the faith was likewise not assigned to bishops but to every believer (Jude 3). It is the church, the assembly of God's elect, which is "the pillar and support of the truth" (1 Timothy 3:15).

With the Holy Spirit as its teacher and the inspired Scriptures as its text, the church of Jesus Christ has no need for the Roman Magisterium. The Holy Spirit, by whom every believer is anointed, is the only authoritative teacher that is needed:

> As for you, the anointing you received from him remains in you, and you do not need anyone to teach you. But as his anointing teaches you about all things and as that anointing is real, not counterfeit—just as it has taught you, remain in him.
>
> —1 John 2:27 NIV

The Bible and the Magisterium

The Roman Catholic Church acknowledges the teaching ministry of the Spirit and the authority of the Bible [101-108, 737-741, 788]. It holds, however, that the Magisterium and not the Bible is the Spirit's primary teaching organ [108, 113, 119]. Father Matthias Premm explains:

> ...the teaching office of the Church is more important than the Bible: only an infallible Church

can tell us what books belong to Scripture, and
only an infallible Church can interpret the true
meaning of Sacred Scripture; no one can do this
for himself. Thus the Catholic can read only one
Bible, the Bible which is published by the Church.
In other words: *The immediate and highest rule of
faith is the living office of the Church.*

—Dogmatic Theology for the Laity[451]

Some believe that the subservient role of the Bible in
Roman Catholicism today is changing. They point to the
teaching of the Second Vatican Council as evidence.
"Ignorance of the Scriptures is ignorance of Christ,"[452]
said the Council, quoting Jerome [133]. It ordered that
"...access to sacred Scripture ought to be open wide to
the Christian faithful"[453] [131, 2653]. The clergy were also
exhorted to "...immerse themselves in the Scriptures by
constant sacred reading and diligent study"[454] [132]. One
Catholic commentator wrote: "Not since the early centuries of the Church has an official document urged the
availability of the Scriptures for all."[455]

Following Vatican II, Catholic parishes began spon-
soring Bible studies and parochial schools started emphasizing Scripture study in their curriculum. As a result,
many Catholics have grown in their appreciation and
knowledge of the Bible.

Nevertheless, the Roman Catholic Bible is still not a
book of the people, but a book of the Church. Revelation,
said Vatican II, has been "entrusted to the Church."[456]
The task of determining the authentic interpretation of
the Word has also "been entrusted to the living teaching
office of the Church alone."[457] Vatican I stated:

...in matters of faith and morals, belonging
as they do to the establishing of Christian doctrine, that meaning of holy scripture must be
held to be the true one, which holy mother
church held and holds, since it is her right to
judge of the true meaning and interpretation of
holy scripture. In consequence, it is not permiss-
ible for anyone to interpret holy scripture in a

sense contrary to this, or indeed against the unanimous consent of the fathers.

—First Vatican Council[458]

Consequently, though Catholics may be encouraged to read the Bible, they are not free to determine what it means [113, 119]. Interpretation is the sole right of the Magisterium [85, 100, 890]. To ensure that Catholics reading the Bible arrive at preapproved conclusions, Vatican II ordered that Bibles with "suitable notes"[459] should be prepared. Canon Law dictates that Roman Catholic Bibles be "annotated with necessary and sufficient explanations."[460]

The same rules apply to Catholic scholars and theologians. They are to work "under the watchful eye of the sacred Magisterium."[461] They may help the Church "towards a better understanding and explanation of the meaning of sacred Scripture,"[462] but it is the Magisterium alone that has the right to form a judgment and interpret the Bible. Pope Pius XII wrote:

> ...the most noble office of theology is to show how a doctrine defined by the Church is contained in the sources of revelation..."in that sense in which it has been defined by the Church."
>
> —*Humani Generis*[463]

In other words, the purpose of Roman Catholic Bible study is not necessarily to understand Scripture in the original sense in which it was written, but to understand it in the sense in which it is understood by the Church. The Catholic scholar is expected to start with the presupposition that the Church's interpretation is correct and then proceed in Bible study to discover why.

A Test Case: Exodus 20:4,5

What is the result of surrendering teaching authority to one group of men and treating their interpretations as authentic and even infallible? The answer can be found by looking at how the Church handles Scriptures that present a challenge to established Roman Catholic beliefs or practices. Consider, for example, this portion of the Ten Commandments:

> You shall not make for yourself an idol, or any likeness of what is in heaven above or on the earth beneath or in the water under the earth. You shall not worship them or serve them . . . .
>
> —Exodus 20:4,5

This commandment forbids the making of images for religious use. It also prohibits the worshiping of such objects. The primary meaning of the Hebrew word translated "worship" (Exodus 20:5) is *to bow down*.[464] Because of this commandment, both Jews and most non-Catholic Christians shun the use of sacred objects such as statues in the practice of their faith.

The Roman Catholic Church has its own interpretation of the commands of Exodus 20:4,5 [2129-2132]: [465]

> They do not forbid images of Christ and the saints. But to make and honor the images of Christ our Lord, of His holy and virginal Mother, and of the Saints, all of whom were clothed with human nature and appeared in human form, is not only not forbidden by this Commandment, but has always been deemed a holy practice and a most sure indication of gratitude. This position is confirmed by the monuments of the Apostolic age, the General Councils of the Church, and the writings of so many among the Fathers, eminent alike for sanctity and learning, all of whom are of one accord upon the subject.
>
> —*The Roman Catechism*[466]

Note how in this explanation the practice of the Church is used to confirm the interpretation of Scripture. The same approach was used by the Second Vatican

Council in its endorsement of the continued use of statues:

> From the very earliest days of the Church there has been a tradition whereby images of our Lord, his holy Mother, and of saints are displayed in churches for the veneration of the faithful.
> —Second Vatican Council[467]

The Catholic interpretation of Exodus 20:4,5 is the product of applying Roman Catholicism's supreme rule for Bible interpretation: The authentic meaning of any verse of Scripture is what the Magisterium of the Church has always said it means [119]. Or, to put it another way: What the Church *believes* and *practices* determines what the Scriptures *teach* or *mean*. Catholics, therefore, are to interpret the Scriptures within "the living Tradition of the whole Church,"[113] "according to the spiritual meaning which the Spirit grants to the Church."[113]

This approach to Scripture study is futile. It can only result in the Church validating itself. Correction is impossible, because the norm of truth is not the plain meaning of Scripture as verified by comparison with other Scriptures, but the authoritative teaching of the Church as confirmed by the beliefs and practices of the Church. The gentle voice of the Holy Spirit speaking through the inspired Scriptures cannot be heard over the dogmatic assertions of the Roman Magisterium.

❖12

SCRIPTURE
AND TRADITION

Rome, November 1, 1950

Pope Pius XII, seated on a red throne in the center of Saint Peter's Square, looked with satisfaction upon the document before him. It represented the culmination of a process that had begun almost 100 years earlier and the fulfillment of a personal promise that he had made to the Blessed Virgin Mary. Over 700,000 Catholics had come to the Vatican to witness the signing of the document.

Born Eugenio Maria Giuseppe Pacelli, Pius XII's election as Pope in 1939 surprised no one. The Pacelli family had served the Vatican for decades. His grandfather had been the Vatican's Under Secretary of the Interior. His father and brother were distinguished Vatican lawyers. Eugenio himself was an expert in canon law and an experienced diplomat. The previous Pope, Pius XI, had chosen him to serve as Vatican Secretary of State. It was soon apparent that the Pope was grooming Eugenio to be his successor. When Pius XI died, the cardinals elected Eugenio as the new Pope in the shortest conclave in modern history. In honor of his mentor, Eugenio took the name of Pius XII.

One of the first goals of the new Pope was to promote devotion to Mary, but the outbreak of World War II delayed his plans. Once the war was over, however, Pius sent an encyclical, *Deiparae Virginis Mariae*, to the bishops of the world in 1946. In it he reviewed how for almost 100 years Catholics had been petitioning the Vatican to formally declare that God had taken Mary bodily into heaven. Pope Pius then asked the bishops for their position on the matter:

> ... We wish to know if you, Venerable Brethren, with your learning and prudence consider that the bodily Assumption of the Immaculate Blessed Virgin can be proposed and defined as a dogma of faith, and whether in addition to your own wishes this is desired by your clergy and people.
>
> —*Deiparae Virginis Mariae*[468]

The response to the letter was beyond the Pope's expectations. Petitions encouraging Pius to move ahead flooded the Vatican.

Nevertheless, Pius' legal training made him hesitant to act. It was a well-established principle of the Roman Catholic Church that doctrine must be contained in the deposit of faith—that is, in Scripture and Tradition. The Bible said nothing about Mary's death, burial, or Assumption. Witnesses to Tradition from the first centuries were also silent. In such a case, it was not clear whether the Pope had the prerogative to define a doctrine. Pius carefully studied the matter and decided that it was too soon to act on the petitions before him. First he would need to clarify the scope of the Church's teaching authority.

On August 12, 1950, Pope Pius XII issued another encyclical to the bishops, *Humani Generis*. It appeared to be a routine pastoral warning of the dangers of modern theological trends. Some Catholic scholars, however, noticed something different:

> It soon became evident that behind the encyclical was a deeper substratum of papal thought. In one passage of the document an apparent leap ahead in doctrinal development was acknowledged.
>
> —*The Papacy Today*[469]

The passage in Pope Pius' letter that caught the attention of theologians was short but significant:

> ...God has given to His Church a living Teaching Authority to elucidate and explain what is contained in the deposit of faith only obscurely and implicitly. This deposit of faith our Divine Redeemer has given for authentic interpretation not to each of the faithful, not even to theologians, but only to the Teaching Authority of the Church.
>
> —*Humani Generis*[470]

Clearly, Pius was preparing to dogmatically define the Assumption of Mary. That is, he was going "to elucidate and explain" that the Assumption of Mary was "contained in the deposit of faith," even though admittedly "only obscurely and implicitly."[471] He would do so despite a lack of clear support either from Scripture or from early witnesses to Tradition.

Three months later, on November 1, 1950, Pope Pius took his seat before an overflow crowd in Saint Peter's Square. In front of him lay the final draft of a document titled *Munificentissimus Deus*, that is, *Most Bountiful God*. It traced the history of widespread Catholic belief in the Assumption of Mary. The document concluded with a declaration stating:

> By the authority of our Lord Jesus Christ, of the Blessed Apostles Peter and Paul, and by our own authority, we pronounce, declare, and define it to be a divinely revealed dogma: that the Immaculate Mother of God, the ever Virgin Mary, having completed the course of her earthly life, was assumed body and soul into heavenly glory.
>
> —*Munificentissimus Deus*[472]

Pope Pius XII, with characteristic precision, signed the document, "I, Pius, Bishop of the Catholic Church, have signed, so defining."[473] The bells of Rome's 400 churches thundered their approval as the crowd cheered and applauded.

On that day Pope Pius not only achieved his goal to honor Mary but in so doing also established a new precedent for the development of doctrine within Roman Catholicism. To grasp the significance of this event, however, we must first consider the Roman Catholic understanding of divine revelation and its transmission down through the ages.

Divine Revelation
[50-141]

Origin in Jesus Christ
[65-67, 73, 75]

According to the Roman Catholic Church, the Lord Jesus Christ, by His presence and self-manifestation, revealed to His apostles the Catholic faith [65, 75]. He did this through His—

> ...words and works, signs and miracles, but above all by his death and glorious resurrection from the dead, and finally by sending the Spirit of truth.
> —Second Vatican Council[474]

Christ was God's final revelation. He "completed and perfected Revelation."[475] "No new public revelation," says the Church, "is to be expected before the glorious manifestation of our Lord, Jesus Christ"[476] [66, 73].

Transmission Through Scripture and Tradition
[74-83]

The Church teaches that in order that the truths revealed by Christ might "...remain in their entirety,

through the ages, and be transmitted to all generations...,"[477] the Lord commanded the apostles to pass
the revelation on to others [74, 75, 96]. This was accomplished in two ways.

First, the apostles passed on the faith in *unwritten*
forms—that is, "...by the spoken word of their preaching, by the example they gave, by the institutions they
established..."[478] [76]. The Roman Catholic Church
refers to revelation handed down by the apostles in
unwritten forms as *Tradition* [81].

The second way was in *written* forms: "...by those
apostles and other men associated with the apostles who,
under the inspiration of the same Holy Spirit, committed
the message of salvation to writing"[479] [76]. These writings became the New Testament Scriptures [81].

Roman Catholic theologians picture divine revelation as a pool. They portray the transmission of revelation to the modern Church as two streams flowing from
the pool. One stream represents Scripture, the other
Tradition. Together they preserve and transmit the revelation that Christ entrusted to the apostles.

One of the goals of the Second Vatican Council
(1962-1965) was to "set forth the true doctrine on divine
Revelation and its transmission."[480] In the first draft of
the Council's decree, "The Dogmatic Constitution on
Divine Revelation," the writers continued to use the pool
and streams metaphor. However, in the final version of
the Constitution the two streams had become one.[481]
Revelation was still pictured as a single pool, a "sacred
deposit,"[482] but the Council had combined Scripture
and Tradition into one stream [84, 86, 97]. In this way the
Church was able to stress the unity of the organs by
which revelation is transmitted to the Church today [80]:

> Sacred Tradition and sacred Scripture, then,
> are bound closely together, and communicate
> one with the other. For both of them, flowing out
> from the same divine well-spring, come together

in some fashion to form one thing, and move towards the same goal.

—Second Vatican Council[483]

The Word of God

[80-85]

The Church calls this "one thing"[484] formed by Scripture and Tradition the *Word of God* [84-85, 97, 182]:

Sacred Tradition and sacred Scripture make up a single sacred deposit of the Word of God, which is entrusted to the Church.

—Second Vatican Council[485]

Here the Church defines Scripture and Tradition *together* as forming the Word of God. When a Roman Catholic theologian refers to the *written* Word of God, he is talking about Scripture. If he speaks of the *unwritten* Word of God, he is talking about Tradition. But if he refers simply to the *Word of God*, he is probably talking about Scripture and Tradition together.

To put it another way, according to the Roman Catholic Church, the Bible alone is not the complete Word of God. There is essential revelation preserved in Tradition that is not clearly taught in Scripture [81-82]. To understand the complete revelation of Jesus Christ, therefore, one must study both Scripture and Tradition [113-114]. In the words of the Magisterium [82]:

...the Church does not draw her certainty about all revealed truths from the holy Scriptures alone. Hence, both Scripture and Tradition must be accepted and honored with equal feelings of devotion and reverence.

—Second Vatican Council[486]

And again:

> [The Church] has always regarded, and continues to regard the Scriptures, taken together with sacred Tradition, as the supreme rule of her faith.
>
> —Second Vatican Council[487]

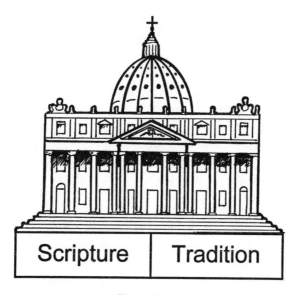

Figure 12:1

The Foundation of the Gospel According to Rome

According to the Second Vatican Council, "Sacred theology relies on the written Word of God, taken together with sacred Tradition, as on a permanent foundation."[488]

A BIBLICAL RESPONSE

This final chapter brings us to the fundamental reason why Roman Catholicism is what it is, and why it differs so significantly from Christianity based solely upon Scripture. To understand the importance of our topic, imagine for a moment a person in some remote corner of the earth. He has no knowledge of Christ, of Christian history, or of Roman Catholicism. Yet, stirred by the Holy Spirit, he longs for a knowledge of God. If such a person were given a Bible and sincerely began to search for God in its pages, what would he uncover?

In the four Gospels, our seeker would find a record of "the exact truth" (Luke 1:4) about Christ's life and teaching. As he continued to study the book of Acts and the epistles he would discover a record of the preaching of the apostles. In a short time he would have obtained "...the wisdom that leads to salvation through faith which is in Christ Jesus" (2 Timothy 3:15).

Assume now that our solitary seeker, having found Christ and salvation by faith in Him, continued his study of Scripture. His goal now was to discover all he could about how to serve and worship God and how to order his life. What would he learn?

In the book of Acts he would read an inspired history of the first 30 years of the church. In the letters of Peter, Paul, John, James, and Jude he would encounter more fully the doctrines of the Christian faith. He would learn how to conduct himself (1 Timothy 3:15), how to minister to others (1 Corinthians 12-14), how the early Christians had worshiped (1 Corinthians 11:17-34; 14:26-40), and how local churches were to be governed (1 Timothy 3:1-13; Titus 1:5-9). In short, he would find everything that he needed to know to live the Christian life. This, writes Paul, is the intended purpose of the Bible:

> All Scripture is given by inspiration of God and is profitable for doctrine, for reproof, for correction, for instruction in righteousness, that the man of God may be complete, thoroughly equipped for every good work.
>
> —2 Timothy 3:16,17 NKJV

Now suppose this new believer, having learned the basics of the Christian faith, set out in search of finding other Christians. After many days' travel, he enters a city early one Sunday morning and finds at its center a large Roman Catholic Church. He finds an empty pew, where he remains for many hours watching priests celebrate the Mass, hear confessions, and lead in the praying of the Rosary before a statue of Mary. Then, having learned all that he could through observation, he asks a priest to explain to him the basic doctrines of Roman Catholicism. What would our new believer conclude?

Certainly our imaginary seeker would find Roman Catholicism very strange. From his study of Scripture, he would have learned absolutely nothing about baptismal regeneration and justification, yearlong programs in preparation for justification, seven sacraments, sanctifying grace, transubstantiation, a continuing sacrifice, confession to a priest, temporal punishment, indulgences, purgatory, merited eternal reward, priestly ordination, the papacy, ruling bishops, the Magisterium, or Mary's Immaculate Conception, Assumption into heaven, co-redemptive work, and mediation of all grace. Realizing that these beliefs were not only not taught in Scripture but actually contradicted God's Word, our seeker would certainly conclude that whatever he had found, it was not what he was looking for, and he would move on.

From the Roman Catholic Church's perspective, the above conclusion by such a person would be meaningless. The man's catechesis, his instruction in the Catholic faith, is terribly lacking [875]. "No one can believe alone," says the Church, "just as no one can live alone"[166] [166-171, 1253]. Regardless of how well he thinks he knows the Scriptures, the man has heard only part of the story [81]. Specifically, he has no knowledge of divine revelation passed on as Tradition. He lacks insight and information necessary to understand Scripture [113]. Consequently, he is unable to appreciate Roman Catholic beliefs and practices not plainly found in the Bible. He is also completely ignorant of the authentic interpretation of revelation assigned to it by God's Magisterium [85]. The man has neither the knowledge nor the authority to judge the Church.

This story presents before us two opposing views on how the faith received from Christ is to be understood and practiced. Roman Catholicism teaches that the Catholic faith is contained in Scripture and Tradition. Together, as interpreted by the Pope and bishops, they are the supreme rule of the Church. Biblical Christianity holds that the plain teaching of Scripture, as illuminated by the Holy Spirit, contains all doctrine essential for salvation and Christian living. It recognizes Scripture alone as the supreme rule of faith. Though it values the information that the study of biblical languages, archaeology, history, and early Christian writers can bring to the study of Scripture, biblical Christianity rejects placing Tradition alongside Scripture as a rule of faith. The reason for this rejection is that Scripture is the inspired Word of God, while Tradition is the fallible words of men.

Scripture Is Inspired; Tradition Is Not

The difference between Scripture and Tradition becomes apparent when one understands what the Roman Catholic Church actually means by Tradition. It is a difficult concept to grasp, yet one which is essential to an understanding of Roman Catholicism. Consider first two things that Roman Catholic Tradition is *not*.

When the Church speaks of Tradition, it is not referring to inherited culture or practices originating from merely human sources or from Church discipline and policy [83]. Sacred Tradition does not refer to matters such as priestly celibacy (obligatory since the eleventh century), the direction in which the priest faces while saying Mass (changed following Vatican II), or whether girls can serve alongside altar boys (approved in 1994). These may rightly be called *traditions* in that they involve practices that have been *handed down* from previous generations, but they are not sacred Tradition, for the Church does not consider them to have their origin in divine revelation. To distinguish human traditions from sacred Tradition, Catholic literature generally capitalizes the latter.

Neither is Roman Catholic Tradition the conclusions of scholars who have studied the documents, history, and archaeology of the first centuries in search of the primitive Christian faith. Tradition is not the writings of early Christian leaders, ancient liturgies, or even the decrees of synods and ecumenical councils. These may be partial *expressions of* or *witnesses to* Tradition, but they are not sacred Tradition itself.

So what exactly *is* Tradition? "Tradition is the word living continuously in the hearts of the faithful,"[489] "the living memorial of God's Word"[113] [78, 113, 2650, 2661]. Roman Catholic Tradition is not something you can read or even lay your hands on.

> [Tradition]... is not an inanimate thing passed from hand to hand; it is not, properly speaking, an assemblage of doctrines and institutions consigned to books or other monuments.... it must be represented as a current of life and truth coming from God through Christ and through the Apostles to the last of the faithful who repeats his creed and learns his catechism.
>
> —*The Catholic Encyclopedia*[490]

Tradition, as explained by Catholic scholars, is not contained in books, but in people, in the life of the Church. It is the *life experience* of the Catholic faithful. It is revelation "... written principally in the Church's heart rather than in documents and records...."[113]

Roman Catholicism describes Tradition as a "living transmission"[78] through which "... the Church, in her doctrine, life and worship, perpetuates and transmits to every generation all that she herself is, all that she believes"[491] [78, 98]. It is the *living faith* produced by "realities and words that are being passed on."[492] This, explains Catholic scholars, is accomplished in a variety of ways:

> The way in which the faith is transmitted can take almost any form in the Church: the sign of the cross that a mother traces on the forehead of her child; teaching the basic prayers of Christianity, especially the "Our Father," in the home

and in religious instruction; living, praying, and singing in the local congregation, into which the young person grows; Christian example in everyday life and Christian action even to the point of martyrdom; the witness given by Christian music (especially hymns and chorales), by architecture and the plastic arts (especially representations of the cross, which is considered a privileged Christian symbol); and, not least, by the liturgy of the Church.

—*The Church's Confession of Faith*[493]

One might reasonably ask: How can any information being passed on for centuries by such informal methods possibly maintain its integrity? The Church answers [77, 81]:

In order that the full and living Gospel might always be preserved in the Church the apostles left bishops as their successors. They gave them "their own position of teaching authority."

—Second Vatican Council[494]

Roman Catholicism teaches that through bishops, Tradition "... was to be preserved in a continuous line of succession until the end of time"[495] [77]. Rather than becoming corrupted with time, the Church teaches that Tradition actually becomes more clear through the Magisterium's teaching [66, 79, 94]:

The Tradition that comes from the apostles makes progress in the Church, with the help of the Holy Spirit. There is a growth in insight into the realities and words that are being passed on.

—Second Vatican Council[496]

The true meaning of Roman Catholic Tradition and the process by which it makes progress in the Church can best be explained by way of example. Consider once more the dogmatic definition of the Assumption of Mary in 1950.

Tradition As a Source of Dogma:
The Assumption of Mary

As we have seen, in 1946 Pope Pius sent a letter to the bishops of the world concerning the Assumption of Mary:

> ... We wish to know if you, Venerable Brethren, with your learning and prudence consider that the bodily Assumption of the Immaculate Blessed Virgin can be proposed and defined as a dogma of faith....
>
> —*Deiparae Virginis Mariae*[497]

This was not a casual invitation for the bishops to express their opinion, but the start of a formal collegial process by which Roman Catholic doctrine develops [877, 888-892]. The Pope wanted to know if the bishops considered it appropriate to classify belief in the Assumption of Mary as a dogma of the Roman Catholic faith, an infallibly defined doctrine which Catholics must believe [88-90].[498] To deny a belief of the Church that has been formally defined is equivalent to falling away from the faith [2089].[499]

To respond to the Pope, the bishops needed to determine the source of belief in the Assumption of Mary. Was it merely a legend believed by a few pious Catholics? Or was it part of the deposit of faith, revelation handed down from the apostles? Only if it proved to be the latter could the Church define it as dogma [88, 891]. So the bishops searched the two channels through which the Church teaches that the apostolic faith has been transmitted: Scripture and Tradition.

First they looked to the Scriptures. There they could find no clear teaching about Mary's death, burial, resurrection, or Assumption.[500]

Next the bishops looked to Tradition. Was Mary's Assumption part of the deposit of faith transmitted in unwritten forms?

This was a more difficult question to answer. Tradition resides in the life of the Church. It transmits revelation as "realities and words,"[501]—*unwritten* words. The bishops could not simply pick up an index of beliefs and practices contained in Tradition and see if the Assumption was there. Rather, the bishops would have to examine the Catholic faith as it had been lived and was being lived by the popes, bishops, and faithful. These three groups are considered to be the *organs* or *instruments* through which Tradition is *expressed* and *described*. The search for evidence of belief in the Assumption would focus in seven areas:

- The dogmatic decrees of the Magisterium
- The creeds of the Church
- The teaching of the Church Fathers
- The teaching of the Church Doctors
- The unanimous teaching of the bishops
- The universal practice of the Church
- The common understanding of the faithful

What did the Pope and bishops discover? Pope Pius XII reviewed the bishops' findings in *Munificentissimus Deus*, the document that finally defined the Assumption of Mary as Church dogma. The results can be summarized as follows:

Was the Assumption part of the dogmatic teaching of the Magisterium?

The answer, of course, was no. The very question that the Magisterium was trying to resolve in 1946 was whether or not Mary's Assumption should become part of the dogmatic teaching of the Church.

Roman Catholicism teaches that the solemn decrees of the bishops meeting in an ecumenical council are infallible and binding upon Catholics everywhere [88, 891]. But none of the first 20 ecumenical councils recognized by the Roman Catholic Church had ever stated that Mary had been assumed into heaven. Neither had any of the popes dogmatically taught the doctrine. These are examples of what the Church calls the *Extraordinary Magisterium*. At that time, therefore, the certainty of the Assumption was unsettled.

Was belief in the Assumption expressed in any of the Church's Creeds?

Creeds are summaries of the fundamental beliefs of the faith [185-192]. The Church gives special recognition to two creeds: the Apostles' Creed and the Nicene Creed [193-195]. Both were silent concerning the Assumption of Mary. The same was true of all other accepted creeds of the early church.

Was the Assumption part of the teaching of the Church Fathers?

Roman Catholicism recognizes 88 men as Fathers of the Church. Most were bishops. Ten were popes. Others were abbots, priests, monks, and apologists. All lived sometime during the first eight centuries and most have been canonized by the Church as saints. Their number includes Clement of Rome, Polycarp, Ignatius, Irenaeus, Tertullian, Origen, Eusebius of Caesarea, Benedict, Pope Leo the Great, and Pope Innocent I.

The Church highly values the writings of the Church Fathers, but does not consider them to be infallible. To the contrary, the Church recognizes that not only do the Fathers sometimes disagree with one another, but occasionally they teach error. Pope Leo XIII wrote that the Church Fathers "... have sometimes expressed the ideas of their own times, and thus made statements which in these days have been abandoned as incorrect."[502]

Of what value, then, are the writings of the Church Fathers? Catholic scholar William A. Jurgens explains [688]:

> The value of the Fathers and Writers is this: that in the aggregate they demonstrate what the Church did and does yet believe and teach. In the

aggregate they provide a witness to the content of Tradition, that Tradition which itself is a vehicle of revelation.

—*The Faith of the Early Fathers*[503]

Or, in the words of the last Council [78]:

The sayings of the Holy Fathers are a witness to the life-giving presence of this Tradition, showing how its riches are poured out in the practice and life of the Church, in her belief and her prayer.

—Second Vatican Council[504]

What did the Church Fathers have to say about the Assumption of Mary? Significantly, the bishops found support for the belief in the writings of only two of the Fathers.[505] Both were from the seventh century: Germanus of Constantinople (634-733) and John Damascene (675-749).

The fact, however, that the bishops could find no evidence of belief in Mary's Assumption in the writings of the other 86 Church Fathers did not dissuade the Pope or the other bishops. Though the Church respects the writings of the Fathers, it nevertheless maintains "... supreme independence towards those writings; she judges them more than she is judged by them."[506] For this same reason, the fact that two of the Church Fathers did believe in the Assumption of Mary did not prove that the belief was authentic doctrine. Jurgens comments:

... we must stress that an isolated patristic text is in no instance to be regarded as a "proof" of a particular doctrine. Dogmas are not "proved" by patristic statements but by the infallible teaching instruments of the Church.

—*The Faith of the Early Fathers*[507]

Was the Assumption part of the teaching of the Church Doctors?

The Roman Catholic Church has honored with the title of *Church Doctor* a few teachers whom it considers exceptionally trustworthy guides to the Catholic faith. Some are from the ranks of the Church Fathers. All are canonized saints.

The first eight men to receive the title of Church Doctor were: Athanasius (297-373), Basil the Great (329-379), Gregory of Nazianzus (330-390), Ambrose (340-397), Jerome (343-420), John Chrysostom (347-407), Augustine of Hippo (354-430), and Pope Gregory the Great (540-604). These eight are the *major Church Doctors*. In the sixteenth century, Thomas Aquinas (1225-1274), the "Angelic Doctor," and Bonaventure (1217-1274), the "Seraphic Doctor," were recognized as *minor Church Doctors*. Today there are a total of 32 Doctors of the Roman Catholic Church, including two women, both mystics: Catherine of Siena (1347-1380) and Teresa of Avila (1515-1582).

As with the Church Fathers, Roman Catholicism does not consider the teaching of the Church Doctors to be infallible or binding upon the Church.

What did the Church Doctors have to say about the Assumption of Mary? The Pope and bishops found no support for the doctrine among any of the major Doctors of the Church. Likewise, none of the minor Doctors of the first 11 centuries taught the doctrine, with one exception: John Damascene (675-749), who, being also one of the Church Fathers, was already mentioned.

Among the Doctors of later centuries, Pope Pius listed support for belief in the Assumption from Anthony of Padua (1195-1231), Albert the Great (1200-1280), Bonaventure (1217-1274), Thomas Aquinas (1225-1274), Robert Bellarmine (1542-1621), Francis De Sales (1567-1622), and Alphonsus de Liguori (1696-1787).[508]

Was the Assumption part of the unanimous teaching of the bishops?

The official teaching of the bishops through normal, everyday means such as catechisms, homilies, and letters, is called the *Ordinary Magisterium* [2032-2034, 2049]. The Church considers the common faith of the bishops expressed by these regular means of instruction to be an infallible guide to the Catholic faith [890, 892].

The primary purpose of Pope Pius's 1946 letter was to poll the opinion of the bishops as the voice of the Ordinary Magisterium. He asked them two questions: "Do you...judge that the bodily Assumption of the Blessed Virgin can be proposed and defined as a dogma of faith? Do you, with your clergy and people, desire it?"[509]

The bishops' reply was clear: "...an almost unanimous affirmative response to both these questions...."[510]

Was belief in the Assumption expressed in the universal practice of the Church?

Since what the Church *does* reflects what the Church *believes*, the universal practice of the Church is also considered a reliable witness to the Roman Catholic faith. In *Munificentissimus Deus*, Pope Pius reviewed how the Church had dedicated "innumerable temples...to the Virgin Mary assumed into heaven," had set up in its churches "sacred images" of the Assumption, and had dedicated regions to "the special patronage and guardianship of the Virgin Mother of God assumed into heaven."[511] Additionally, the fourth glorious mystery of the Rosary commemorated Mary's Assumption,[512] and the Church's calendar honored the feast of Mary's Assumption, August 15.[513]

Moreover, the Church's liturgy made several references to Mary's Assumption into heaven.[514] Liturgy, the public worship of the Church, is considered an especially trustworthy expression of the Catholic faith, for it requires the approval of the Magisterium [1069-1070, 1124-1125]. Pope Pius XII wrote that the Liturgy "...has the Catholic faith for its content, inasmuch as it bears public witness to the faith of the Church."[515]

Together these practices demonstrated a belief in the Assumption of Mary among Roman Catholics going back several centuries.

Was the Assumption part of the common understanding of the faithful?

In 1946, devotion to Mary among Catholics was at an all-time high. Accounts of her appearances and associated miracles had captured the imagination of the people. Recent Church teaching had emphasized Mary's role in the redemption. Additionally, the definition of Mary's Immaculate Conception in 1854 had encouraged Catholics devoted to Mary to begin petitioning the Vatican to declare that the Assumption was also part of the faith.

From the Church's perspective, these developments were a healthy progression in the faithful's understanding of Tradition [94]. The people were not inventing some new doctrine about Mary. To the contrary, they were getting in touch with an old belief, one that had been living within the Church for centuries. Now, through new insight, the belief was coming to light and being expressed [66, 93, 99]. This, says the Church, is one of the ways in which Tradition makes progress in the Church [94]:

> It comes through the contemplation and study of believers who ponder these things in their hearts (cf. Luke 2:19,51). It comes from the intimate sense of spiritual realities which they experience.
> —Second Vatican Council[516]

The fact that so many Catholics had already embraced the Assumption of Mary as part of their faith was significant. Roman Catholicism teaches that the faithful have a "supernatural appreciation of the faith."[517] This is called the *sensus fidelium*, the *consensus of faith* [67, 91-93, 785, 904]. It is an "...instinctive sensitivity and discrimination which the members of the Church possess in matters of faith."[518] In that which the faithful hold in common to be the true Catholic faith, they are infallible and "cannot err in matters of belief"[519] [889].

How the faithful are able to infallibly recognize truth is not clear. Most lay Catholics have no more than a cursory knowledge of either Scripture or Roman Catholic theology.

Nevertheless, Pope Pius, in accordance with Roman Catholic belief, considered the piety of the people to be a trustworthy witness to the authentic Catholic faith. For this reason, in his 1946 letter, the Pope also asked the bishops to inform him as to "...the devotion of your clergy and people (taking into account their faith and piety) toward the Assumption of the most Blessed Virgin Mary."[520] The Pope's goal here was to determine the common sentiment of the people.

Encouraged by his request for their input, clergy and laity responded enthusiastically. By 1950, totaled with previous petitions, the Vatican had received responses from 32,000 priests and brothers, 50,000 nuns, and 8,000,000 laypeople![521] Pope Pius found the response "truly remarkable."[522]

After considering all of the evidence for belief in Mary's Assumption and the research of the Church's theologians, Pope Pius concluded:

> These studies and investigations have brought out into even clearer light the fact that the dogma of the Virgin Mary's Assumption into heaven is contained in the deposit of Christian faith entrusted to the Church.
>
> —*Munificentissimus Deus*[523]

In making this decision, the Pope was aware that Scripture clearly taught that as a consequence of sin, God had declared to Adam and his descendants, "You are dust, and to dust you shall return" (Genesis 3:19). Nevertheless, Pius determined that "God has willed that the Blessed Virgin Mary should be exempted from this general rule."[524] And so, on November 1, 1950, as the supreme teacher of the Church, he declared that the Assumption of Mary was "a divinely revealed dogma."[525]

Scripture, Tradition, and the Magisterium

The process by which the Assumption of Mary became dogma demonstrates three important points. The first is that Catholic definitions equating Tradition with the oral teachings of the apostles are misleading [81, 83, 96]. For example, the Second Vatican Council described Tradition as revelation that the apostles passed on "... by the spoken word of their preaching, by the example they gave, by the institutions they established ..."526 [76]. In support of this definition, the Council referred to Paul's instruction to the Thessalonians:527

> So then, brethren, stand firm and hold to the traditions which you were taught, whether by word of mouth or by letter from us.
>
> —2 Thessalonians 2:15

In citing this verse, the Church would have us believe that Roman Catholic Tradition is equivalent to the apostle Paul's oral teachings. This is misleading, however, for, as we have seen, Roman Catholic Tradition is a far more complex concept. It is not the direct oral teaching of the apostles as referred to in 2 Thessalonians 2:15. Rather, Roman Catholic Tradition is "a current of life and truth."528 It can be as ethereal as an idea that, after having lain dormant for centuries, as in the case of Mary's Assumption, can spring to life in modern times through pious contemplation. No reasonable comparison can be drawn between Roman Catholic Tradition and the apostle Paul personally and directly instructing the Thessalonians in the Christian faith. (See Appendix D for an overview of each of the references to Tradition in the New Testament.)

Second, Scripture and Roman Catholic Tradition are not equals. The Roman Catholic Church teaches that "... both Scripture and Tradition must be accepted and honored with equal feelings of devotion and reverence"529 [82]. But the Scriptures are a *written* record of revelation. They are tangible, unalterable, and accessible to all. Moreover, they are an *inspired* record, "God-breathed" (2 Timothy 3:16 NIV), the writings of "... men moved by the Holy Spirit [who] spoke from God" (2 Peter 1:21). Scripture, therefore, is rightly called the Word of God.

Roman Catholic Tradition, on the other hand, is an amorphous body of beliefs and practices which the Church claims has been handed down for some 60 generations in "human formulas":[530] a bishop teaching, a priest delivering a Sunday's homily, a theologian writing, a mother reciting prayers with her children, a hymn, a stained-glass window, or the unspoken "spiritual realities"[531] shared by the faithful. Though a child could see the difference between this and Scripture, the Church cannot or will not.

Third, the Magisterium, claiming to speak for God Himself, is a law unto itself. It is accountable to no one on earth. What *it* says is the only rule of faith that most Catholics know, for the Magisterium has placed itself between the Word of God and the Catholic people:

> The *Catholics* admit a two fold rule of faith, a remote rule and a proximate rule. The *remote* rule is the word of God, written or handed down by tradition. The *proximate* rule is the living and infallible magisterium of the Church, which magisterium sets forth the word of God in an authoritative and trustworthy manner.
>
> —*A Manual of Dogmatic Theology*[532]

In other words, since Catholics are expected to submit to the official teaching of the Church, the Magisterium itself is a rule of faith [119, 169-171, 182]. It is the *proximate* rule, for it is more available and closer to the people than the *remote* rule, the Word of God.

The Magisterium is neither accountable to man nor to the plain teaching of Scripture. In his encyclical preparing the way for the defining of Mary's Assumption as dogma, Pope Pius XII wrote that the Magisterium is able

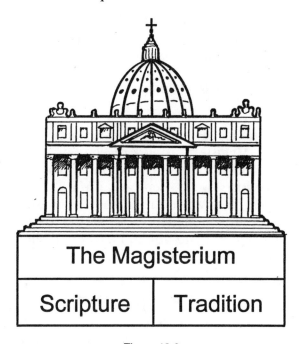

The Magisterium	
Scripture	Tradition

Figure 12:2

The Full Foundation of the Gospel According to Rome

According to the Second Vatican Council, "...sacred Tradition, sacred Scripture and the Magisterium of the Church are so connected and associated that one of them cannot stand without the others. Working together, each in its own way under the action of the one Holy Spirit, they all contribute effectively to the salvation of souls"[533] [95].

"...to elucidate and explain what is contained in the deposit of faith only obscurely and implicitly"[534] [66, 88, 2035, 2051]. Catholic scholar Father John Hardon comments:

> The degree of obscurity, we may add, is unimportant. Given this faculty by her founder, whose Spirit of truth abides with her at all times, the Church can infallibly discern what belongs to revelation no matter how cryptic the contents may be.
>
> Consequently, when Pius XII defined the Assumption, he did more than propose the doctrine for acceptance by the faithful or give them

a new motive for devotion to the Blessed Mother. He indicated the Church's right to authorize a legitimate development in doctrine and piety that scandalizes Protestants and may even surprise believing Catholics.

—*The Catholic Catechism*[535]

Here we see the true relationship between the teaching of the Magisterium and revelation. Though both Scripture and documentary evidence from before the seventh century were silent as to Mary's Assumption, nevertheless, as an act of the Extraordinary Magisterium of the Church, Pope Pius XII declared it to be a divinely revealed dogma. In so doing, he asserted the Church's independence both from Scripture and from the catholic faith of the early church.

A Biblical Verdict

Significant parallels can be drawn between the authority structure of Roman Catholicism today and that of first-century Judaism. Similar to Rome's Pope and Bishops, Jerusalem, the central city of Jewish authority, was the base of a "Council of the elders of the people" (Luke 22:66), "the Senate of the sons of Israel" (Acts 5:21), known as the *Sanhedrin*. The Jewish high priest presided over this body and served as its head (Matthew 26:3, 57, 62-65; Acts 5:21, 27; 7:1; 9:1; 22:5; 23:2-5). With some restrictions, the Roman government allowed the Sanhedrin to function as the supreme political, religious, and judicial body of the Jews in Judea (Matthew 5:22; John 3:1; 7:26; 7:48; Acts 3:17; 4:5,8).

At least two schools of thought were represented among the membership of the Sanhedrin (Acts 23:6-8). The aristocratic high-priestly families and their associates were of the sect of the Sadducees (Acts 5:17). Others were of the party of the Pharisees. Known for their strict and detailed interpretation of the law (Matthew 5:20; 23:23), the Pharisees were accustomed to receiving "the front seats in the synagogues, and respectful greetings in the market places" (Luke 11:43). Some of their number were scribes who copied, interpreted, and taught the law (Matthew 5:20; 12:38; 15:1; 22:35; 23:2; Mark 2:16; Luke 5:17, 21). Much the same as the Roman Magisterium, the scribes and Pharisees considered themselves to be the authoritative teachers of the law and sought to dictate to the common people the proper observance of every aspect of the Jewish faith (Matthew 9:11; 12:2; 23:2-36).

As in Roman Catholicism today, the scribes and Pharisees also held to the joint authority of Scripture and Tradition (Matthew 15:2; Mark 7:3,5,9,13). They taught that Moses had handed down the law received on Mount Sinai in two ways. The first was through his oral teaching. They called this the *unwritten Torah* or *oral Tradition*.[536] The second was the *written Torah* or *Scripture*. They taught that the written law and the unwritten law together made up the complete Torah, the Word of God.

The scribes and Pharisees had not received their authority from God. To the contrary, Jesus said, "The scribes and the Pharisees have seated themselves in the chair of Moses" (Matthew 23:2). Nowhere did the Hebrew Scriptures instruct the Jews to set up the Sanhedrin, to submit to the teaching of the scribes and Pharisees, or to recognize the authority of oral Tradition alongside Scripture. Nevertheless, in the first century, this is the way it was, and most Jews submitted to it without question.

Jesus was an exception. He refused to subject His ministry to the Sanhedrin, the scribes and the Pharisees, or Tradition. As His popularity grew among the people, a showdown became inevitable.

It occurred during the last year of the Lord's ministry in Galilee, and is recorded in Matthew 15:1-9 and in Mark 7:1-13. A group of scribes and Pharisees came from Jerusalem to confront Jesus, apparently on behalf of the Sanhedrin. In order to enter into controversy with Christ, they challenged Him with a question: "Why do Your disciples not walk according to the tradition of the elders, but eat their bread with impure hands?" (Mark 7:5).

Dirty hands were not the issue but the observance of a strict procedure that the oral law, or Tradition, dictated. Preserved today in the Mishna, the Tradition of the elders specified every detail as to how one's hands were to be washed before eating. The Pharisees had seen some of Christ's disciples "eating their bread with impure hands, that is, unwashed" (Mark 7:2). Now the authoritative teachers of the Jewish nation were demanding an explanation.

Jesus was not intimidated. Rather than submitting to their authority as they expected, He rebuked them for their hypocrisy:

> Rightly did Isaiah prophesy of you hypocrites, as
> it is written,
> "This people honors Me with their lips,
> But their heart is far away from Me.
> But in vain do they worship Me,
> Teaching as doctrines the precepts of men."
> —Mark 7:6,7

The scribes and Pharisees appeared devout in their zeal for the proper observance of Tradition, but the Lord knew it was a pious deception. Their hearts were far from God. Their worship was vain, worthless in the sight of God.

The Lord accused the Pharisees of "teaching as doctrine the precepts of men" (Mark 7:7). The Scriptures said absolutely nothing about washing one's hands before eating. Nonetheless, the Pharisees enforced ceremonial handwashing as if God Himself had ordained it. In this way they had elevated the teachings of men to the same level of authority as God's inspired Scriptures.

With intentional sting, the Lord continued His rebuke, labeling the oral Torah as "the tradition of men" (Mark 7:8). Jesus accused them of putting men's words before God's Word: "Neglecting the commandment of God, you hold to the tradition of men.... You nicely set aside the commandment of God in order to keep your tradition" (Mark 7:8,9). In other words, when the Pharisees disobeyed Scripture, they did it with style. They did it "nicely" (Mark 7:9). Jesus gave them credit for how cleverly they could slip God's commandments to the side to clear the way for strict obedience to their own Traditions. By their Traditions, Jesus said, they were "invalidating

---

Sola Scriptura!

"Scripture Alone!" was the battle cry of the Reformation. None championed the cause better than Martin Luther. He was an Augustinian priest and professor of Catholic theology at the University of Wittenberg. Luther objected to papal representatives selling pardons from purgatory to help finance the building of St. Peter's Basilica. In 1517 he made a list of 95 reasons why this was wrong and nailed it to the church door at Wittenberg. When ordered to recant, Luther responded, "My conscience is captive to the Word of God." He rejected Tradition and the teaching authority of the Pope and bishops as infallible guides to the Christian faith. He proclaimed Scripture alone as the rule or standard for the Christian faith. (For a reply to some of the modern challenges to *Sola Scriptura*, see Appendix E.)

---

the word of God" (Mark 7:13), stamping the Scriptures null and void.

In this way, Jesus rejected the manmade authority structure of the first-century Jews. He refused to submit to Tradition, the teaching authority of the Scribes and Pharisees, or the ruling authority of the Sanhedrin they represented.

What Jesus rejected the Roman Catholic Church has now restored. It has elevated Tradition to the same level of authority as God's inspired Scriptures. Its Pope and bishops have laid claim to universal jurisdiction and sole teaching authority. All the while, the Roman Catholic hierarchy, even as the Pharisees, honors God with its lips, claiming [86]:

> ...this Magisterium is not superior to the Word of God, but is its servant. It teaches only what has been handed on to it.
>
> —Second Vatican Council[537]

Spiritual Authority: Error Versus Truth

The Catholic Church Teaches	The Bible Teaches
1. Peter was the head of the apostles [552, 765, 880].	Christ was the head of the apostles (John 13:13).
2. The bishops are the successors of the apostles [861-862, 938].	The apostles had no successors, for to succeed them one needed to be a witness of Christ's resurrection (Acts 1:21,22).
3. The Pope, as the Bishop of Rome, is the successor of Peter [882, 936].	Peter had no successor.
4. The bishops, with the Pope as their head, rule the universal Church [883, 894-896].	Christ, the head of the body, rules the universal church (Colossians 1:18).
5. God has entrusted revelation to the Roman Catholic bishops [81, 86].	God has entrusted revelation to the saints (Jude 3).
6. The Magisterium is the authoritative teacher of the Church [85-87].	The Holy Spirit is the authoritative teacher of the church (John 14:26; 16:13; 1 John 2:27).
7. The Magisterium is the infallible interpreter of Scripture [890-891, 2034-2035].	Scripture is the only infallible interpreter of Scripture (Acts 17:11).

8. The Pope is infallible in his authoritative teaching [891].

God alone is infallible (Numbers 23:19).

9. The Magisterium alone has the ability and the right to interpret Scripture [85, 100, 939].

Every Christian, aided by the Holy Spirit, has the ability and the right to interpret Scripture (Acts 17:11; 1 Corinthians 2:12-16).

10. Scripture is to be interpreted in the sense in which it has been defined by the Magisterium [113, 119].

Scripture must be interpreted in the original sense intended by the Holy Spirit (2 Peter 3:14-16).

11. The Magisterium has the right to define truth found only obscurely or implicitly in revelation [66, 88, 2035, 2051].

No one has the right to go beyond what is written in Scripture (1 Corinthians 4:6; Proverbs 30:6).

12. Scripture and Tradition together are the Word of God [81, 85, 97, 182].

Scripture is the Word of God (John 10:35; 2 Timothy 3:16,17; 2 Peter 1:20,21). Tradition is the words of men (Mark 7:1-13).

13. Scripture and Tradition together are the Church's supreme rule of faith [80, 82].

Scripture is the church's only rule of faith (Mark 7:7-13; 2 Timothy 3:16,17).

THE JUNCTION

To the Catholic Reader

Almost 20 years ago I stood at a junction where you may now stand or may soon find yourself. Before me lay the most difficult decision of my life. In one direction there was the faith of my youth, my religious heritage, and my church. In the other there was Christianity as I had come to know it from the Word of God. Complicating the decision was the knowledge that my family would be terribly hurt if I left the Church. Yet, no longer believing that the Roman Catholic Church was the one, holy, catholic, and apostolic Church founded by Christ, I knew I had to leave. I had to obey God rather than men (Acts 4:19; 5:29).

My prayer is that God will guide you even as He did me at that most difficult time. I offer the following biblical principles to guide you as you weigh the matter for yourself.

Follow the example of the Bereans, whom the Bible commends as "noble-minded ... for they received the word with great eagerness, examining the Scriptures daily, to see whether these things were so" (Acts 17:11). In faith, ask God to give you the wisdom to understand the Bible (James 1:5-8). If you are willing to do God's will, He promises to provide the information and insight that you will need (John 7:17). Whenever you learn something from God's Word, act upon it immediately (James 1:22-25). As you do, the Lord will teach you further truth (Luke 19:26). I recommend that you start by reading the Gospel of John, the Acts of the Apostles, and Paul's letters to the Galatians and to the Romans.

Believe God and His promises (Hebrews 11:6). Most importantly, place your trust completely in Christ to save you (Romans 10:8-13). Renounce dependence upon the Church, the sacraments, your good works, and Mary for salvation (Acts 4:12; Philippians 3:7-11).

Do not think that by staying in the Roman Catholic Church you can change it. Though every error cataloged in this book has been pointed out by others long ago, the Church refuses to listen. It has never acknowledged a single doctrinal error. Indeed, it cannot, lest people realize that the Church's claim to infallibility is a charade. Far from admitting error, the Roman Catholic Church has shamelessly opposed its critics, staining its hands with their blood down through the centuries.

God's counsel to a Christian who finds himself in an unbiblical religious institution is to leave:

> Come out of her, my people, that you may not
>   participate in her sins
> and that you may not receive of her plagues;
> for her sins have piled up as high as heaven,
> and God has remembered her iniquities.
>   —Revelation 18:4-5

> "Therefore, come out from their midst and be
>   separate," says the Lord,
> "And do not touch what is unclean."
>   —2 Corinthians 6:17

To those who obey, the Lord adds this promise:

> "And I will welcome you.
> "And I will be a father to you,
> And you shall be sons and daughters
>   to Me,"

Says the Lord Almighty.
—2 Corinthians 6:17,18

Once you escape the fog of Roman Catholicism, you will see more clearly the truths of Scripture. Find church fellowship among Christians who love the Lord and recognize the Bible alone as their supreme authority. There you will progress in your knowledge of God unhindered by false teaching. You will also find opportunities to serve the Lord and make Him known.

What about your Catholic family and friends? The best thing you can do for them is to leave the Roman Catholic Church yourself and become part of a strong, biblically based church. As you learn to live more like Christ, your life will become an exhibit of the transforming power of the gospel. You will grow in your understanding of the truth and your ability to explain it. You will also be in a position to minister to others who are seeking God. When you leave the Catholic Church, your family and friends will want to know why. Use the opportunity to explain what you have found, but do so "with gentleness and reverence" (1 Peter 3:15), "speaking the truth in love" (Ephesians 4:15).

To the Non-Catholic Christian Reader

High above the main altar of Saint Peter's Basilica there is an inscription around the inside base of the great central dome. Large enough for all to read, it is the banner verse of Roman Catholicism: "Thou art Peter; and upon this rock I will build my church" (Matthew 16:18 Douay Rheims).

How fitting that the distinctive claim of the Roman Catholic Church should be that it is an institution built upon a man! And so it is. Let us grant the Church this status that it seeks. As its theology demonstrates, Roman Catholicism rests upon a very human foundation, a combination of God's way and man's way, a mixture of truth and error. It is a belief system based upon Scripture (the Word of God) plus Tradition (the words of men). It offers atonement through the sacrifice of Jesus plus the sacrifices of priests. It teaches salvation by the work of Christ plus the works of men. It tells people to approach God through the mediation of the Lord Jesus Christ plus that of the Blessed Virgin Mary. In each of its distinctive doctrines, Roman Catholicism is "a way which seems right to a man, but its end is the way of death" (Proverbs 14:12). Appropriately, the Church has built the main altar of Saint Peter's Basilica upon a crypt full of dead men's bones, allegedly including those of Peter himself.

Yet, one might ask, how can so much error coexist alongside so much Christian truth? The prospect should not shock us. Biblical prophecy warns that apostasy, a falling away or departure from the Christian faith, will precede the second coming of Christ (2 Thessalonians 2:3). In the last days, say the Scriptures, there will arise "false teachers among you who will secretly introduce destructive heresies, even denying the Master who bought them..." (2 Peter 2:1). These false teachers will not openly oppose the Christian faith. Quite to the contrary, they will offer prayers in the name of Christ, use the Scriptures in their ceremonies, and promise salvation to those who follow their teaching. They will hold "to a form of godliness, although they have denied its power" (2 Timothy 3:5), opposing the truth even "as Jannes and Jambres opposed Moses" (2 Timothy 3:8). These were the two magicians of Pharaoh's court who challenged Moses' authority by mimicking what he did (Exodus 7:11,22; 8:7). Similarly, the false teachers of the end times will lead many people astray with an insidious imitation of Christianity. The Bible says that "many will follow their sensuality, and because of them the way of the truth will be maligned; and in their greed they will exploit you with false words..." (2 Peter 2:2,3).

Who is behind this great deception? According to the Bible, "the Spirit explicitly says that in later times some will fall away from the faith, paying attention to deceitful spirits and doctrines of demons..." (1 Timothy 4:1). Ultimately, the lie can be traced to Satan himself, the deceiver of old, "the father of lies" (John 8:44).

This is not to say that the Pope, bishops, and priests of the Roman Catholic Church are consciously aware that they are serving Satan's purposes. Many are undoubtedly sincere. For the most part, they, even as Paul before his conversion, are acting "ignorantly in unbelief" (1 Timothy 1:13); they are "deceived" (Titus 3:3). Nevertheless, they are responsible before God, for they have failed to take heed to God's Word. Having believed a false gospel, they remain in their sins. Consequently, but for a great outpouring of the Holy Spirit in these last days, the vast majority of Roman Catholics alive on earth today, clergy and laity alike, will die in their sins.

To God we must cry out. To the lost we must reach out.

Pray for Catholics

The Bible tells us that the gospel "... is veiled to those who are perishing, in whose case the god of this world has blinded the minds of the unbelieving, that they might not see the light of the gospel of the glory of Christ, who is the image of God" (2 Corinthians 4:3,4). Pray that God would open the eyes of Roman Catholics, that "if perhaps God may grant them repentance leading to the knowledge of the truth, and they may come to their senses and escape from the snare of the devil, having been held captive by him to do his will" (2 Timothy 2:25,26).

Develop Friendships

Since Catholicism tends to run along family and ethnic lines, many Catholics do not have even one non-Catholic Christian friend. Relatively few have ever heard a clear presentation of the gospel.

Ask God to increase your love and compassion for Catholics. Then look for ways to nurture friendships with them. You will find that your greatest opportunities to share your faith usually come early in a new relationship, so don't let them pass. Catholics are more open today than most people realize. Each year thousands are turning to Christ. And don't be afraid to reach out to priests and nuns. Many are lonely and searching for answers.

Stimulate Thought

Many Catholics are more dutiful than devout. They don't ask much of the Church, and the Church doesn't ask much of them. Family expectations are met and the conscience soothed in an equilibrium of peaceful coexistence with the Church.

If the love of God abides in us, we cannot sit by idly. Take the initiative. Get your Catholic friend thinking about his spiritual condition. Try, for example, offering your friend some Christian literature or a videotape. Ask him (or her) if he knows with certainty what will happen to his soul when he dies.

Don't be paralyzed by the fear of offending. Confronting your Catholic friend with the errors of the Church may be the best thing you can do for him. Some Catholics will get angry before they get saved, but later they will thank you for having loved them enough to present the truth to them.

Promote Bible Study

The average Catholic is trusting the Church to care for his soul and to tell him what to believe about God and salvation. In coming to Christ, such a person must learn to think for himself, to take personal responsibility for his soul, and to base his faith upon God's Word. This requires a major shift in his thinking.

You can help your Catholic friend to start the process by encouraging him to read the Scriptures. Make sure he has a Bible that is readable and convenient to use, not an oversized family edition. Explain how the Bible is structured and how to find a Bible passage. Suggest a place to start reading. Invite your friend to a Bible study. A discussion-style study (where visitors can simply observe if they so desire) is best. Once a person seeking God discovers that he can learn directly from the Scriptures, there will be no stopping him.

Address the Real Problem

Your friend's greatest problem is not the Roman Catholic Church; it is his sin. So don't let Roman Catholicism become the focus of your discussions. As discussed in Chapter 4, many Catholics have a deficient understanding of the seriousness of sin and its consequences. They think that because they have been baptized and are living relatively moral lives, everything is just fine. Help your friend to see what God says about sin in the Bible. Pray that he would become genuinely convicted of his sins.

Explain the way of salvation. Do so directly from the Scriptures. This will help your Catholic friend to see that the authority for what you are saying does not rest with you or with your church, but on God's inspired Word. Make sure that he understands what the Bible is saying by asking him to explain it to you. Since Catholics and non-Catholics use many of the same words but with different meanings, be careful to define your terms.

Go slowly! Do not prematurely lead your friend in a prayer to accept Christ. As we have seen, Catholicism is an endless series of rites and prayers. The more the better, or so they think. Your friend may interpret your invitation to pray to receive Christ as just one more rite, and repeat your words whether he understands what he is doing or not. Wait until the person is clearly under conviction of sin and understands the gospel. Then encourage him to make a decision for Christ, speaking to God in his own words.

Encourage a Clean Break

The Lord Jesus has commissioned us to make disciples, to baptize them, and to thoroughly instruct them in the Christian faith (Matthew 28:19,20). The work of evangelism, therefore, is not completed until your Catholic friend is saved, baptized, and incorporated into a sound, Bible-teaching church.

Encourage a clean break with the Roman Catholic Church. A thorough housecleaning may also be in order. Explain the value of disposing of everything associated with unbiblical beliefs and practices: statues, Rosaries, scapulars, miraculous medals, holy cards, holy water, etc. (Acts 19:17-20; Jude 23). Do not underestimate how ingrained Roman Catholicism can be even in lapsed Catholics. Pray for spiritual liberation and encourage the individual regularly.

If a newly saved Catholic is having trouble leaving the Roman Catholic Church, try explaining more fully what Roman Catholicism teaches and why it is unbiblical. Start with the Mass. If the person is truly saved, he will soon realize that he should no longer participate in a continuing sacrifice of Christ or in the worship of bread and wine. If devotion to Mary is the problem, emphasize the glories of the Lord Jesus Christ and His sufficiency. As when coaxing an infant to release a harmful object clutched in his hand, the best method is to offer something better in exchange.

Anticipate Trials

Jesus taught that following Him often involves opposition, particularly from family members (Matthew 10:34-39). Prepare a newly saved Catholic to expect trials. They usually start when the person leaves the Roman Catholic Church or decides to get baptized. Counsel the person to avoid harsh arguments and constant, unwelcome attempts at trying to convert family members. Rather, exhort the newly saved Catholic to witness to his family by living like Christ, by doing acts of kindness, and by being humble and patient.

Continue to Learn

The better you understand Roman Catholicism, the better you will be able to effectively communicate the gospel to Catholics. Consider reading the new *Catechism of the Catholic Church*. Then use it in evangelism to point out to Catholics what Roman Catholicism teaches and to contrast it with biblical truth. You may also wish to obtain a simplified catechism and a Catholic dictionary. Finally, consider subscribing to a Catholic newspaper or magazine to keep abreast of current trends within the Roman Catholic Church.

Oppose Ecumenism

One of the principal objectives of the Second Vatican Council was the promotion of ecumenism, the restoration of unity among Christian churches of every kind. The Council set forth three principles to guide the Church's ecumenical movement. First, Catholics were to be aware that Christ established the Roman Catholic Church and gave it the Eucharist, the Holy Spirit, and bishops with the Pope as their head to rule, so that the Church might be unified.[538] Second, it taught that non-Catholic Christians who have been justified by baptism are to be considered as *separated brethren* [818, 1271]. They have a valid means of salvation, said the Church, but not in its fullness as in the Roman Catholic Church [819, 824].[539] Third, the Council stated that all Catholics should promote ecumenism by avoiding unfair criticism of other Christians. To promote understanding and cooperation, competent experts were to engage in dialogue [821].[540]

The Council stated that the goal of the Church's ecumenical strategy was the unity of all Christian churches through common communion with the Roman Catholic Church [820-822, 855]:

> The results will be that, little by little, as the obstacles to perfect ecclesiastical communion are overcome, all Christians will be gathered, in a common celebration of the Eucharist, into the unity of the one and only Church, which Christ bestowed on his Church from the beginning.

> This unity, we believe, subsists in the Catholic Church as something she can never lose, and we hope that it will continue to increase until the end of time.
>
> —Second Vatican Council[541]

Though Rome has yet to achieve its ultimate purpose, it has succeeded in undermining the commitment of many Christians to the evangelization of Catholics. Consider, for example, the 1994 signing in the U.S. of an accord titled *Evangelicals & Catholics Together: The Christian Mission in the Third Millennium.*[542] In it leading evangelicals and Roman Catholics stated that "evangelicals and Catholics are brothers and sisters in Christ." They labeled the evangelization of active members of each other's flocks as illegitimate theology and "sheep stealing," and resolved "to explore patterns of working and witnessing together in order to advance the one mission of Christ."

Such ecumenical compromise must be opposed. There is no room in biblical Christianity for unity or cooperation with Rome and its false gospel, its continuing sacrifice, and its idolatrous devotion to Mary. As long as the Roman Catholic Church continues "to regard the Scriptures, taken together with sacred Tradition, as the supreme rule of her faith,"[543] there is not even a common basis for dialogue.

APPENDICES
NOTES
SCRIPTURE INDEX
SUBJECT INDEX

INFANT BAPTISMAL JUSTIFICATION

Roman Catholicism teaches that the sacrament of baptism is the "instrumental cause"[544] of justification. The Church, however, cannot cite a single verse of Scripture that explicitly states this belief. It must therefore resort to indirect methods in its attempt to demonstrate a biblical basis. In general the approach taken is to cite passages from the Bible that speak of baptism in the same context as the effects of justification (the removal of guilt by divine forgiveness, a right standing before God) and the effects of regeneration (new birth, new life, and ultimately eternal life). The Church then equates baptism as the instrumental cause of these effects. The following are the primary texts that Roman Catholicism uses in arguing its case for infant baptismal justification.

Mark 16:16

> He who has believed and has been baptized shall be saved; but he who has disbelieved shall be condemned.

The Roman Catholic Church says that here Jesus is teaching that baptism is necessary for salvation [977, 1257]. One must be baptized to be saved.

On the contrary, the second half of the verse clarifies the actual intended emphasis: "but he who has disbelieved shall be condemned" (Mark 16:16). The contrast is between the one who believes and the one who disbelieves. The believer shall be saved. The unbeliever shall be condemned. Jesus says nothing about the one who believes but is unbaptized. He links believing and baptism here because true believers in the New Testament were baptized believers. First they believed, then they were baptized.

This last point provides a good opportunity for us to refocus our topic. There is no question about whether those who decide to follow Jesus should be baptized. The New Testament is clear: Every Christian is to be baptized (Matthew 28:19). The question is whether baptism is the *means of receiving* justification. More specifically: Can the sacrament of baptism justify an infant?

Luke 18:16,17

Some argue that to prohibit the baptismal justification of infants would be to disobey a command of the Lord. When some parents tried to bring their children to Jesus, the Lord's disciples tried to stop them. Jesus rebuked His own disciples, saying:[545]

> Permit the children to come to Me, and do not hinder them, for the kingdom of God belongs to such as these. Truly I say to you, whoever does not receive the kingdom of God like a child shall not enter it at all.
>
> —Luke 18:16,17

We can sympathize with Catholic parents who want to bring their children to Jesus. However, this passage does not teach that baptismal justification is the way to do it. The Jewish parents were bringing their children to Jesus that He might "lay His hands on them and pray" (Matthew 19:13). And that is exactly what Jesus did. He did not baptize them or anyone else (John 4:2).

John 3:5

Jesus answered, "Truly, truly, I say to you, unless one is born of water and the Spirit, he cannot enter into the kingdom of God."

There are four common interpretations of this verse.

Born of Baptism

This is the interpretation taught by the Roman Catholic Church [782, 1215, 1225, 1238, 1257, 1262]. It says that "born of water" (John 3:5) is a reference to the sacrament of baptism. Through it an infant is born again and made fit for heaven.

The weakness of this interpretation is that it distorts God's clear message of salvation found throughout the Scriptures. The Bible teaches that for Jew and Gentile alike salvation has always been through faith (Genesis 15:6; Habakkuk 2:4; Acts 20:21). In John 3, Jesus is speaking to a Jew named Nicodemus, a Pharisee and member of the Sanhedrin. Jesus tells Nicodemus, "God so loved the world that He gave His only begotten Son, that whoever *believes in Him* should not perish but have eternal life" (John 3:16, emphasis added). Faith, the fundamental response that God requires, is the missing ingredient in infant baptism. Furthermore, in that Christian baptism was not practiced until three years later, the Roman Catholic interpretation renders Jesus' instruction to Nicodemus rather meaningless.

Born Naturally and Spiritually

This interpretation understands being "born of water" (John 3:5) as a reference to physical birth, and being "born of the Spirit" (John 3:5) as a reference to spiritual birth. It is supported by the fact that Nicodemus thought that Jesus was speaking about physical birth (John 3:4). Jesus also went on to say, "That which is born of the flesh is flesh, and that which is born of Spirit is spirit" (John 3:6). Here Jesus is clearly speaking of physical and spiritual birth. Though this interpretation may have some merit, it does not appear to account for the full meaning of Jesus' words.

Born of Water, Even the Spirit

In the phrase "born of water and the Spirit" (John 3:5), the Greek word translated "and" can be translated "even." The phrase would then read "born of water, even the Spirit" or "born of water, namely the Spirit." This view is supported by the fact that water is used to symbolize the Holy Spirit in John 7:38,39.

Born of Repentance and Faith

Earlier in John's gospel we read that John the Baptist said that he came to baptize "in water" (John 1:31), but another was coming, Christ, "who baptizes in the Holy Spirit" (John 1:33). These previous references to water and the Spirit would support interpreting Jesus' words in John 3:5 as referring to the need to respond to the messages of John and Jesus. John called the Jews to repentance (Matthew 3:2). Jesus called them to repent and to believe (Mark 1:15). And so Jesus' message to Nicodemus that one must be "born of water and the Spirit" (John 3:5) could be understood as saying that repentance followed by faith was necessary for new birth and entry into the kingdom of God. This is the same message that the apostles preached: They solemnly testified "...to both Jews and Greeks of repentance toward God and faith in our Lord Jesus Christ" (Acts 20:21).

Christians differ as to which of these last three interpretations best fits the context.

Acts 2:38

And Peter said to them, "Repent, and let each of you be baptized in the name of Jesus Christ for the forgiveness of your sins; and you shall receive the gift of the Holy Spirit."

Roman Catholic scholars argue from this passage that the apostles considered baptism the rite of Christian initiation [1226, 1262, 1287, 1427]. Through it infants receive "... a regenerative grace by which all sins and the punishments due to sins are fully remitted."[546]

Peter, however, was not speaking to infants but to Jews who had just been told that they had crucified the Messiah. The Bible says that "they were pierced to the heart, and said to Peter and the rest of the apostles, 'Brethren, what shall we do?'" (Acts 2:37).

It is in this context that Peter responded, "Repent, and let each of you be baptized in the name of Jesus Christ for the forgiveness of your sins..." (Acts 2:38). In other words, Peter was promising that God would forgive them of their sins, even of having crucified Christ, if they genuinely believed, if they were willing to make a public statement of faith in Jesus Christ by being baptized in His name. All realized that making such a declaration might result in severe persecution at the hands of the ruling Jews, family, and friends. Nevertheless, "those *who had received his word* were baptized; and there were added that day about three thousand souls" (Acts 2:41, emphasis added). Peter's promise in Acts 2:38 is just as true today as it was on Pentecost, if it is applied in the same context.

Acts 10, 16, 18, and Other Household Baptisms

The Roman Catholic Church also argues for infant baptismal justification by citing New Testament examples of individuals and their household receiving baptism [1226, 1252]. Paul and his associates baptized Cornelius and his household (Acts 10:48; 11:14), Lydia "and her household" (Acts 16:15), the Philippian jailer "and all his household" (Acts 16:33), Crispus "with all his household" (Acts 18:8), and "the household of Stephanas" (1 Corinthians 1:16).

This argument assumes that there were infants in each of these households. The conclusion that Paul baptized infants, therefore, is also an assumption—and not a very good one at that. Luke provides details about the conversion of the jailer that would suggest that infants were not included. Luke writes that Paul and Silas "spoke the word of the Lord to him [the jailer] together with all who were in his house" (Acts 16:32). The jailer "believed in God with his whole household" (Acts 16:34). The jailer's household heard the gospel and believed—hardly activities that Luke would attribute to infants. The Scriptures state that personal faith also preceded the baptisms of Cornelius' household (Acts 10:44-48) and Crispus' household (Acts 18:8).

Acts 22:16

> And now why do you delay? Arise, and be baptized, and wash away your sins, calling on His name.

Proponents of baptismal justification argue that this verse teaches that baptism is the means by which original and personal sins are washed away. You must "be baptized" in order to "wash away your sins" (Acts 22:16).

The grammar of this verse, however, says otherwise. "Be baptized" and "wash away" are both commands in the imperative mood. "Arise" and "calling" are both participles. The verse can be translated: "Rising up, be baptized, and wash away your sins by calling on His name." The remission of sin is associated not with baptism, but with calling on the name of Christ. The same truth is found elsewhere in the New Testament. For example: "Whoever will call upon the name of the Lord will be saved" (Romans 10:13).

Romans 6:3,4

> Or do you not know that all of us who have been baptized into Christ Jesus have been baptized into His death? Therefore we have been buried with Him through baptism into death, in order that as Christ was raised from the dead through the glory of the Father, so we too might walk in newness of life.

Referring to this passage, the Second Vatican Council stated that through the sacred rite of baptism "...fellowship in Christ's death and resurrection is symbolized and is brought about..."[547] [628, 1214, 1227, 1987].

All agree that baptism *symbolizes* the Christian's union with Christ in His death and resurrection. The claim that it is by the rite of baptism that this union is *brought about*, however, must be rejected because of the context of Romans 6.

Paul opens the doctrinal section of his letter to the Romans by presenting mankind's problem: All are under the condemnation of God because of sin (Romans 1:18–3:18). He then explains God's solution: justification through faith in Jesus Christ (Romans 3:19–5:21). In Romans 6:1-8:39, the section containing the passage under examination, the subject changes to sanctification: how the justified are to live the Christian life. In Romans 6:1-14 Paul teaches that a knowledge of one's union with Christ, as symbolized in baptism, is essential to victory over sin.[548] The Roman Catholic Church's interpretation of Romans 6:3,4, that the sacrament of baptism is the instrument by which infants and adults are justified, is foreign to the context.

Colossians 2:11,12

> ...in Him you were also circumcised with a circumcision made without hands, in the removal of the body of the flesh by the circumcision of Christ; having been buried with Him in baptism, in which you were also raised up with Him through faith in the working of God, who raised Him from the dead.

Roman Catholicism teaches that circumcision prefigures baptism [527]. As circumcision removed original sin in Old Testament times, says the Church, baptism removes it today.

Jewish circumcision, however, did not remove sin from a child, but brought him into God's covenant with

Abraham (Genesis 17:11). Roman Catholicism holds that baptism justifies the infant in virtue of the rite performed. Furthermore, in Colossians 2:11,12 Paul is speaking neither of water baptism nor of Jewish circumcision. He is referring to the baptism of the Holy Spirit (1 Corinthians 12:13; Galatians 3:27; Ephesians 4:5), "a circumcision made without hands" (Colossians 2:11), a spiritual work of the Holy Spirit upon the inner person of the believer.

Titus 3:5

> He saved us, not on the basis of deeds which we have done in righteousness, but according to His mercy, by the washing of regeneration and renewing by the Holy Spirit....

The Roman Catholic Church uses Titus 3:5 to teach that the sacrament of baptism is the "laver of regeneration"[549] [1215]. The Catholic *New American Bible* goes so far as to translate the second part of this verse "He saved us through the baptism of new birth and renewal by the Holy Spirit" (Titus 3:5 NAB). Here the translation of the text has been skewed in order to support the Church's doctrine of baptismal regeneration. The English word "baptism" is a transliteration of the Greek word *baptisma*. Consequently, when one reads the word "baptism" in the New Testament, one would expect the Greek text to read *baptisma*. But in this Catholic translation the Greek word *loutron*, meaning *bath*, *laver*, or *washing*, is translated *baptism*.

Had Paul wanted to teach that salvation is by the "baptism of new birth" (Titus 3:5 NAB), as the Catholic Bible puts it, he would surely have used the Greek word *baptisma*. Instead he refers to the "washing of regeneration" (Titus 3:5), using the word *loutron*. This speaks of the cleansing of guilt that accompanies salvation. It is an act of "God our Savior" (Titus 3:4). "He saved us" (Titus 3:5). It is not the result of a sacramental rite.

1 Peter 3:21

And corresponding to that, baptism now saves
you—not the removal of dirt from the flesh, but
an appeal to God for a good conscience—through
the resurrection of Jesus Christ.

This verse is part of one of the most difficult passages in the New Testament to interpret. Nevertheless, this much is clear: It does not support the Roman Catholic doctrine that baptism is the instrument of justification. Peter does not say that "baptism now justifies you," but that "baptism now saves you" (1 Peter 3:21). According to Roman Catholic doctrine, baptism does not save, it justifies. As explained in Chapter 5, *Final Destiny*, Roman Catholic salvation is not the direct or immediate result of baptism or any other sacrament. It is the goal of a lifelong process of cooperating with grace.

It is also clear that when Peter says that "baptism now saves you" (1 Peter 3:21), he is speaking of the typological, or symbolic, significance of baptism. This is communicated by the Greek word *antitupos*, which means *a corresponding type* or *figure*, and is translated "corresponding to that" (1 Peter 3:21). It tells us that what follows, "baptism now saves you" (1 Peter 3:21), is a figurative illustration that complements the symbolism of a preceding figure. In the previous verse, we find that figure. There we read of Noah and "the construction of the ark, in which a few, that is eight persons, were brought safely through the water" (1 Peter 3:20).

To understand how these pieces fit together, it is necessary to examine the greater context of the passage. The first letter of Peter was written to Christians who were being persecuted because of their faith (1 Peter 1:6-9). Peter's goal in writing was to instruct these believers on how they were to respond. Specifically, they were to abstain from fleshly passions such as revenge (1 Peter 2:11,12); to submit to God-ordained authority (1 Peter 2:13-3:7); to show love when wronged (1 Peter 3:8-14); and to not be fearful (1 Peter 3:14,15).

In all of their behavior, these Christians were to "keep a good conscience" (1 Peter 3:16). As a result, those persecuting them would be put to shame (1 Peter 3:16). If it is God's will that they are to suffer, it would be better for them to do so for having done what is right than for what is wrong (1 Peter 3:17). Such was Christ's example (1 Peter 3:18).

Peter then reinforces his teaching with two figurative illustrations. The first is the ark, by which God brought eight persons safely through the perils of the flood (1 Peter 3:20). Apparently Peter's point is that just as God was able to preserve Noah and his family through their trial, so He would now see Peter's readers through theirs.

The second figure has to do with baptism, which likewise illustrates God's way of deliverance. Baptism, Peter explains, is "... the pledge of a good conscience toward God" (1 Peter 3:21 NIV). Maintaining that good conscience now in a time of persecution would result in their salvation or deliverance through the present trial.

Admittedly, the passage is difficult. But lest anyone get the wrong idea, Peter inserts an important aid to interpretation within the verse. Baptism, he writes, is "not the removal of dirt from the flesh" (1 Peter 3:21). The waters of baptism cannot cleanse the flesh, the seat of sin in man (Galatians 5:16-21; 1 John 2:16), of dirt, filth, and moral defilement. Contrary to Roman Catholic doctrine, baptism does not free sinners from original sin and regenerate the soul. It is "... the pledge of a good conscience toward God" (1 Peter 3:21 NIV), not the instrument or source of a good conscience toward God. Significantly, the context of the passage is not about how to be saved from eternal punishment, but about how to be victorious in a time of intense persecution.

THE SEVEN ROMAN CATHOLIC SACRAMENTS

The Three Sacraments of Initiation

Baptism [1213-1284]

According to the Roman Catholic Church, the purpose of the sacrament of baptism is to reverse the effects of Adam's sin. Baptism is said to accomplish this by removing original sin from the soul and infusing sanctifying grace back into it [1262-1266]. This justifies the recipient, making the person holy before God, a participant in the life of grace, and a member of the Roman Catholic Church [1265-1270].

Eucharist [1322-1419]

The Eucharist is the central act of Roman Catholicism. It is the "Sacrament of sacraments,"[1211] and "all the other sacraments are ordered to it as to their end"[1211] [1113]. Catholics receive the sacrament of Holy Eucharist during the Mass. It is believed to provide the body and blood of Christ as spiritual food [1392]. Commonly called Holy Communion, this sacrament is said to unite the Catholic more closely with God [1391]. The Church considers the Eucharist the greatest of the seven sacraments, the *Blessed Sacrament*, and encourages Catholics to receive it frequently [1389]. Many devout Catholics go to Mass and receive the Eucharist daily.

Confirmation [1285-1321]

Confirmation is a special strengthening by the Holy Spirit to enable the Catholic to resist temptation, and to both defend and promote the Roman Catholic Church [1285, 1302-1305]. Catholics usually receive confirmation at about age 12 after completing a preparatory course on doctrine [1306-1311]. A bishop or his delegate administers the sacrament. The minister of the sacrament dips his right thumb in holy oil and anoints the person on the forehead with the sign of the cross, saying, "Be sealed with the gift of the Holy Spirit"[1300] [1300, 1312-1314]. Confirmation is sometimes referred to as a personal Pentecost [1288, 1302].

The Two Sacraments of Healing

Penance [1422-1498]

Commonly referred to as confession, this sacrament is for the forgiveness of serious sins committed after baptism [1446]. It is normally first received at about age eight just before First Holy Communion [1457]. Penance restores sanctifying grace to the baptized Catholic who has fallen because of serious sin. For this reason it is also called the Sacrament of Reconciliation [1424].

Today there are three different rites for the sacrament of penance [1482-1484, 1497]. The first and probably still most common is the traditional form in which an individual receives the sacrament privately, as portrayed in the introduction to Chapter 4, *Rejustification.* In the second form of the rite, several persons receive the first part of the sacrament together. Then they individually and privately confess their sins to a priest and receive absolution. The third form is also designed for several penitents. In this variation, the participants receive the entire sacrament as a group. Rather than individually confessing their sins to a priest, they recite a prayer in which they acknowledge their general guilt in thought, word, and deed. The priest proposes a common penance and declares absolution over the entire group. However, if a person who is guilty of a serious sin receives absolution by this third rite, he is still required to privately confess the sin to a priest within one year.[550]

Anointing of the Sick [1499-1532]

Older Catholics know this sacrament as *extreme unction* [1512]. The purpose of this sacrament is to provide spiritual and physical strength to individuals who are seriously ill or in danger of death [1499, 1511, 1514-1515, 1520-1523, 1532]. In the case of a person threatened by death, it prepares the soul for heaven. Under some circumstances, this sacrament also promises physical healing [1512]. The anointing of the sick is usually received with two other sacraments: penance and Eucharist [1524-1525]. These three together are called the *last rites*.

The Two Sacraments of Service

Holy Orders [1536-1600]

Holy Orders is the sacrament by which men are incorporated into the episcopate as bishops, the presbyterate as priests, or the diaconate as deacons. These are the three degrees of Roman Catholic ordination [1536-1537].

Matrimony [1601-1666]

The sacrament of matrimony is the Roman Catholic marriage ceremony [1601]. Through this sacrament the union is made holy and the couple receives special grace to help in married life [1638-1642].

THE ROMAN CATHOLIC BIBLE

Old Testament

[120-123, 138]

The Roman Catholic Old Testament is about 20 percent larger than that of non-Catholic Bibles. The additions, over 4000 verses, come from a group of 15 writings known since antiquity as the *Apocrypha*, meaning *hidden* or *hard to understand.*

The Apocrypha contains valuable historical information of the 400 years between the Old and New Testaments. Early Christian writers quote the Apocrypha; and some, such as Augustine, considered portions of it to be inspired Scripture. Fourth-century A.D. manuscripts of the Septuagint, a Greek translation of the Old Testament made in the third century before Christ, also include the Apocrypha. When the Apocrypha was appended to this translation is unknown.

In 1546 the Roman Catholic Church officially declared that God had inspired 12 of the 15 writings of the Apocrypha, specifically, seven books:

- Tobit
- Judith
- 1 Maccabees
- 2 Maccabees

- Wisdom of Solomon
- Sirach (Ecclesiasticus)
- Baruch

and five passages:

- The Letter of Jeremiah, which became Baruch chapter 6
- A 107-verse expansion of the Book of Esther
- The Prayer of Azariah, which became Daniel 3:24-90
- Susanna, which became Daniel 13
- Bel and the Dragon, which became Daniel 14

The Roman Catholic Church's claim that these writings of the Apocrypha are inspired must be rejected for the following reasons:

1. The Apocrypha does not present itself as inspired. The author of 2 Maccabees says that his book is the abridgement of another man's work (2 Maccabees 2:23). He concludes the book by saying, "If it is well written and to the point, that is what I wanted; if it is poorly done and mediocre, that is the best I could do" (2 Maccabees 15:38, NAB). Mediocre is a good description of the Apocrypha. Despite its historical value, it promotes questionable ethics (Judith 9-11), fanciful legends (Tobit), and doctrine that contradicts Scripture (Tobit 4:10; 12:9).

2. The Jews of Palestine never accepted the Apocrypha as part of sacred Scripture. Neither was there a Jewish prophet living during the time in which the Apocrypha was written (300-30 B.C.).

3. Jesus and the New Testament writers did not treat the Apocrypha as inspired. Though the New Testament quotes virtually every book of the Old Testament, there is not a single quotation from the Apocrypha.

4. The early church as a whole never accepted the Apocrypha as inspired. Moreover, many Christian leaders

spoke against the Apocrypha, including Jerome, Origen, Athanasius, and Cyril of Jerusalem.

5. Even the Roman Catholic Church did not dogmatically declare the Apocrypha to be inspired until the Council of Trent in the sixteenth century. Roman Catholic priest Father. H. J. Schroeder, a translator of the decrees of the Council of Trent, writes, "The Tridentine list or decree was the first infallible and effectually promulgated declaration on the Canon of the Holy Scriptures."[551] The purpose of the Council of Trent was to counteract the Protestant Reformation. Protestants had rejected the Apocrypha. Rome reacted by dogmatically declaring most of the Apocrypha to be inspired. The Apocrypha also included teachings that could help Rome defend its doctrine against growing Protestant criticism. For example, Martin Luther had forcefully argued against Rome's practice of selling pardons from purgatory. But Tobit 12:9 supports the practice, stating, "... almsgiving saves one from death and expiates every sin." Even some Catholic writers acknowledge that Trent's decision to accept the Apocrypha as inspired is problematic.[552]

New Testament
[120, 124-127, 138-139]

The books of the Roman Catholic New Testament are the same as those of the Protestant Bible and the translations are generally reliable. However, some verses are translated with a noticeably Catholic slant. For example, the Catholic *New American Bible* translates a warning of Jesus to the Jews as saying: "But I tell you, you will all come to the same end unless you reform" (Luke 13:5 NAB). Here the Greek word *metanoeō*, meaning *to change one's mind* or *to repent*, is translated to "reform," meaning *to change into a new and improved form*. Making matters worse, the chapter title to Luke 13 added by the editors of the Catholic *New American Bible* reads: "Providential Calls to Penance."

NEW TESTAMENT REFERENCES TO TRADITION

The word translated *tradition* in the New Testament refers to something *handed down* or *handed over*. It occurs 13 times.

Jewish Tradition

Ten of the 13 references to tradition in the New Testament refer to Jewish tradition. Eight of these are found in the parallel accounts of a confrontation between Jesus and the Pharisees (Matthew 15:2,3,6; Mark 7:3,5,8,9,13). This incident is discussed in the conclusion of Chapter 12, *Scripture and Tradition*.

The other two references to Jewish tradition are:

Galatians 1:14

Paul, referring to his life before he became a Christian, wrote:

> I was advancing in Judaism beyond many of my contemporaries among my countrymen, being more extremely zealous for my ancestral traditions.

Here Paul was speaking of his experience as a member of the Pharisees (Philippians 3:5). The traditions to which he was referring are the Jewish regulations *handed down* by the rabbis that ruled his life. Through Christ he found liberation from these.

Colossians 2:8

Paul instructed the Christians of Colosse:

> See to it that no one takes you captive through philosophy and empty deception, according to the tradition of men, according to the elementary principles of the world, rather than according to Christ.

In this verse Paul is speaking of deceptive doctrines that false teachers were trying to introduce into the church in Colosse. From the context we know that these traditions of men (Colossians 2:8) were a mixture of Jewish legalism and Greek philosophy. Paul warned the Colossians that the result of following the traditions of men is spiritual slavery.

Paul's Teachings

The remaining three references to tradition in the New Testament refer to the teaching of Paul.

1 Corinthians 11:2

> Now I praise you because you remember me
> in everything, and hold firmly to the traditions,
> just as I delivered them to you.

This verse introduces a passage on the topic of whether or not it is proper to cover one's head when praying or prophesying (1 Corinthians 11:2-16). Paul praised the Corinthians for continuing to practice that which he had previously *handed down* by his oral teaching.

2 Thessalonians 2:15

> So then, brethren, stand firm and hold to the traditions which you were taught, whether by word of mouth or by letter from us.

From the context of 2 Thessalonians 2:15, we know that the traditions of which Paul was speaking refer to aspects of the Lord's second coming. Paul called these "traditions" to stress that they were truths he had received by revelation from the Lord and *had handed down* to the church in Thessalonica. They did not originate with him. Since they were from the Lord, Paul wanted the Thessalonians to hold fast to them.

2 Thessalonians 3:6

> Now we command you, brethren, in the name of our Lord Jesus Christ, that you keep aloof from every brother who leads an unruly life and not according to the tradition which you received from us.

The context of this verse explains that some of the Thessalonians had misunderstood an earlier letter from Paul. They had stopped working for a living and had become troublesome busybodies. Paul told them here to discipline their lives and follow his example of hard work. His personal example of a disciplined lifestyle is what he had *handed down* to the Thessalonians while he was with them.

These last three verses demonstrate that Paul *handed down* the Christian faith to the early church not only by his letters but also by his oral teaching and example. To know the content of Paul's oral teaching, we need not invent a second font of revelation such as Roman Catholic Tradition. Paul's 13 epistles provide an inspired transcript of what God revealed to Paul and he passed on to

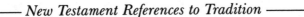

the early church. Moreover, to equate these three references to Paul's oral teaching with Roman Catholic
Tradition is unjustified. The former refers to direct apostolic teaching. The latter refers to beliefs and practices
residing in the spirit and heart of the Roman Catholic
Church today, having been transmitted by fallible means
for some 2000 years. Clearly, these are not the same.

SOLA SCRIPTURA

Today, even as in the time of the Reformation, thousands of Catholics worldwide are leaving Roman Catholicism for biblical Christianity. And once again the rallying cry of the sixteenth century, *Sola Scriptura*, Scripture Alone, is being heard.

Roman Catholic defenders have responded to this challenge by going on the offensive. A typical argument sounds something like this:

> The Bible cannot be the sole rule of faith because the first Christians didn't have the New Testament. Initially Tradition, the oral teachings of the apostles, was the Church's rule of faith. The New Testament came later, when a portion of Tradition was put to writing. It was the Roman Catholic Church that produced the New Testament, and it was the Church that infallibly told us what books belong in the Bible. It is the Church, therefore, that is the authoritative teacher of Scripture. *Sola Scriptura* is not even taught in the Bible. The rule of faith of the Roman Catholic Church, therefore, is rightly Scripture and Tradition together.

Christians confronted with such arguments should keep the following points in mind.

Christians Have Never Been Without the Scriptures

The unforgettable experience of two early disciples shows the fallacy of thinking that the first Christians were ever without Scripture as their rule of faith. Three days after the crucifixion, two of Jesus' disciples were walking home. A fellow traveler, whom they took for a stranger, joined them along the way. The conversation quickly turned to the events that had just taken place in Jerusalem. With deep sorrow the disciples told the story of how the chief priests and rulers of the nation had sentenced Jesus to death and had Him crucified by the civil authorities.

To the disciples' shock, the stranger rebuked them: "How foolish you are, and how slow of heart to believe all that the prophets have spoken!" (Luke 24:25 NIV). Then, beginning with Moses and proceeding through the prophets, the stranger explained to them the truths concerning Jesus in the Old Testament Scriptures.

Eventually the two disciples realized that their fellow traveler was no stranger at all but the Lord Jesus Himself! Later they recalled, "Were not our hearts burning within us while He was speaking to us on the road, while He was explaining the Scriptures to us?" (Luke 24:32).

The experience of those two early disciples was not unique. With the Holy Spirit's coming at Pentecost, and with the aid of the apostles' teaching, Jewish Christians rediscovered their own Scriptures. Their common conviction was that the Old Testament, properly understood, was a revelation of Christ. There they found a prophetic record of Jesus' life, teaching, death, and resurrection.

The Old Testament Scriptures served as the standard of truth for the infant church, Jew and Gentile alike. Within a short time the New Testament Scriptures took their place alongside those of the Old Testament. Consequently the early church was never without the written Word of God.

Scripture Is Not Simply Written Tradition

Roman Catholic descriptions of the origin of the New Testament stress that the oral teachings of the apostles, Tradition, preceded the written record of those teachings, Scripture. Often the New Testament is presented as little more than a written record of Tradition, the writer's recollections, and a partial explanation of Christ's teaching [126].[553] This, of course, elevates Tradition to the same level of authority as Scripture—or, more precisely, drops Scripture to the level of Tradition.

But the New Testament Scriptures are much more than a written record of the oral teaching of the apostles; they are an *inspired* record. A biblical understanding of inspiration makes clear the significance of this distinction. Peter writes:

> Above all, you must understand that no prophecy of Scripture came about by the prophet's own interpretation. For prophecy never had its origin in the will of man, but men spoke from God as they were carried along by the Holy Spirit.
>
> —2 Peter 1:20,21 NIV

Here we see that Scripture is not "the prophet's own interpretation" (2 Peter 1:20 NIV). The word translated "interpretation" means *to solve* or *to explain*. Peter is saying that no writer of the New Testament simply recorded his own explanation of what he had heard Jesus teach and had seen Him do. Scripture does not have "its origin in the will of man" (2 Peter 1:21 NIV). The writers of the Bible did not decide that they would write a prophetic record or what would be included in Scripture. Rather, they were "carried along by the Holy Spirit" (2 Peter 1:21 NIV).

The word translated here "carried along" is found in the New Testament in Mark 2:3. There it is used with reference to the paralytic whose friends *carried* him to Jesus for healing. Just as the paralytic did not walk by his own power, a true prophet does not write by his own impulse. He is "carried along by the Holy Spirit" (2 Peter 1:21 NIV). Men wrote the New Testament; "men spoke" (2 Peter 1:21 NIV). Their writings reflect their individual personalities and experiences, but these men "spoke from God" (2 Peter 1:21). Men wrote but God was the author.

For these reasons Scripture is revelation perfectly communicated in God-given words:

> All Scripture is given by inspiration of God, and is profitable for doctrine, for reproof, for correction, for instruction in righteousness, that the man of God may be complete, thoroughly equipped for every good work.
>
> —2 Timothy 3:16,17 NKJV

The phrase "inspired by God" is the translation of a compound term made up of the words *God* and *to breathe*. The verse can be translated: "All Scripture is God-breathed..." (2 Timothy 3:16 NIV). Scripture is therefore rightly called the *Word of God*.

In reducing Scripture to simply written Tradition, Catholic proponents are able to boost the importance of Tradition. But in doing so they distort the meaning of biblical inspiration and minimize the primary difference between Scripture and Tradition.

The Roman Catholic Church Did Not Give Us the Bible

Some defenders of the Roman Catholic Church argue that the Magisterium is the rightful interpreter and authoritative teacher of Scripture because the Church gave Christianity the Bible. If it were not for the Church, they argue, no one could know with certainty even which books belong in the Bible.

This argument is based on faulty assumptions. The early Christians did not receive the Bible from the Roman Catholic Church. They received the Bible from the Holy Spirit, who inspired it. Catholics who argue to the contrary are not representing the official teaching of the Roman Catholic Church. Speaking of the books of both Testaments, the First Vatican Council stated:

> These books the church holds to be sacred and canonical not because she subsequently approved them by her authority after they had been composed by unaided human skill, nor simply because they contain revelation without error, but because, being written under the inspiration of the holy Spirit, they have God as their author, and were as such committed to the church.
>
> —First Vatican Council[554]

The process of writing and recognizing the New Testament books began long before the Roman Catholic Church even existed. The night before the Lord was crucified, He told His disciples that they, empowered by the Holy Spirit, would bear witness to His life and teaching:

> When the Helper comes, whom I will send to you from the Father, that is the Spirit of truth, who proceeds from the Father, He will bear witness of Me, and you will bear witness also, because you have been with Me from the beginning.
>
> —John 15:26,27

Through the Holy Spirit the disciples would also receive further revelation:

> I have many more things to say to you, but you cannot bear them now. But when He, the Spirit of truth, comes, He will guide you into all the truth; for He will not speak on His own initiative, but whatever He hears He will speak; and He will disclose to you what is to come. He shall glorify Me, for He shall take of Mine and shall disclose it to you.
>
> —John 16:12-14

In certain writings of the apostles and their associates, the first Christians recognized the prophetic and authoritative teaching of the Holy Spirit. Jesus had taught, "My sheep hear My voice ... and they follow Me" (John 10:27). In these writings the early Christians heard the Savior's voice. They compared the doctrinal content of these new writings to that of the Old Testament Scriptures and found agreement. They applied the teaching to their lives and experienced its transforming power. In these writings they recognized the dynamic interaction between book and reader that is unique to Scripture:

> For the word of God is living and active and sharper than any two-edged sword, and piercing as far as the division of soul and spirit, of both joints and marrow, and able to judge the thoughts and intentions of the heart.
>
> —Hebrews 4:12

The writings were self-authenticating.[555] They demonstrated by their uniquely divine wisdom and power that God was their author.

Consequently the early Christians read, copied, and circulated the books widely. Teachers began to quote the books as authoritative in their own sermons and letters. Within the lifetime of the apostles, some of the writings were already considered God-given "wisdom" (2 Peter 3:15) on a par with "the rest of the Scriptures" (2 Peter 3:16).

The history of the events leading to the universal acceptance of the 27 books of the New Testament as inspired Scripture spans several centuries and is beyond the scope of this book. However, it should be noted that the role which church councils played in the process is often overstated by Roman Catholics.

The first councils to have addressed the question as to which books were inspired and were rightfully part of the Bible appear to have been the North African Councils of Hippo (393) and Carthage (397). The list of books accepted by the Council of Hippo no longer exists. The Council of Carthage, however, is believed to have repeated the same list and its decree on the matter still exists.

Both councils were regional synods. They were not universal or ecumenical councils. About 50 bishops from the provinces of Africa attended each. These councils did not have authority to speak for the whole fourth-century church.

It is also important to note that by the time these councils addressed the matter at the close of the fourth century, the canon or list of books recognized as forming the New Testament was well-established. F. F. Bruce comments:

> What is particularly important to notice is that the New Testament canon was not demarcated by the arbitrary decree of any Church Council. When at last a Church Council—the Synod of Carthage in A.D. 397—listed the twenty-seven books of the New Testament, it did not confer upon them any authority which they did not already possess, but simply recorded their previously established canonicity.
>
> —*The Books and the Parchments*[556]

Furthermore, the decision reached by these councils has never been universally accepted. The controversy centers around writings referred to by Roman Catholic scholars as the *deuterocanonicals* and by Protestant scholars as the *Apocrypha*. In that non-Catholics have never accepted the decision of the councils to accept the Apocrypha as part of the Bible, it can hardly be argued that were it not for the Roman Catholic Church no one would know with certainty which books belong in the Bible. (See Appendix C for an explanation on why the Apocrypha is not considered inspired by non-Catholics.)

The Bible Contains All Essential Revelation

It is true that the New Testament does not contain a record of everything that Jesus did. John makes this clear in the conclusion of his Gospel:

> There are also many other things which Jesus did, which if they were written in detail, I suppose that even the world itself would not contain the books which were written.
>
> —John 21:25

John's point in concluding his Gospel with this comment was to acknowledge that the life of the Lord Jesus was far too wonderful to be fully contained in any book. He was not commenting on the general purpose of Scripture or the need for Tradition. Neither was he implying that he had left out of his book essential revelation received from Christ. Indeed, earlier in his Gospel John implies the opposite:

> Many other signs therefore Jesus also performed in the presence of the disciples, which are not written in this book; but these have been written that you may believe that Jesus is the Christ, the Son of God; and that believing you may have life in His name.
>
> —John 20:30,31

We can infer from this statement that John included in his Gospel all the essential teachings of Christ necessary for salvation. Significantly, he makes no reference to seven sacraments, the Sacrifice of the Mass, sanctifying grace, penance, purgatory, or an institution such as the Roman Catholic Church—all necessary for salvation according to Roman Catholicism.

The Scriptures achieve their stated purpose: "that the man of God may be thoroughly equipped for every good work" (2 Timothy 3:17 NIV). They are the perfect guide to the Christian faith. Unlike Tradition, the Scriptures are accessible and open to all. Translations of the entire Bible have been made into all the primary languages of the world, 276 in total.[557] It is the most widely distributed and read book in all of history.

To define Roman Catholic Tradition as a font of extrabiblical revelation is to add to God's Word. Scripture warns us "not to exceed what is written" (1 Corinthians 4:6). "Do not add to His words lest He reprove you, and you be proved a liar" (Proverbs 30:6). The last book of the New Testament ends with this solemn warning:

> I testify to everyone who hears the words of the prophecy of this book: if anyone adds to them, God shall add to him the plagues which are written in this book; and if anyone takes away from the words of the book of this prophecy, God shall take away his part from the tree of life and from the holy city, which are written in this book.
>
> —Revelation 22:18,19

At Question Is the Authority of Tradition, Not Scripture

There are hundreds of verses in the Bible establishing the truth that the Word of God is the church's sufficient and supreme rule of faith. Psalm 119 alone dedicates 176 verses to the unparalleled value of God's Word. The Lord Jesus taught:

> Man shall not live on bread alone, but on every word that proceeds out of the mouth of God.
>
> —Matthew 4:4

Though Scriptures can be multiplied on this theme, it is not necessary to do so. The Roman Catholic Church agrees that the Bible teaches that the Word of God is the supreme rule of faith and that all theology must rest upon it.[558] There is no question as to the sufficiency or authority of the Word of God.

The controversy revolves around the *identity* of God's Word. Namely, is the Word of God Scripture plus Tradition? Or is the Word of God Scripture alone?

In the ongoing debate, Roman Catholic proponents enjoy taking the offensive by challenging non-Catholics to prove that God intended that the Scriptures alone were to serve as the church's rule of faith. "Where does the Bible teach *Sola Scriptura?*" they demand.

Though this tactic is effective in putting their opponents on the defensive, it is in fact misleading. Both sides agree that the *Scriptures* are the Word of God and that as such they speak with divine authority. The Lord Jesus Himself, in John 10:35, clearly identifies the Word of God as Scripture.

The point of controversy is *Tradition.* The Roman Catholic Church asserts that Tradition is also the Word of God.

The question which the Roman Catholic Church must answer, therefore, is: Where do Jesus, the prophets, or the apostles teach that Tradition is the Word of God? Or, more precisely: Where in the Bible can it be found that Scripture and Tradition together, as interpreted by the Pope and bishops of the Roman Catholic Church, are to be the church's rule of faith? This is what Roman Catholicism is really asserting and should be the topic of debate. And since the Roman Catholic Church is the one asserting the authority of Tradition and the Magisterium, the burden of proof lies with Rome.

Notes

1. "What Happens When Christians Use Bad Language" (February 21, 1994 news release from the Barna Research Group, Ltd.).
2. Pope John Paul II, "Pope Approves Universal Catechism," in *L'Osservatore Romano*, July 1, 1992, p. 1.
3. Pope John Paul II, *Letter to Priests for Holy Thursday 1993*, published in *L'Osservatore Romano*, March 31, 1993, p. 1.
4. Some of the documents referenced in this book to the Second Vatican Council (1962-1965) are postconciliar documents. These documents reflect developments that were authorized by the council but not implemented by the Church's hierarchy until after the council's close.
5. Pope Pius XII, *Humani Generis*, no. 20.
6. See Pope Pius XII, *Humani Generis*, no. 20; Second Vatican Council, "Dogmatic Constitution on the Church," no. 25.
7. Pope Pius XII wrote, "...since the Liturgy is also a profession of eternal truths, and subject as such to the Supreme Teaching Authority of the Church, it can supply proofs and testimony, quite clearly of no little value, towards the determination of a particular point of Christian doctrine" (Pope Pius XII, *Mediator Dei*, no. 48). The liturgy of the Church according to the Roman Rite will be used in this book.
8. The Code of Canon Law, canon 252, section 3.
9. The Catholic rite of baptism is abridged in this introduction. For the full rite, see *The Rites of the Catholic Church* (New York: Pueblo Publishing Co., 1990), vol. 1, pp. 394-407.
10. The Roman Catholic Church holds that baptism can be conferred "either by immersion or by pouring" (Canon Law 854). Sprinkling an infant with water is no longer considered appropriate.
11. Council of Trent, session 6, "Decree on Justification," chapter 2.
12. Council of Trent, session 6, "Decree on Justification," chapter 3.
13. Thomas Aquinas, *Summa Theologica*, translated by the Fathers of the English Dominican Province (Westminster, MD: Christian Classics, 1981), Appendix 1, question 1, article 1.
14. *The Rites of the Catholic Church* (New York: Pueblo Publishing Co., 1990), vol. 1, p. 398.
15. *The Rites of the Catholic Church* (New York: Pueblo Publishing Co., 1990), vol. 1, p. 399.
16. Council of Trent, session 6, "Decree on Justification," chapter 4.

17. Council of Trent, session 6, "Decree on Justification," chapter 7.
18. Council of Trent, session 5, "Decree on Original Sin," no. 3.
19. Council of Trent, session 6, "Decree on Justification," chapter 7.
20. Council of Trent, session 6, "Decree on Justification," chapter 7.
21. This principle is referred to in Roman Catholic theology by the term *ex opere operato*, meaning *from the work performed*. It will be discussed further in Chapter 3, *Increasing and Preserving Justification*.
22. *The Rites of the Catholic Church* (New York: Pueblo Publishing Co., 1990), vol. 1, p. 400.
23. Sacred Congregation for Divine Worship, *Introduction to the Rite of Christian Initiation* (Washington, D.C.: United States Catholic Conference, 1977), p. 17.
24. Lyrics by Charlotte Elliott, *Just As I Am.*
25. Council of Trent, session 6, "Decree on Justification," chapter 5.
26. Council of Trent, session 6, "Decree on Justification," chapter 6.
27. Council of Trent, session 6, "Decree on Justification," canon 9.
28. Council of Trent, session 6, "Decree on Justification," chapter 6.
29. Council of Trent, session 6, "Decree on Justification," chapter 7.
30. Council of Trent, session 6, "Decree on Justification," chapter 7.
31. The Roman Catholic *Rite of Christian Initiation* is abridged in the explanation that follows. For the full rite, see *The Rites of the Catholic Church* (New York: Pueblo Publishing Co., 1990), vol. 1, pp. 15-244.
32. *The Rites of the Catholic Church* (New York: Pueblo Publishing Co., 1990), vol. 1, p. 56.
33. *The Rites of the Catholic Church* (New York: Pueblo Publishing Co., 1990), vol. 1, p. 60.
34. *The Rites of the Catholic Church* (New York: Pueblo Publishing Co., 1990), vol. 1, p. 70.
35. *The Rites of the Catholic Church* (New York: Pueblo Publishing Co., 1990), vol. 1, p. 70.
36. *The Rites of the Catholic Church* (New York: Pueblo Publishing Co., 1990), vol. 1, p. 71.
37. *The Rites of the Catholic Church* (New York: Pueblo Publishing Co., 1990), vol. 1, p. 94.
38. *The Rites of the Catholic Church* (New York: Pueblo Publishing Co., 1990), vol. 1, pp. 99-100.
39. *The Rites of the Catholic Church* (New York: Pueblo Publishing Co., 1990), vol. 1, p. 101.
40. *The Rites of the Catholic Church* (New York: Pueblo Publishing Co., 1990), vol. 1, p. 109.
41. Council of Trent, session 6, "Decree on Justification," chapter 4.
42. Council of Trent, session 6, "Decree on Justification," chapter 8.
43. Catholic theologians divide merit into two categories. *Merit de condigno* is a true merit in which the reward is the just and deserving value of the work performed. *Merit de congruo* is an improper kind of merit in which the reward received exceeds the value of the work, because of the generosity of God. This latter merit contributes to the reception of a benefit, but does not fully earn it.

     Some Catholic theologians, including Thomas Aquinas, teach that first actual grace can be merited by an already justified person on behalf of a sinner. They say, for example, that Stephen, the first martyr of the church, congruously merited the conversion of Paul, who observed the stoning of

Stephen. Also, Monica congruously merited first grace for her son Augustine. Additionally, some Catholic theologians hold that the unjustified sinner acting under the influence of first actual grace can congruously merit for himself an increase of actual grace, which further helps prepare him for justification. Since in both these cases the merit is *de congruo*, Catholic justification can still be said to be completely dependent on pure grace. At least, that is how Catholic theologians see it. (For further explanation, see A. Tanquerey, *Manual of Dogmatic Theology* (New York: Desclee Co, 1959), vol. 2, pp. 181-182).

44. *The Rites of the Catholic Church* (New York: Pueblo Publishing Co., 1990), vol. 1, p. 71.
45. Council of Trent, session 6, "Decree on Justification," canon 12.
46. Council of Trent, session 6, "Decree on Justification," canon 9.
47. Council of Trent, session 6, "Decree on Justification," chapter 8.
48. *The Rites of the Catholic Church* (New York: Pueblo Publishing Co., 1990), vol. 1, p. 70.
49. *The Rites of the Catholic Church* (New York: Pueblo Publishing Co., 1990), vol. 1, p. 90.
50. *The Rites of the Catholic Church* (New York: Pueblo Publishing Co., 1990), vol. 1, p. 94.
51. *The Rites of the Catholic Church* (New York: Pueblo Publishing Co., 1990), vol. 1, pp. 99-100.
52. *The Rites of the Catholic Church* (New York: Pueblo Publishing Co., 1990), vol. 1, pp. 99-100.
53. *The Rites of the Catholic Church* (New York: Pueblo Publishing Co., 1990), vol. 1, p. 71.
54. *The Rites of the Catholic Church* (New York: Pueblo Publishing Co., 1990), vol.1, p. 71.
55. This story is based on an event described by Joan Carrol Cruz, *Eucharistic Miracles* (Rockford, IL: Tan Books, 1987), pp. 38-46.
56. Council of Trent, session 6, chapter 7.
57. Council of Trent, session 7, "Canons on the Sacraments in General," canon 6.
58. Tanquerey, *A Manual of Dogmatic Theology* (New York: Desclee, 1959), vol. II, p. 197.
59. Council of Trent, session 7, "Canons on the Sacraments in General," canon 8. The principle spoken of here is often referred to by the Latin phrase of which this quote is the translation: *"ex opere operato."*
60. Council of Trent, session 7, "Canons on the Sacraments in General," canon 4.
61. Since Roman Catholic theology teaches that baptism is essential for attaining to the enjoyment of eternal life in the presence of God, the Church has found it necessary to define three kinds of valid baptism:

   • *Baptism of water* is the normal form of the sacrament [1257].

   • *Baptism of blood* applies to individuals who were martyred for the Catholic faith before receiving the sacrament of baptism. Martyrdom itself is said to bring the benefits of the sacrament [1258, 1281].

   • *Baptism of desire* applies to individuals who have no opportunity to receive the sacrament of baptism, but would do so if they could [1259-1260, 1281]. "For *catechumens* who die before their Baptism, their explicit desire to receive it, together with repentance for their sins, and charity, assures them the salvation that they were not able to receive through the sacrament."[1259]

The Bible makes no mention of a baptism of blood or a baptism of desire.

62. Second Vatican Council, "Liturgy," chapter 1, no. 11.

63. Council of Trent, session 6, "Decree on Justification," chapter 10. Translation from H. J. Schroeder, translator, *Canons and Decrees of the Council of Trent* (Rockford, IL: Tan Books and Publishers, 1978).

64. This summary is based on an analysis by A. Tanquerey, *A Manual of Dogmatic Theology* (New York: Desclee, 1959), vol. II, p. 177.

65. Council of Trent, session 6, "Decree on Justification," chapter 10. Translation from H. J. Schroeder, translator, *Canons and Decrees of the Council of Trent* (Rockford, IL: Tan Books and Publishers, 1978).

66. Second Vatican Council, "Dogmatic Constitution on the Church," no. 42.

67. Council of Trent, session 6, chapter 7.

68. John A. McHugh, O.P., and Charles J. Callan, O.P., translators, *The Roman Catechism: The Catechism of the Council of Trent* (Rockford, IL: Tan Books and Publishers, 1982), p. 255.

69. Ludwig Ott, *Fundamentals of Catholic Dogma* (Rockford, IL: Tan Books and Publishers, 1960), p. 255.

70. Cf. Thomas Aquinas, *Summa Theologica*, Parts I-II, Question 110, articles 1-4.

71. Council of Trent, session 6, "Decree on Justification," canon 32.

72. Council of Trent, session 7, "Canons on the Sacraments in General," canon 8.

73. The Second Vatican Council, "Dogmatic Constitution on the Church," no. 14.

74. Council of Trent, session 6, "Decree on Justification," chapter 10. Translation from H. J. Schroeder, translator, *Canons and Decrees of the Council of Trent* (Rockford, IL: Tan Books and Publishers, 1978).

75. Council of Trent, session 6, "Decree on Justification," canon 24.

76. Quoted by William J. Cogan, *A Catechism for Adults* (Youngtown, AZ: Cogan Productions, 1975), p. 30.

77. The Catholic rite of penance is abridged in this introduction. For the full rite see *The Rites of the Catholic Church* (New York: Pueblo Publishing Co., 1990), pp. 517-548.

78. Matthias Premm, *Dogmatic Theology for the Laity* (Rockford, IL: Tan Books, 1967), p. 373.

79. Matthias Premm, *Dogmatic Theology for the Laity* (Rockford, IL: Tan Books, 1967), p. 374.

80. As explained in Chapter 1, according to Roman Catholic theology, with the infusion of sanctifying grace come the gifts of the Holy Spirit and the infusion of virtue, most notably charity [1803-1845]. To be in possession of charity, therefore, is equated in Catholic theology with being in a state of grace. Conversely, one who has lost charity through mortal sin has lost sanctifying grace in his soul. For example, the *Catechism of the Catholic Church* states that mortal sin "...results in the loss of charity and the privation of sanctifying grace, that is, of the state of grace."[1861] At other times the *Catechism* simply states, "*Mortal sin* destroys charity in the heart of man...."[1855]

81. Though two words used in this book, *dejustification* and *rejustification*, are not used in Roman Catholic documents, equivalent expressions are found. The Council of Trent stated:

Those who through sin have forfeited the received grace of justification can again be justified when, moved by God, they exert themselves to obtain through the sacrament of penance the recovery, by the merits of Christ, of the grace lost. (See Council of Trent, session 6, "Decree on Justification," chapter 14. Translation by H. J. Schroeder, *Canons and Decrees of the Council of Trent* [Rockford, IL: Tan Books and Publishers, 1978], p. 39.)

The process by which baptized Catholics "through sin have forfeited the received grace of justification" is summarized in this book as *dejustification*. The process by which Catholics "can again be justified" is expressed here as *rejustification*.

Dejustification should not be understood as a return to that state in which the person existed before baptism. The Church teaches that baptism imprints an indelible character upon the soul [1272-1274, 1280]. Additionally, the sacrament is conferred principally to remove original sin. When a person commits a mortal sin, though he loses justifying grace in his soul, original sin does not return and the imprint of baptism is not removed. Therefore a person can be baptized only once, and grace forfeited after baptism must be restored through the sacrament of penance.

Similarly, *rejustification* should not be understood to mean the removal of original sin, the imprinting of the character of baptism, and other effects unique to baptism. Rather, it is used here to refer to the restoration to the life of grace through the sacrament of penance. (Cf. Council of Trent, session 7, "Canons on the Sacraments in General," canon 9; Thomas Aquinas, *Summa Theologica*, part III, question 66, article 9.)

82. The Code of Canon Law, canon 960, states the requirement for individual confession while at the same time allowing for exception: "Individual and integral confession and absolution constitute the only ordinary way by which the faithful person who is aware of serious sin is reconciled with God and with the Church; only physical or moral impossibility excuses the person from confession of this type, in which case reconciliation can take place in other ways."

Perfect contrition, explains the Church, is one such way: "When it arises from a love by which God is loved above all else, contrition is called 'perfect' (contrition of charity). Such contrition remits venial sins; it also obtains forgiveness of mortal sins if it includes the firm resolution to have recourse to sacramental confession as soon as possible"[1452] [1492].

83. Council of Trent, session 6, "Decree on Justification," chapter 14. Translation by H. J. Schroeder, *Canons and Decrees of the Council of Trent* (Rockford, IL: Tan Books and Publishers, 1978), p. 39.

84. Council of Trent, session 14, "The Most Holy Sacraments of Penance and Extreme Unction," chapter 5. Translation from H. J. Schroeder, translator, *Canons and Decrees of the Council of Trent* (Rockford, IL: Tan Books and Publishers, 1978).

85. The Code of Canon Law defines the role of the priest in the confessional as one of judge: "In hearing confessions the priest is to remember that he acts as a judge as well as a healer and is placed by God as the minister of divine justice as well as of mercy, concerned with the divine honor and the salvation of souls" (canon 978, section 1). "If the confessor has no doubt

about the disposition of a penitent who asks for absolution, absolution is not to be refused or delayed" (canon 980).

86. Council of Trent, session 14, "Teaching Concerning the Most Holy Sacraments of Penance and Last Anointing," chapter 3.

87. Council of Trent, session 14, "Canons Concerning the Most Holy Sacrament of Penance," canon 9.

88. Council of Trent, session 14, "The Most Holy Sacraments of Penance and Extreme Unction," chapter 8. Translation from H. J. Schroeder, translator, *Canons and Decrees of the Council of Trent* (Rockford, IL: Tan Books and Publishers, 1978).

89. William J. Cogan, *A Catechism for Adults* (Youngtown, AZ: Cogan Productions, 1975), p. 80.

90. Code of Canon Law, canon 989.

91. The Code of Canon Law, canon 960.

92. There are special circumstances in which a Christian may also need to admit his guilt before another person. For example, if a Christian were to wrongfully offend another person, he should not only confess the sin to God, but he should go and be reconciled to the other person (Matthew 5:23,24). Another example might be the case of a person who because of ongoing sin has been put under church discipline (Matthew 18:15-20; 1 Corinthians 5:1-13). In order to be restored to church fellowship, the guilty party would need to confess his sin to the church's leadership. In response to the sinner's repentance, the church is to "forgive and comfort him" (2 Corinthians 2:7). A final case might be a person under direct chastisement from God for some secret sin. Possibly God has struck him with a serious sickness (James 5:14). The Scriptures say that this person should call for the elders of the church and confess his sin to them (James 5:14). God promises that "the prayer offered in faith will restore the one who is sick, and the Lord will raise him up, and if he has committed sins, they will be forgiven him" (James 5:15). In this context, the Scriptures exhort, "confess your sins to one another, and pray for one another" (James 5:16).

93. H. E. Dana and Julius R. Mantey, *A Manual Grammar of the Greek New Testament* (Toronto: Macmillan Company, 1955), p. 200.

94. A. Tanquerey, *A Manual of Dogmatic Theology* (New York: Desclee, 1959), vol. II, p. 330.

95. A. Tanquerey, *A Manual of Dogmatic Theology* (New York: Desclee, 1959), vol. II, p. 330.

96. Some Catholic scholars point to 1 John 5:17 as a biblical basis for dividing sin into categories of mortal and venial [1854]. John writes, "All unrighteousness is sin, and there is a sin not leading to death" (1 John 5:17). The "sin not leading to death," they say, is venial sin. The sin that leads to death is mortal sin.

This interpretation ignores the context of the passage. The epistle is written to Christians influenced by the heresy of Gnosticism. False prophets were teaching that only the spiritual realm mattered. One's behavior in the flesh was irrelevant. They even denied that Jesus had come in the flesh.

John exhorts the Christians to hold fast to the truth. He assures them that they can pray with confidence that God will hear and answer their requests (1 John 5:14,15). John, however, does make one exception to this promise: "If anyone sees his brother committing a sin not leading to death, he shall ask and God will for him give life to those who commit sin not leading to death. There is a sin leading to death; I do not say that he should make request for this" (1 John 5:16). The Christians were not to intercede in prayer for those who had renounced Christ and embraced Gnosticism. The reason for this restriction is that there is no forgiveness for those who reject God's only provision for sin, Jesus Christ the Savior (Hebrews 6:4-8).

First John 5:17, therefore, is not speaking about different punishments for sin, but rather, a special condition when intercessory prayer is inappropriate. If a person commits a "sin leading to death" (1 John 5:16), here the sin of apostasy, no intercession is to be made, for God is not willing to grant that request.

97. Matthias Premm, *Dogmatic Theology for the Laity* (Rockford, IL: Tan Books, 1967), pp. 373-374.

98. Melvin L. Farrell, *A Catholic Catechism for Parents and Teachers* (Milwaukee: Hi-Time Publishers, 1977), p. 133.

99. The Catholic rite of anointing for emergencies is abridged in this introduction. For the full rite, see *The Rites of the Catholic Church* (New York: Pueblo Publishing Co. 1990), pp. 883-886.

100. *The Rites of the Catholic Church* (New York: Pueblo Publishing Co., 1990), pp. 885-886.

101. Council of Florence, session 6.

102. Council of Trent, session 6, "Decree on Justification," chapter 9.

103. Second Vatican Council, "Sacred Liturgy," Apostolic Constitution on the Revision of Indulgences, no. 2.

104. Matthias Premm, *Dogmatic Theology for the Laity* (Rockford, IL: Tan Books, 1967), p. 434.

105. Council of Florence, 6 July 1439, session 6.

106. Thomas Aquinas, *Summa Theologica*, App. 1, Q. 2, Art. 6.

107. Second Vatican Council, "Sacred Liturgy," "Apostolic Constitution on the Revision of Indulgences," no. 5.

108. See A. Tanquerey, *A Manual of Dogmatic Theology* (New York: Desclee Company, 1959), vol. 2, pp. 321-322.

109. Council of Trent, session 6, "Decree on Justification," canon 32.

110. Council of Trent, session 6, "Decree on Justification," chapter 16.

111. Second Vatican Council, "Dogmatic Constitution on the Church," no. 48

112. A full explanation of the events recorded in Matthew 25:31-46 and how they fit into biblical end-time prophecy is beyond the scope of this book. It can be said, however, that *doctrinal* sections of the Bible should be used to interpret *prophetic* events, not vice versa. The Roman Catholic Church uses Matthew 25:31-46, a prophetic event, to deduce its doctrine of salvation. The result is the Church's doctrine of salvation based upon faith and works.

113. Council of Trent, session 6, "Decree on Justification," canon 32.

114. Thomas Aquinas, *Summa Theologica*, Pts. 1-11, Q. 114, Art. 3.

115. Thomas Aquinas, *Summa Theologica*, Pts. 1-11, Q. 114, Art. 3.

116. A. Tanquerey, *A Manual of Dogmatic Theology* (New York: Desclee Company, 1959), vol. 2, p. 174.

117. Council of Trent, session 6, "Decree on Justification," chapter 16.

118. Matthias Premm, *Dogmatic Theology for the Laity* (Rockford, IL: Tan Books, 1967), p. 262.

119. The Second Vatican Council addressed the relationship of the Catholic Church to non-Christian religions in two documents: "Dogmatic Constitution on the Church," no. 16; and "The Declaration on the Relation of the Church to Non-Christian Religions," nos. 1-5.

120. Second Vatican Council, "Dogmatic Constitution on the Church," no. 16.

121. Though the Roman Catholic Church teaches that baptism is necessary for salvation, its theology nevertheless leaves room for unbaptized members of non-Christian faiths to be saved: "Baptism is necessary for salvation for those to whom the Gospel has been proclaimed and who have had the possibility of asking for this sacrament."[1257] "Every man who is ignorant of the Gospel of Christ and of his Church, but seeks the truth and does the will of God in accordance with his understanding of it, can be saved. It may be supposed that such persons would have *desired Baptism explicitly* if they had known its necessity."[1260]

122. Second Vatican Council, "Dogmatic Constitution on the Church," no. 16.

123. Second Vatican Council, "Dogmatic Constitution on the Church," no. 14.

124. Council of Trent, session 6, "Decree on Justification," chapter 12.

125. Council of Trent, session 25, "Decree Concerning Purgatory."

126. First Vatican Council, session 2, "Profession of Faith."

127. Second Vatican Council, "Dogmatic Constitution on the Church," no. 49 and no. 51.

128. Second Vatican Council, "Sacred Liturgy," "Apostolic Constitution on the Revision of Indulgences," no. 2.

129. Council of Lyons II, session 4.

130. Second Vatican Council, "Sacred Liturgy," "Apostolic Constitution on the Revision of Indulgences," no. 3.

131. Pope John Paul II offers Mass for John Paul I and Paul VI on September 28, the anniversary of the death of John Paul I. ("The Lord Gives Us Confidence," in *L'Osservatore Romano*, October 7, 1992, p. 1.)

132. John A. McHugh, O.P., and Charles J. Callan, O.P., translators, *The Roman Catechism: The Catechism of the Council of Trent* (Rockford, IL: Tan Books and Publishers, 1982), p. 255.

133. The Roman Catholic Liturgy of the Mass is abridged in this introduction. For the full rite, see *The Vatican II Sunday Missal* (Boston: Daughters of St. Paul, 1974), pp. 583-627.

134. Second Vatican Council, "Sacred Liturgy," "On Holy Communion and the Worship of the Eucharistic Mystery Outside of Mass," no. 6.

135. Second Vatican Council, "Sacred Liturgy," "On Holy Communion and the Worship of the Eucharistic Mystery Outside of Mass," no. 6.

136. Second Vatican Council, "Sacred Liturgy," "On Holy Communion and the Worship of the Eucharistic Mystery Outside of Mass," no. 6.

137. John A. McHugh, O.P., and Charles J. Callan, O.P., translators, *The Roman Catechism: The Catechism of the Council of Trent* (Rockford, IL: Tan Books and Publishers, 1982), p. 228.

138. Second Vatican Council, "Sacred Liturgy," "On Holy Communion and the Worship of the Eucharistic Mystery Outside of Mass," no. 6.

139. In the words of the Church: "Hence it is entirely true that as much is contained under one of the forms as under both; for Christ exists whole and entire under the form of bread and under any part of that form, and likewise whole under the form of wine and under its parts." (Council of Trent, session 13, "Decree on the Eucharist," chapter 3.)

140. Second Vatican Council, "Sacred Liturgy," "On Holy Communion and the Worship of the Eucharistic Mystery Outside of Mass," no. 6.

141. Second Vatican Council, "Sacred Liturgy," "General Instruction on the Roman Missal," no. 268.

142. Council of Trent, session 13, "Decree on the Most Holy Sacrament of the Eucharist," chapter 2.

143. Second Vatican Council, "Sacred Liturgy," "Instruction on the Worship of the Eucharistic Mystery," no. 7; quoting Leo the Great, *Sermones*, 63, 7.

144. The Code of Canon Law, canon 1246, establishes Sunday as "the foremost holy day of obligation in the universal Church." Canon 1247 states, "On Sundays and other holy days of obligation the faithful are bound to participate in the Mass...." Canon 1248 allows for the obligation to attend Mass to be satisfied by attending on the evening of the preceding day.

145. The Code of Canon Law, canon 920.

146. Pope Paul VI, *Mysterium Fidei*, no. 39.

147. The Code of Canon Law, canon 898.

148. Second Vatican Council, "Sacred Liturgy," "On Holy Communion and the Worship of the Eucharistic Mystery Outside of Mass," no. 21.

149. Second Vatican Council, "Sacred Liturgy," "Second Instruction on the Proper Implementation of the Constitution on the Sacred Liturgy," no. 3ff.; quoting the Council of Trent, session 13, "Decree on the Eucharist," chapter 5.

150. Albert Tesniere, *Saint Peter Julian Eymard* (Cleveland: Emmanuel Publications, 1962), p. 90.

151. John J. Cardinal Carberry, *Reflections and Prayers for Visits with Our Eucharistic Lord* (Boston: St. Paul Books and Media, 1992), p. 15.

152. Council of Trent, session 13, "Canons on the Most Holy Sacrament of the Eucharist," canon 1.

153. Council of Trent, session 13, "Decree on the Eucharist," chapter 4.

154. John A. McHugh, O.P., and Charles J. Callan, O.P., translators, *The Roman Catechism: The Catechism of the Council of Trent* (Rockford, IL: Tan Books and Publishers, 1982), p. 228.

155. Second Vatican Council, "Sacred Liturgy " "Instruction on the Worship of the Eucharistic Mystery," no. 1.

156. John A. McHugh, O.P., and Charles J. Callan, O.P., translators, *The Roman Catechism: The Catechism of the Council of Trent* (Rockford, IL: Tan Books and Publishers, 1982), p. 239.

157. John A. McHugh, O.P., and Charles J. Callan, O.P., translators, *The Roman Catechism: The Catechism of the Council of Trent* (Rockford, IL: Tan Books and Publishers, 1982), p. 239.

158. John A. McHugh, O.P., and Charles J. Callan, O.P., translators, *The Roman Catechism: The Catechism of the Council of Trent* (Rockford, IL: Tan Books and Publishers, 1982), p. 228.

159. John A. McHugh, O.P., and Charles J. Callan, O.P., translators, *The Roman Catechism: The Catechism of the Council of Trent* (Rockford, Illinois: Tan Books and Publishers, 1982), p. 228.

160. Pope Paul VI, *Mysterium Fidei*, no. 5.

161. Second Vatican Council, "Sacred Liturgy," *On Holy Communion and the Worship of the Eucharistic Mystery Outside of Mass*, no. 79.

162. Second Vatican Council, "Sacred Liturgy," *General Instruction on the Roman Missal*," no. 55.

163. Second Vatican Council, "Sacred Liturgy," "Instruction on the Worship of the Eucharistic Mystery," no. 6; quoting "Decree on the Ministry and Life of the Priests," no. 5.

164. The Code of Canon Law, canon 898.

165. The Roman Catholic Liturgy of the Mass is abridged in this introduction. For the full rite, see *The Vatican II Sunday Missal* (Boston: Daughters of St. Paul, 1974), pp. 583-627.

166. Prayer After Communion, August 15, Feast of the Assumption.

167. Council of Trent, session 22, "Teaching and Canons on the Most Holy Sacrifice of the Mass," chapter 1.

168. Council of Trent, session 22, "Teaching and Canons on the Most Holy Sacrifice of the Mass," chapter 1.

169. Council of Trent, session 22, "Decree and Canons on the Most Holy Sacrifice of the Mass," chapter 1.

170. Council of Trent, session 22, "Teaching and Canons on the Most Holy Sacrifice of the Mass," chapter 1.

171. Council of Trent, session 22, "Teaching and Canons on the Most Holy Sacrifice of the Mass," canon 1.

172. Second Vatican Council, "Sacred Liturgy," "Instruction on the Worship of the Eucharistic Mystery," no. 9.

173. Second Vatican Council, "Sacred Liturgy," "General Instruction on the Roman Missal," chapter 2, section 55.

174. Pope John Paul II, *On the Mystery and Worship of the Eucharist*, no. 9.

175. Second Vatican Council, "Sacred Liturgy," "General Instruction on the Roman Missal," no. 2.

176. Pope Pius XI, "Ad Catholici Sacerdotii," December 20, 1935.

177. Rev. Matthias Premm, *Dogmatic Theology for the Laity* (Rockford, IL: Tan Books and Publishers, 1977), p. 354.

178. Second Vatican Council, "Sacred Liturgy," "The Constitution on the Sacred Liturgy," no. 47.

179. Second Vatican Council, "Sacred Liturgy," "General Instruction on the Roman Missal," no. 2.

180. Council of Trent, session 22, "Teaching and Canons on the Most Holy Sacrifice of the Mass," chapter 1.

181. John A. McHugh, O.P., and Charles J. Callan, O.P., translators, *The Roman Catechism: The Catechism of the Council of Trent* (Rockford, IL: Tan Books and Publishers, 1982), p. 227.

182. Pope Pius XII, *Mediator Dei*, no. 70.

183. Second Vatican Council, "Sacred Liturgy," "Instruction on the Worship of the Eucharistic Mystery," no. 3b; quoting Paul VI, *Mysterium Fidei.*

184. Pope Pius XII, *Mediator Dei*, no. 68.

185. John A. McHugh, O.P., and Charles J. Callan, O.P., translators, *The Roman Catechism: The Catechism of the Council of Trent* (Rockford, IL: Tan Books and Publishers, 1982), p. 258.

186. The Code of Canon Law, canon 899.

187. The Memorial Prayer of the First Eucharistic Prayer.

188. Pope Pius XII, *Mediator Dei*, no. 68.

189. Second Vatican Council, "Sacred Liturgy," "General Instruction on the Roman Missal," no. 270.

190. Pope Pius XII, *Mediator Dei*, no. 79.

191. Second Vatican Council, "Instruction on the Manner of Distributing Holy Communion," no. 55.

192. Eucharistic Payer, Memorial Acclamation.

193. John A. McHugh, O.P., and Charles J. Callan, O.P., translators, *The Roman Catechism: The Catechism of the Council of Trent* (Rockford, IL: Tan Books and Publishers, 1982), p. 255.

194. Council of Trent, session 22, "Teaching and Canons on the Most Holy Sacrifice of the Mass," chapter 2.

195. Council of Trent, session 22, "Teaching and Canons on the Most Holy Sacrifice of the Mass," chapter 2.

196. Council of Trent, session 22, "Teaching and Canons on the Most Holy Sacrifice of the Mass," chapter 2.

197. John A. McHugh, O.P., and Charles J. Callan, O.P., translators, *The Roman Catechism: The Catechism of the Council of Trent* (Rockford, IL: Tan Books and Publishers, 1982), p. 259; quoting the Secret Prayer of the Ninth Sunday after Pentecost.

198. Third Eucharistic Prayer, The Memorial Prayer.

199. Third Eucharistic Prayer, The Prayer of Intercession for the Church.

200. Council of Trent, session 22, "Teaching and Canons on the Most Holy Sacrifice of the Mass," chapter 1.

201. Harris, Archer, and Waltke, editors, *Theological Wordbook of the Old Testament* (Chicago: Moody, 1980), vol. II, pp. 796.

202. Council of Trent, session 22, "Teaching and Canons on the Most Holy Sacrifice of the Mass," chapter 1.

203. This principle applies to all sacraments. The Church teaches that a sacrament is valid if the priest properly observes all the essential elements of the rite. It is not required that he himself be in a state of grace (Council of Trent, session 7, "First Decree On the Sacraments " canon 12).

204. Rev. Matthias Premm, *Dogmatic Theology for the Laity* (Rockford, IL: Tan Books and Publishers, 1967), p. 355.

205. Liturgy of the Eucharist, Eucharistic Prayer I.

206. A. Tanquerey, *A Manual of Dogmatic Theology* (New York: Desclee Company, 1959), vol. II, pp. 267-268.

207. H. E. Dana and Julius R. Mantey, *A Manual Grammar of the Greek New Testament* (Toronto: Macmillan Company, 1955), p. 230.

208. Dana and Mantey describe the futuristic present as follows:

> This use of the present tense denotes an event which has not yet occurred, but which is regarded as so certain that in thought it may be contemplated as already coming to pass. (H. E. Dana and Julius R. Mantey, *A Manual Grammar of the Greek New Testament* [Toronto: Macmillan Company, 1955], p. 185.)

An example of this is found in Matthew 26:2. There the Lord Jesus uses the present tense to speak of His yet future betrayal, literally saying, "...after two days the Passover is coming, and the Son of Man is delivered up for crucifixion." The context makes it clear that He is using the *futuristic* present, and that is how most Bible translators handle the verse: "...after two days the Passover is coming, and the Son of Man is *to be delivered up* for crucifixion" (Matthew 26:2, emphasis added).

209. A. Tanquerey, *A Manual of Dogmatic Theology* (New York: Desclee Company, 1959), vol. II, p. 268.

210. Council of Trent, session 22, "Teaching and Canons on the Most Holy Sacrifice of the Mass," chapter 1.

211. Second Vatican Council, "Dogmatic Constitution on the Church," no. 3.

212. In 1 Corinthians 5:7 the verb "has been sacrificed" is in the indicative mood and the aorist tense.

213. Council of Trent, session 22, "Teaching and Canons on the Most Holy Sacrifice of the Mass," chapter 1.

214. Colin Brown, editor, *New International Dictionary of New Testament Theology*, vol. 2, p. 520.

215. H. E. Dana and Julius R. Mantey, *A Manual Grammar of the Greek New Testament* (Toronto: Macmillan Company, 1955), p. 200.

216. Kenneth S. Wuest, *The New Testament, An Expanded Translation* (Grand Rapids: Eerdmans Publishing Company, 1956), p. 262.

217. Pope Pius XII, *Mediator Dei*, no. 79.

218. Pope Pius XI, *Quas Primas*, December 11, 1925.

219. This figure is based upon each of the 404,031 Roman Catholic priests of the world offering the Mass 300 times each year. The annual total would be 121.2 million Masses. (Number of priests based on figures from *1994 Catholic Almanac* [Huntington, IN: Our Sunday Visitor Publishing Division, 1993], p. 367. Figure is as of December 31, 1991.)

220. Pope Pius XII, *Mediator Dei*, no. 68.

221. Pope Pius XII, *Mediator Dei*, no. 68.

222. Third Eucharistic Prayer.

223. Second Vatican Council, "Sacred Liturgy," "General Instruction on the Roman Missal," no. 2.

224. First Eucharistic Prayer, The Memorial Prayer.

225. Council of Trent, session 22, "Decree and Canons on the Most Holy Sacrifice of the Mass," chapter 2.

226. A. Tanquerey, *A Manual of Dogmatic Theology* (New York: Desclee Company, 1959), vol. II, p. 279. Also compare Ludwig Ott, *Fundamentals of Catholic Dogma*, (Rockford, IL: Tan Books and Publishers, 1960), p. 414.

227. Council of Trent, session 22, "Teaching and Canons on the Most Holy Sacrifice of the Mass," chapter 2.

228. Council of Trent, session 22, "Teaching and Canons on the Most Holy Sacrifice of the Mass," chapter 2.

229. Pope Pius XII, *Mediator Dei*, no. 79.

230. Pope Paul VI, *Mysterium Fidei*, no. 33.

231. Council of Trent, session 22, "Decree on Things to Be Observed and Avoided in Celebrating Mass."

232. Catholic scholar Father A. Tanquerey provides this explanation of the Roman Catholic position:

> It is not inappropriate that *the body of Christ at the same time be in heaven and upon all the altars on which the bread and the wine are consecrated*. It is indeed inconsistent that the same body be at the same time in many places according to local presence: for it would be locally distant from itself and divided from itself. But any contradiction vanishes when the body is *locally* in one place only, and in another place according to the *mode of substance*; for then it is not distant or divided from itself. Now Christ's body is *locally* in heaven certainly, but it is not in the Eucharist locally, but according to the mode of substance (*A Manual of Dogmatic Theology* [New York: Desclee Company, 1959], vol. II, p. 262).

233. John A. Hardon, S.J., *The Catholic Catechism* (Garden City, NY: Doubleday, 1975), p. 467.

234. Second Vatican Council, "Life of Priests," no. 13. See also the Code of Canon Law, canon 904.

235. Pope Pius XII, *Mediator Dei*, no. 73.

236. *Roman Missal*, "Prayer Over the Offerings," ninth Sunday after Pentecost. This prayer is cited by the Second Vatican Council, "Life of Priests," no. 13, footnote 14.

237. Pope Pius XII, *Mediator Dei*, no. 79.

238. Second Vatican Council, "Decree on the Ministry and Life of Priests," no. 2.

239. Second Vatican Council, "Dogmatic Constitution on the Church," no. 10; Second Vatican Council, "Decree on the Ministry and Life of Priests," no. 2.

240. Second Vatican Council, "Decree on the Ministry and Life of Priests," no. 2.

241. Council of Trent, session 23, "Canons on the Sacrament of Order," canon 1.

242. John A. Hardon, S.J., *Pocket Catholic Dictionary* (New York: Image Books, 1985), p. 256.

243. *The Catechism of the Catholic Church* also cites Titus 1:5 [1577, 1590] and James 5:14 [1510, 1516, 1519, 1526] in support of the ministerial priesthood.

244. Second Vatican Council, "Dogmatic Constitution on the Church," no. 8.

245. Second Vatican Council, "Dogmatic Constitution on the Church," no. 8.

246. Second Vatican Council, "The Church in the Modern World," no. 44.

247. First Vatican Council, session 4, "First Dogmatic Constitution of the Church of Christ," chapter 1.

248. Council of Trent, session 13, "Decree on the Most Holy Sacrament of the Eucharist," chapter 3.

249. Council of Trent, session 23, "The True and Catholic Doctrine of the Sacrament of Order," chapter 1.

250. Council of Trent, session 22, "Teaching and Canons on the Most Holy Sacrifice of the Mass," chapter 1.

251. Second Vatican Council, "Dogmatic Constitution on the Church," no. 53.

252. Second Vatican Council, "Dogmatic Constitution on the Church," no. 53.

253. Second Vatican Council, "Dogmatic Constitution on the Church," no. 53.

254. Reported by Virgilio Levi, *L'Osservatore Romano*, May 18, 1991, p. 7.

255. The motto *Totus Tuus* comes from a Latin prayer by Saint Louis de Montfort (1673-1716): *Tuus totus ego sum, et omnia mea tua sunt, O Virgo super omnia benedicta*, meaning: "I belong to you entirely, and all that I possess is yours, Virgin blessed above all" (Arthur Burton Calkins, *Totus Tuus* [Libertyville, IL: Academy of the Immaculate, 1992], p. 27).

256. Dialogue is based on an interview with Monsignor Stanislaus conducted and recorded by Andre Frossard, *Be Not Afraid!* (New York: St. Martin's Press, 1982), p. 226.

257. Alphonsus De Liguori, *The Glories of Mary* (Brooklyn, NY: Redemptorist Fathers, 1931), p. 235.

258. Pope Pius IX, *Ineffabilis Deus*.

259. Pope Pius IX, *Ineffabilis Deus*.

260. Pope Pius IX, *Ineffabilis Deus*.

261. Pope Pius IX, *Ineffabilis Deus*.

262. Pope Pius IX, *Ineffabilis Deus*.

263. John A. McHugh, O.P., and Charles J. Callan, O.P., translators, *The Roman Catechism: The Catechism of the Council of Trent* (Rockford, IL: Tan Books and Publishers, 1982), p. 46.

264. John A. McHugh, O.P., and Charles J. Callan, O.P., translators, *The Roman Catechism: The Catechism of the Council of Trent* (Rockford, IL: Tan Books and Publishers, 1982), p. 46.

265. John A. McHugh, O.P., and Charles J. Callan, O.P., translators, *The Roman Catechism: The Catechism of the Council of Trent* (Rockford, IL: Tan Books and Publishers, 1982), pp. 45-46.

266. John A. McHugh, O.P., and Charles J. Callan, O.P., translators, *The Roman Catechism: The Catechism of the Council of Trent* (Rockford, IL: Tan Books and Publishers, 1982), pp. 45-46.

267. Litany of the Blessed Virgin Mary, approved by Pope Sixtus V.

268. Litany of the Blessed Virgin Mary, approved by Pope Sixtus V.

269. Pope Pius XII, *Munificentissimus Deus*, no. 44.

270. The Roman Catholic Church says that Mary is foreshadowed in the woman of Genesis 3:15. The immediate context, however, speaks of Eve, not Mary.

271. Some Roman Catholic scholars understand "the woman" of Revelation 12:1 to be a reference to Mary (for example, Pope John Paul II, *Redemptoris Mater*, no. 24). Others see "the woman" as a reference to Israel. The latter appears to fit the context better.

272. Council of Ephesus, "Third Letter of Cyril to Nestorius," canon 1.

273. John A. McHugh, O.P., and Charles J. Callan, O.P., translators, *The Roman Catechism: The Catechism of the Council of Trent* (Rockford, IL: Tan Books and Publishers, 1982), p. 46.

274. Thomas Aquinas, Summa, part III, q. 28, A.3.

275. Thomas Aquinas, Summa, part III, q. 28, A.3.

276. Thomas Aquinas, Summa, part III, q. 28, A.3.

277. Thomas Aquinas, Summa, part III, q. 28, A.3.

278. Thomas Aquinas, Summa, part III, q. 28, A.3.

279. Thomas Aquinas, Summa, part III, q. 28, A.3.

280. Thomas Aquinas, Summa, part III, q. 28, A.3.

281. Matthias Premm, *Dogmatic Theology for the Laity* (Rockford, IL: Tan Books, 1967), p. 313.

282. John A. McHugh, O.P., and Charles J. Callan, O.P., translators, *The Roman Catechism: The Catechism of the Council of Trent* (Rockford, IL: Tan Books and Publishers, 1982), pp. 371-372, quoting Augustine.

283. Pope Pius IX, *Ineffabilis Deus*.

284. Pope Pius IX, *Ineffabilis Deus*.

285. Pope Pius XII, *Mystici Corporis*.

286. Pope Pius IX, *Ineffabilis Deus*.

287. Some Roman Catholic documents avoid stating that Mary actually died. Instead they use ambiguous euphemisms such as "when the course of her earthly life was completed,"[974] "at the end of her earthly life" (Pope Paul VI, *The Credo of the People of God*, no. 15), and "when her earthly life was over" (Second Vatican Council, "Dogmatic Constitution on the Church," no. 59). In the dogmatic definition of the Assumption of Mary, Pope Pius XII chose not to settle the question. Rather, he wrote of Mary "having completed the course of her earthly life" (Pope Pius XII, *Munificentissimus Deus*, no. 44). Though some continue to debate the issue, most modern Catholic theologians teach that Mary died.

288. Alphonsus de Liguori, *The Glories of Mary* (Brooklyn, NY: Redemptorist Fathers, 1931), p. 407.

289. Genesis 3:15; Psalm 131:8; 44:10-14; Song of Solomon 3:6; 4:8; 6:9; 8:5; Isaiah 61:13; Luke 1:28; Romans 5,6; 1 Corinthians 15:21-26,54-57; Revelation 12.

290. Pope Pius XII, *Munificentissimus Deus*, no. 26.

291. John Paul II, *Portugal: Message of Fatima* (Boston: St. Paul's Editions, 1983), p. 74.

292. John Paul II, *Portugal: Message of Fatima* (Boston: St. Paul's Editions, 1983), pp. 49-50.

293. Based on an interview with Monsignor Stanislaus conducted and recorded by Andre Frossard, *Be Not Afraid!* (New York: St. Martin's Press, 1982), p. 251.

294. This was not the first time that a pope had consecrated the world to Mary, nor the last. For a history from a Roman Catholic viewpoint of John Paul's program of Marian consecration, see Arthur Burton Calkins, *Totus Tuus* (Libertyville, IL: Academy of the Immaculate, 1922).

295. Pope John Paul II, *L'Osservatore Romano*, May 24, 1982, pp. 5, 12.

296. Second Vatican Council, "Dogmatic Constitution on the Church," no. 56.

297. Pope Benedict XV, *Inter Sodalicia*. This quote and some of the others which follow can be found in a collection of statements by recent popes compiled by Francis J. Ripley, *Mary, Mother of the Church* (Rockford, IL: Tan Books, 1969).

298. Pope Pius XII, *Mystici Corporis*.

299. Second Vatican Council, "Dogmatic Constitution on the Church," no. 58.

300. Pope Pius XI, *Explorata Res*.

301. Pope Benedict XV, *Inter Sodalicia*.

302. Pope Pius XII, *Ad Coeli Reginam*.

303. Pope Leo XIII, *Ubi Primum*.

304. Decree of the Sacred Congregation of the Holy Office, "Indulgences," June 26, 1913, published in *Acta Apostolicae Sedis*. Also refer to Henry Denzinger, *Sources of Catholic Dogma* (St. Louis: Herder Book Co., 1957),

p. 502, article 1978a and footnote 2; A. Tanquerey, *A Manual of Dogmatic Theology* (New York: Desclee Company, 1959), vol. 2, pp. 108-109; and Ludwig Ott, *Fundamentals of Catholic Dogma* (Rockford, IL: Tan Books and Publishers, 1960), pp. 212-213.

305. Pope Pius IX, *Ineffabilis Deus*.

306. Pope Leo XIII, *Adiutricem Populi*.

307. Pope Pius XII, *Ad Coeli Reginam*.

308. Pope Pius X, *Ad Diem Illum Laetissimum*, no. 12.

309. Pope Benedict XV, *Fausto Appetente Die*.

310. Pope Leo XIII, *Octobri Mense*.

311. Pope Pius IX, *Ineffabilis Deus*.

312. Pope Pius IX, *Ineffabilis Deus*.

313. Pope Leo XIII, *Octobri Mense*.

314. Pope Pius X, *Ad Diem Illum Laetissimum*, no. 13.

315. Pope Leo XIII, *Octobri Mense*.

316. Second Vatican Council, "Dogmatic Constitution on the Church," no. 66.

317. Pope Pius XII, *Mystici Corporis*.

318. Pope Benedict XV, *Inter Sodalicia*.

319. Pope John Paul II, *Salvifici Doloris*, no. 25.

320. Pope John Paul II, *Salvifici Doloris*, no. 25.

321. Second Vatican Council, "Dogmatic Constitution on the Church," no. 61.

322. Pope Pius IX, *Ineffabilis Deus*.

323. Second Vatican Council, "Dogmatic Constitution on the Church," no. 57.

324. Pope John Paul II, *Salvifici Doloris*, no. 25.

325. Pope John Paul II, *Salvifici Doloris*, no. 25.

326. Roman Catholic theology fails to make a clear distinction between the redemptive sufferings of Christ for our salvation and the personal sufferings of men and women [618, 964, 1505, 1521, 1532]. Consider, for example, Pope John Paul II's treatment of human suffering in his apostolic letter *Salvifici Doloris*, "On the Christian Meaning of Human Suffering," published in 1984. His theme is developed around Colossians 1:24, where Paul writes:

> Now I rejoice in my sufferings for your sake, and in my flesh I do my share on behalf of His body (which is the church) in filling up that which is lacking in Christ's afflictions.

The Pope says that Paul here is "declaring the power of salvific suffering...." (*Salvifici Doloris*, no. 1). Of Mary he writes:

...She truly has a special title to be able to claim that she "completes in her flesh"—already in her heart—"what is lacking in Christ's afflictions."

—*Salvifici Doloris*, no. 25

Likewise, according to Pope John Paul II, all human suffering contributes to the redemption:

Every man has his own share in the Redemption.... In bringing about the Redemption through suffering, Christ has also raised human suffering to the level of the Redemption. Thus each man, in his suffering, can also become a sharer in the redemptive suffering of Christ.

—*Salvifici Doloris*, no. 19

The context of Colossians 1:24, however, says nothing about Paul suffering for salvation or participating in the redemption. Rather, he is speaking of his suffering for the sake of righteousness in the course of fulfilling his ministry. When Christians, Christ's body on earth, suffer, the Lord in heaven shares their suffering (Acts 9:4; 1 Corinthians 12:26). It is in this sense that the church completes the sufferings of Christ. These sufferings of Christians should not be confused with redemptive suffering and death of Christ for our sins on the cross.

327. Pope Benedict XV, *Inter Sodalicia*.

328. Pope Leo XII, *Jucunda Semper*.

329. Second Vatican Council, "Dogmatic Constitution on the Church," no. 58.

330. Pope Benedict XV, *Fausto Appetente Die*.

331. Second Vatican Council, "Dogmatic Constitution on the Church," no. 60.

332. Second Vatican Council, "Dogmatic Constitution on the Church," no. 62.

333. Second Vatican Council, "Dogmatic Constitution on the Church," no. 60.

334. The Code of Canon Law, canon 1186.

335. Pope Leo XIII, *Ubi Primum*.

336. Pope Leo XIII, *Adiutricem Populi*.

337. Pope Leo XIII, *Supreme Apostolatus*.

338. Pope Leo XIII, *Octobri Mense*.

339. Pope Benedict XV, *Fausto Appetente Die*.

340. Pope Leo XIII, *Superiore Anno*.

341. Pope Pius XII, allocution given on April 21, 1940.

342. Pope Pius IX, *Exultavit Cor Nostrum*.

343. Pope Benedict XV, *Fausto Appetente Die*.

344. Pope Leo XIII, *Octobri Mense*.

345. Pope Pius X, *Tanto Studio*.

346. Pope Leo XIII, *Octobri Mense.*

347. Second Vatican Council, "Dogmatic Constitution on the Church," no. 60.

348. Pope Pius X, *Ad Diem Illum Laetissimum,* no. 14.

349. Second Vatican Council, "Sacred Liturgy," "Apostolic Constitution on the Revision of Indulgences," no. 5.

350. Second Vatican Council, "Sacred Liturgy," "Apostolic Constitution on the Revision of Indulgences," no. 5.

351. Pope Pius X, *Ad Diem Illum Laetissimum,* no. 12.

352. Pope Pius X, *Ad Diem Illum Laetissimum,* no. 14.

353. Second Vatican Council, "Dogmatic Constitution on the Church," no. 60.

354. Pope Pius IX, *Ineffabilis Deus.*

355. Pope Pius IX, *Ubi Primum.*

356. Pope Pius X, *Ad Diem Illum Laetissimum,* no. 14.

357. Pope Leo XIII, *Fidentem Piumque.*

358. Pope Leo XIII, *Octobri Mense.*

359. Pope Leo XIII, *Augustissimae.*

360. Pope Leo XIII, *Jucunda Semper.*

361. Pope Pius XI, *Ingravescentibus Malis.*

362. Pope Leo XIII, *Jucunda Semper.*

363. Pope Leo XIII, *Parta Humano Generi.*

364. Pope Leo XIII, *Adiutricem Populi.*

365. Pope Pius X, *Ad Diem Illum Laetissimum,* no. 13.

366. Translation of the Hebrew of "before Me" (Exodus 20:3) by C. F. Keil and F. Delitzsch, *Commentary on the Old Testament* (Grand Rapids: Eerdmans, reprinted 1985), The Pentateuch, vol. 2, p. 114.

367. Pope Pius IX, *Ineffabilis Deus.*

368. Pope Pius IX, *Ineffabilis Deus.*

369. Pope Pius IX, *Ineffabilis Deus.*

370. Pope Leo XIII, *Jucunda Semper.*

371. Pope Leo XIII, *Fidentem Piumque.*

372. Pope Benedict XV, *Inter Sodalicia.*

373. Pope Pius IX, *Ineffabilis Deus.*

374. Alphonsus de Liguori, *The Glories of Mary* (Brooklyn, NY: Redemptorist Fathers, 1931), p. 407.

375. Cf. Pope Pius XII, *Munificentissimus Deus,* no. 39.

376. Pope Pius XII, *Munificentissimus Deus,* no. 17.

377. Pope Paul VI, *The Credo of the People of God,* no. 15.

378. Second Vatican Council, "Dogmatic Constitution on the Church," no. 59.

379. Pope Pius X, *Ad Diem Illum Laetissimum*, no. 14.

380. Pope Pius XII, *Munificentissimus Deus*, no. 20.

381. Pope Leo XII, *Magnae Dei Matris*.

382. Pope Pius XII, *Munificentissimus Deus*, no. 14.

383. Second Vatican Council, "Dogmatic Constitution on the Church," no. 62.

384. *Catechism of the Catholic Church*, no. 722. Compare 2 Corinthians 9:15.

385. Litany of the Blessed Virgin Mary, approved by Pope Sixtus V. Compare John 15:11.

386. Litany of the Blessed Virgin Mary, approved by Pope Sixtus V. Compare Revelation 22:16.

387. Litany of the Blessed Virgin Mary, approved by Pope Sixtus V. Compare John 10:9; 14:6.

388. Litany of the Blessed Virgin Mary, approved by Pope Sixtus V. Compare Matthew 11:19, 28.

389. The veneration of Mary under the title of "Our Lady of Perpetual Help" or "Our Lady of Perpetual Succor" was officially sanctioned by Pope Pius IX (1846-1878). Compare Hebrews 7:25; 13:5,6.

390. Pope Leo XIII, *Parta Humano Generi*. Compare 1 Peter 2:25.

391. Pope Benedict XV, *Inter Sodalicia*. Compare Romans 10:13.

392. Pope Pius VIII, *Praestantissiumum Sane*.

393. Thomas Aquinas, *Summa Theologica*, part III, question 28, article 3.

394. Litany of the Blessed Virgin Mary, approved by Pope Sixtus V.

395. Pope Leo XIII, *Octobri Mense*.

396. Pope Leo XIII, *Adiutricem Populi*.

397. Litany of the Blessed Virgin Mary, approved by Pope Sixtus V. See also *Catechism of the Catholic Church*, no. 721.

398. Second Vatican Council, "Dogmatic Constitution on the Church," no. 56. See also *Catechism of the Catholic Church*, no. 726.

399. Pope Pius IX, *Ineffabilis Deus*.

400. The Roman Catholic Church recognizes Miltiades (311-314) as the Bishop of Rome at the time of Constantine's supposed conversion. Sylvester (314-335) was the first bishop to enjoy the full benefits of imperial favor.

401. Some historians recognize June 19, 325, as the opening date of the council.

402. Figures are as of December 31, 1991. Published by Felician A. Foy, editor, *1994 Catholic Almanac* (Huntington, IA: Our Sunday Visitor Publishing Division, 1993), p. 367.

403. Second Vatican Council, "Decree on the Pastoral Office of Bishops in the Church," no. 8.

404. Second Vatican Council, "Dogmatic Constitution on the Church," no. 20.

405. Second Vatican Council, "Decree on the Pastoral Office of Bishops in the Church," no. 2.

406. Second Vatican Council, "Decree on the Pastoral Office of Bishops in the Church," no. 2.

407. Second Vatican Council, "Decree on the Pastoral Office of Bishops in the Church," no. 4.

408 First Vatican Council, session 4, "First Dogmatic Constitution of the Church of Christ," chapter 1.

409. The Eastern Catholic Church should not be confused with the Eastern Orthodox Church. The latter's full communion with Rome ended with the Schism of 1054. Eastern Orthodox bodies include the Greek Orthodox, Russian Orthodox, and others. The Orthodox Churches do not accept the supremacy of the Bishop of Rome. They are not, therefore, Roman Catholics [838, 1399].

410. Figures are as of December 31, 1991. Published by Felician A. Foy, editor, *1994 Catholic Almanac* (Huntington, IA: Our Sunday Visitor Publishing Division, 1993), p. 367.

411. First Vatican Council, session 4, "First Dogmatic Constitution of the Church of Christ," chapter 1.

412. First Vatican Council, session 4, "First Dogmatic Constitution of the Church of Christ," chapter 3.

413. First Vatican Council, session 4, "First Dogmatic Constitution of the Church of Christ," chapter 1.

414. The *Catechism of the Catholic Church* states that Peter is the rock upon which Christ would build His church [552, 586, 881]. This is the official Roman Catholic position. Curiously, however, it also states:

> Moved by the grace of the Holy Spirit and drawn by the Father, we believe in Jesus and confess: "You are the Christ, the Son of the living God." On the rock of this faith confessed by St. Peter, Christ built his Church.
>
> —*Catechism of the Catholic Church*[424]

415. G. Campbell Morgan, *The Gospel According to Matthew* (New York: Fleming H. Revell Co.), p. 211.

416. Examples of Aramaic words in the Greek New Testament include *raca* (Matthew 5:22), *Eloi* (Mark 15:34), and *Rabboni* (John 20:16).

417. John 1:42; 1 Corinthians 1:12; 3:22; 9:5; 15:5; Galatians 1:18; 2:9,11,14.

418. A. Tanquerey, *A Manual of Dogmatic Theology* (New York: Desclee Company, 1959), vol. 1, p. 120.

419. The Roman Catholic doctrine of apostolic succession is the belief that the apostles ordained bishops as their successors and gave to them their threefold power of teaching, sanctifying, and ruling. It is not the belief that the bishops are new apostles [860]. The Church, therefore, does not appeal to Acts 1:15-26, the choosing of Matthias to replace Judas Iscariot as one of the Twelve, to substantiate its claims.

420. A. Tanquerey, *A Manual of Dogmatic Theology* (New York: Desclee Company, 1959), vol. 1, p. 104.

421. Philip Schaff, *History of the Christian Church* (Grand Rapids: Eerdmans, 1910), vol. 2, pp. 164-165.

422. Michael Walsh, *An Illustrated History of the Popes: Saint Peter to John Paul II* (New York: St. Martin's Press, 1980), p. 9.

423. Bruce L. Shelley, *Church History in Plain Language* (Waco, TX: Word, 1982), p. 151.

424. For a full explanation of how Leo I applied Roman Law to the claims of the papacy, refer to F. A. Sullivan, "Papacy," in *The New Catholic Encyclopedia* (New York: McGraw-Hill, 1967), vol. 10, pp. 952-953.

425. Will Durant, *The Story of Civilization*, "The Age of Faith," (New York: Simon and Schuster, 1950), vol. 4, p. 50.

426. Will Durant, *The Story of Civilization*, "The Age of Faith," (New York: Simon and Schuster, 1950), vol. 4, p. 525.

427. Richard P. McBrien, *Catholicism* (San Francisco, CA: Harper Collins, 1994), vol. 2, p. 622. Though the author is a Roman Catholic priest and the Chairman of the Department of Theology at the University of Notre Dame, this book does not carry the official declarations of the Church *Nihil Obstat* and *Imprimatur*.

428. Pope Boniface VIII, *Unam Sanctam*.

429. Second Vatican Council, "Dogmatic Constitution on the Church," no. 18.

430. This account is based upon records of the event by James T. O'Conner, *The Gift of Infallibility* (Boston: Daughters of St. Paul, 1986), and by Dom Cuthbert Butler, *The Vatican Council* (Westminster, MD: Newman Press, 1962).

431. James T. O'Conner, *The Gift of Infallibility* (Boston: Daughters of St. Paul, 1986), p. 19.

432. James T. O'Conner, *The Gift of Infallibility* (Boston: Daughters of St. Paul, 1986), pp. 19-20.

433. Second Vatican Council, "Dogmatic Constitution on Divine Revelation," no. 7; quoting Irenaeus, *Against Heresies*, III, 3, 1.

434. Second Vatican Council, "Dogmatic Constitution on Divine Revelation," no. 10.

435. Second Vatican Council, "Dogmatic Constitution on the Church," no. 20.

436. Second Vatican Council, "Dogmatic Constitution on the Church," no. 25.

437. First Vatican Council, session 3, "Dogmatic Constitution on the Catholic Faith," chapter 4, "On Faith and Reason."

438. First Vatican Council, session 3, "Dogmatic Constitution on the Catholic Faith," chapter 4, "On Faith and Reason."

439. Second Vatican Council, "Dogmatic Constitution on the Church," no. 25.

440. First Vatican Council, "First Dogmatic Constitution on the Church of Christ," session 4, chapter 4.

441. Second Vatican Council, "Dogmatic Constitution on the Church," no. 25.

442. Second Vatican Council, "Dogmatic Constitution on the Church," no. 25; see also Canon Law 752.

443. Second Vatican Council, "Dogmatic Constitution on the Church," no. 25.

444. *National Catholic Reporter*, February 4, 1994, p. 14.

445. Second Vatican Council, "Dogmatic Constitution on Divine Revelation," no. 7; quoting Irenaeus, *Against Heresies*, III, 3, 1.

446. The primary verses used by the Church in arguing for the infallibility of Peter and the apostles are: Isaiah 59:21; Matthew 16:18,19; 28:18-20; Mark 16:20; Luke 10:16; 22:31,32; John 14:16-26; 16:13; 21:15-17; Acts 1:8; 5:32; 15:28; 2 Corinthians 10:5,6; 1 Timothy 3:15; 6:20,21; 2 Timothy 1:13,14; 2 Thessalonians 2:14.

447. Ignatius, Letter to the Smyrneans, 8, 2.

448. See, for example, A. Tanquerey, *A Manual of Dogmatic Theology* (New York: Desclee Company, 1959), vol. 1, pp. 99-103.

449. A. Tanquerey, *A Manual of Dogmatic Theology* (New York: Desclee Company, 1959), vol. 1, p. 103.

450. Michael J. Wrenn, *Catechisms and Controversies* (San Francisco: Ignatius Press, 1991), pp. 144-147.

451. Matthias Premm, *Dogmatic Theology for the Laity* (Rockford, IL: Tan Books, 1967), p. 29.

452. Second Vatican Council, "Dogmatic Constitution on Divine Revelation," no. 25.

453. Second Vatican Council, "Dogmatic Constitution on Divine Revelation," no. 22.

454. Second Vatican Council, "Dogmatic Constitution on Divine Revelation," no. 25.

455. Walter M. Abbott, S.J., editor, *The Documents of Vatican II* (New York: 1966), p. 125, footnote 50.

456. Second Vatican Council, "Dogmatic Constitution on Divine Revelation," no. 10.

457. Second Vatican Council, "Dogmatic Constitution on Divine Revelation," no. 10.

458. First Vatican Council, session 3, "Dogmatic Constitution on the Catholic Faith," chapter 2, "On Revelation."

459. Second Vatican Council, "Dogmatic Constitution on Divine Revelation," no. 25.

460. The Code of Canon Law, canon 825.

461. Second Vatican Council, "Dogmatic Constitution on Divine Revelation," no. 23.

462. Second Vatican Council, "Dogmatic Constitution on Divine Revelation," no. 12.

463. Pope Pius XII, *Humani Generis*, no. 21; quoting Pope Pius IX.

464. Harris, Archer, Waltke, editors, *Theological Wordbook of the Old Testament* (Chicago: Moody, 1980), vol. ii, pp. 914-915.

465. Protestants consider Exodus 20:4-6, "You shall not make for yourself an idol..." the second commandment. The Catholic Church treats this command as part of the first commandment, "I am the Lord your God.... You shall have no other gods before Me" (Exodus 20:2,3) [2066, 2084-2141].

The Roman Catholic grouping of the commandments deemphasizes the prohibition against the making of graven images such as statues. As a result, many Catholic catechisms completely ignore Exodus 20:4-6. Those catechisms which do comment on Exodus 20:4-6, such as the *Catechism of the Catholic Church*, explain how it does not apply to Catholic practices [2129-2132, 2141]:

> The Christian veneration of images is not contrary to the first commandment which proscribes idols. Indeed, "the honor rendered to an image passes to its prototype," and "whoever venerates an image venerates the person portrayed in it."
>
> —*Catechism of the Catholic Church*[2132]

Since the first two commandments of Exodus 20 are counted as only one commandment in Roman Catholicism, the Church must divide Exodus 20:17 into two commandments in order to have a total of ten. Exodus 20:17 states:

> You shall not covet your neighbor's house; you shall not covet your neighbor's wife or his male servant or his female servant or his ox or his donkey or anything that belongs to your neighbor.

By Roman Catholic reckoning, the ninth commandment is "You shall not covet your neighbor's wife," and the tenth commandment is "You shall not covet your neighbor's goods" [2514-2557].

466. John A. McHugh, O.P., and Charles J. Callan, O.P., translators, *The Roman Catechism: The Catechism of the Council of Trent* (Rockford, IL: Tan Books and Publishers, 1982), pp. 375-376.

467. Second Vatican Council, "Sacred Liturgy," "A General Instruction on the Roman Missal," no. 278.

468. Pope Pius XII, *Deiparae Virginis Mariae*, no. 4.

469. Francis X. Murphy, *The Papacy Today* (New York: Macmillan, 1981), p. 69.

470. Pope Pius XII, *Humani Generis*, no. 21.

471. Pope Pius XII, *Humani Generis*, no. 21.

472. Pope Pius XII, *Munificentissimus Deus*, no. 44.

473. Pope Pius XII, *Munificentissimus Deus*, no. 48.

474. Second Vatican Council, "Dogmatic Constitution on Divine Revelation," no. 4.

475. Second Vatican Council, "Dogmatic Constitution on Divine Revelation," no. 4.

476. Second Vatican Council, "Dogmatic Constitution on Divine Revelation," no. 4.

477. Second Vatican Council, "Dogmatic Constitution on Divine Revelation," no. 7.

478. Second Vatican Council, "Dogmatic Constitution on Divine Revelation," no. 7.

479. Second Vatican Council, "Dogmatic Constitution on Divine Revelation," no. 7.

480. Second Vatican Council, "Dogmatic Constitution on Divine Revelation," no. 1.

481. The writing of the Dogmatic Constitution on Divine Revelation resulted in some of the most heated debates of the Second Vatican Council. Pope John XXIII finally had to mediate the dispute. For an account of this event refer to two volumes by Xavier Rynne, *Letters from Vatican City* (New York: Farrar, Straus and Co., 1963), pp. 140-173; and *The Third Session* (New York: Farrar, Straus and Giroux, 1965), pp. 35-48.

482. Second Vatican Council, "Dogmatic Constitution on Divine Revelation," no. 10.

483. Second Vatican Council, "Dogmatic Constitution on Divine Revelation," no. 9.

484. Second Vatican Council, "Dogmatic Constitution on Divine Revelation," no. 9.

485. Second Vatican Council, "Dogmatic Constitution on Divine Revelation," no. 10.

486. Second Vatican Council, "Dogmatic Constitution on Divine Revelation," no. 9.

487. Second Vatican Council, "Dogmatic Constitution on Divine Revelation," no. 21. Stated also at the Council of Trent: "...truth and rule are contained in written books and unwritten traditions..." (Council of Trent, session 4, "First Decree: Acceptance of the Sacred Books and Apostolic Traditions").

488. Second Vatican Council, "Dogmatic Constitution on Divine Revelation," no. 24.

489. The German Bishops' Conference, *The Church's Confession of Faith* (San Francisco: Ignatius Press, 1987), p. 45, quoting J. A. Möhler. See also the Second Vatican Council, "Dogmatic Constitution on Divine Revelation," no. 8; and the Council of Trent, session 4, "First Decree: Acceptance of the Sacred Books and Apostolic Traditions."

490. Jean Bainvel, *The Catholic Encyclopedia* (New York: Robert Appleton Co., 1912), "Tradition," vol. 15, p. 9.

491. Second Vatican Council, "Dogmatic Constitution on Divine Revelation," no. 8.

492. Second Vatican Council, "Dogmatic Constitution on Divine Revelation," no. 8.

493. The German Bishop's Conference, *The Church's Confession of Faith* (San Francisco: Ignatius Press, 1987), p. 46, quoting J. A. Möhler.

494. Second Vatican Council, "Dogmatic Constitution on Divine Revelation," no. 7; quoting Irenaeus, *Against Heresies*, III, 3, 1.

495. Second Vatican Council, "Dogmatic Constitution on Divine Revelation," no. 8.

496. Second Vatican Council, "Dogmatic Constitution on Divine Revelation," no. 8.

497. Pope Pius XII, *Deiparae Virginis Mariae*, no. 4.

498. The Code of Canon Law states:

> All that is contained in the written word of God or in tradition, that is, in the one deposit of faith entrusted to the Church and also proposed as divinely revealed either by the solemn magisterium of the Church or by its ordinary and universal magisterium, must be believed with divine and catholic faith; it is manifested by the common adherence of the Christian faithful under the leadership of the sacred magisterium; therefore, all are bound to avoid any doctrines whatever which are contrary to these truths.
>
> —Canon 750

499. The Code of Canon Law states:

> Heresy is the obstinate post-baptismal denial of some truth which must be believed with divine and catholic faith, or it is likewise an obstinate doubt concerning the same; apostasy is the total repudiation of the Christian faith; schism is the refusal of submission to the Roman Pontiff or of communion with the members of the Church subject to him.
>
> —Canon 751

See also: Pius XII, *Munificentissimus Deus*, no. 45.

500. For a fuller discussion of biblical arguments put forth for the Assumption of Mary, refer to the presentation of the Assumption in Chapter 8, *The Mother of God*.

501. Second Vatican Council, "Dogmatic Constitution on Divine Revelation," no. 8.

502. Pope Leo XIII, *On the Study of Sacred Scripture*, St. Paul Editions, p. 24.

503. W. A. Jurgens, *The Faith of the Early Fathers* (Collegeville, MN: The Liturgical Press, 1970), vol. 3, p. 359.

504. Second Vatican Council, "Dogmatic Constitution on Divine Revelation," no. 8.

505. Pope Pius XII, *Munificentissimus Deus*, nos. 21-22.

506. Jean Bainvel, *The Catholic Encyclopedia* (New York: Robert Appleton Co., 1912), "Tradition," vol. 15, p. 10.

507. W. A. Jurgens, *The Faith of the Early Fathers* (Collegeville, MN: The Liturgical Press, 1970), vol. 3, p. 359.

508. Pope Pius XII, *Munificentissimus Deus*, nos. 27-35.

509. Pope Pius XII, *Munificentissimus Deus*, no. 11.

510. Pope Pius XII, *Munificentissimus Deus*, no. 12.

511. Pope Pius XII, *Munificentissimus Deus*, no. 15.

512. Pope Pius XII, *Munificentissimus Deus*, no. 15.

513. Pope Pius XII, *Munificentissimus Deus*, no. 19.

514. Pope Pius XII, *Munificentissimus Deus*, nos. 16-18.

515. Pope Pius XII, *Mediator Dei*, no. 47.

516. Second Vatican Council, "Dogmatic Constitution on Divine Revelation," no. 8.

517. Second Vatican Council, "Dogmatic Constitution on the Church," no. 12.

518. Christopher O'Donnell, O. Carm., translator's note, Austin Flannery, editor, *Vatican Council II: The Conciliar and Post Conciliar Documents, Study Edition* (Northport, NY: Costello Publishing Company, 1986), p. 363.

519. Second Vatican Council, "Dogmatic Constitution on the Church," no. 12.

520. Pope Pius XII, *Deiparae Virginis Mariae*, no. 4.

521. Michael O'Carroll, C.S.Sp., *Theotokos: A Theological Encyclopedia of the Blessed Virgin Mary* (Wilmington, DE: Michael Glazier, Inc., 1982), p. 56.

522. Pope Pius XII, *Munificentissimus Deus*, no. 9.

523. Pope Pius XII, *Munificentissimus Deus*, no. 8.

524. Pope Pius XII, *Munificentissimus Deus*, no. 5.

525. Pope Pius XII, *Munificentissimus Deus*, no. 44.

526. Second Vatican Council, "Dogmatic Constitution on Divine Revelation," no. 7.

527. Second Vatican Council, "Dogmatic Constitution on Divine Revelation," no. 8.

528. Jean Bainvel, *The Catholic Encyclopedia* (New York: Robert Appleton Co., 1912), "Tradition," vol. 15, p. 9.

529. Second Vatican Council, "Dogmatic Constitution on Divine Revelation," no. 9.

530. Jean Bainvel, *The Catholic Encyclopedia* (New York: Robert Appleton Co., 1912), "Tradition," vol. 15, p. 11.

531. Second Vatican Council, "Dogmatic Constitution on Divine Revelation," no. 8.

532. A. Tanquerey, *A Manual of Dogmatic Theology* (New York: Desclee Company, 1959), vol. 1, p. 102.

533. Second Vatican Council, "Dogmatic Constitution on Divine Revelation," no. 10.

534. Pope Pius XII, *Humani Generis*, no. 21.

535. John A. Hardon, S. J., *The Catholic Catechism* (Garden City, NY: Double-day and Company, 1975), p. 161.

536. Following the destruction of Jerusalem in 70 A.D., the surviving Jews, realizing that their national heritage was threatened, started a movement to make a written record of their oral Tradition. This was completed about 200 A.D. and is known today as the *Mishna*.

537. Second Vatican Council, "Dogmatic Constitution on the Church," no. 10.

538. Second Vatican Council, "Decree on Ecumenism," no. 2.

539. Second Vatican Council, "Decree on Ecumenism," no. 3.

540. Second Vatican Council, "Decree on Ecumenism," no. 4.

541. Second Vatican Council, "Decree on Ecumenism," no. 4.

542. Among the initial evangelical signers were Charles Colson (Prison Fellowship), Bill Bright (Campus Crusade for Christ), J. I. Packer (Regent College), Pat Robertson (Regent University), Richard Land (Christian Life Commission of the Southern Baptist Convention), Larry Lewis (Home Mission Board of the Southern Baptist Convention), Os Guinness (Trinity Forum), Richard Mouw (Fuller Theological Seminary), Jesse Miranda (Assemblies of God), Brian O'Connell (Word Evangelical Fellowship), Kent Hill (Eastern Nazarene College), Thomas Oden (Drew University), and Mark Noll (Wheaton College).

543. Second Vatican Council, "Dogmatic Constitution on Divine Revelation," no. 21.

544. Council of Trent, session 6, "Decree on Justification," chapter 7.

545. See also parallel accounts in Matthew 19:13-15 and Mark 10:13-16.

546. A. Tanquerey, *A Manual of Dogmatic Theology* (New York: Desclee Company, 1959), vol. 2, p. 221.

547. Second Vatican Council, "Dogmatic Constitution on the Church," no. 7.

548. Some Bible commentators understand Romans 6:3,4 to be speaking of the Christian's baptism into the body of Christ by the agency of the Holy Spirit (1 Corinthians 12:13).

549. Council of Trent, session 6, "Decree on Justification," chapter 4. Translation from H. J. Schroeder, translator, *Canons and Decrees of the Council of Trent* (Rockford, IL: Tan Books and Publishers, 1978). The Catholic Douay Rheims Bible translates the verse: "Not by works of justice, which we have done, but according to his mercy, he saved us, by the laver of regeneration, and renovation of the Holy Ghost..." (Titus 3:5 Douay Rheims).

550. Code of Canon Law, canons 960, 962, 963.

551. H. J. Schroeder, translator, *Canons and Decrees of the Council of Trent* (Rockford, IL: Tan Books and Publishers, 1978), p. 17, footnote 4.

552. For a candid discussion of the Apocrypha by Roman Catholic scholars, see Raymond E. Brown, Joseph A. Fitzmyer, S.J., Roland E. Murphy, O. Carm., editors, *The Jerome Biblical Commentary* (Englewood Cliffs, NJ: Prentice Hall, 1968), vol. 2, pp. 523-524.

553. Compare: Second Vatican Council, "Dogmatic Constitution on Divine Revelation," no. 19.

554. First Vatican Council, session 3, chapter 2.

555. F. F. Bruce commented:

> Divine authority is by its very nature self-evidencing; and one of the profoundest doctrines recovered by the Reformers is the doctrine of the inward witness of the Holy Spirit, by which testimony is borne within the believer's heart to the divine character of the Holy Scripture (F. F. Bruce, *The Books and the Parchments* [London: Pickering Inglis, 1950], p. 111).

Calvin wrote:

> Let this point therefore stand: that those whom the Holy Spirit has inwardly taught truly rest upon Scripture, and that Scripture indeed is self-authenticated; hence, it is not right to subject it to proof and reasoning. And the certainty it deserves with us, it attains by the testimony of the Spirit. For even if it wins reverence for itself by its own majesty, it seriously affects us only when it is sealed upon our hearts through the Spirit. Therefore, illumined by his power, we believe neither by our own nor by anyone else's judgment that Scripture is from God; but above human judgment we affirm with utter certainty (just as if we were gazing upon the majesty of God himself) that it has flowed to us from the very mouth of God by the ministry of men (John Calvin, *Institutes of the Christian Religion*, book 1, chapter 7, no. 5. Published by John T. McNeill, editor, The Library of Christian Classics [Philadelphia: Westminster Press, 1960], vol. 20, p. 80).

556. F. F. Bruce, *The Books and the Parchments* (London: Pickering Inglis, 1950), p. 111.

557. Patrick Johnstone, *Operation World* (Grand Rapids: Zondervan, 1993), p. 22.

558. Second Vatican Council, "Dogmatic Constitution on Divine Revelation," nos. 21,24.

Scripture Index

Subject Index

A

Abbot 248
Absolution 77-78
Apocrypha 337-339, 351
Apostolic succession
  bishops not new apostles, note 419
  four primary arguments for 248-252
  necessary for preservation of Tradition 292
  teaching, sanctifying, and ruling power 234-235
Aquinas, Thomas
  on limbo 26
  on Mary's perpetual virginity 192-193
  patron saint of students 195
  Summa Theologica 18
Ashes placed on forehead 58
Augustine 264, 297
Authority (biblical)
  apostolic submission to Scripture 271
  Christ head of church 248
  deacons 255
  elders 255
  Holy Spirit living teaching authority 275
  Paul claimed no infallibility 270
Authority (Catholic) *(see also Bishops, Magisterium, Pope, Scripture, Tradition)*
  Error v. Truth 308-309
  spiritual and temporal swords 259

B

Baptism (biblical)
  cannot cleanse flesh 332
  of households 327-328
  to be received by all Christians 324
Baptism (Catholic)
  adult 39, 44
  benefits of Christ's death received through 25
  emergency baptism 32
  first step in plan of salvation 28
  incorporation into church through 25
  infant 21-29

  modes of, note 10
  of blood, note 61
  of desire 57, note 61, note 121
  original sin removed through 25-26
  sacrament of faith 31
  sacrament of regeneration 25
  sanctifying grace received through 26-28
  wonder-working water 32
Beatific vision 93
Bishops
  appointed teachers of Catholic faith 265
  must be obeyed as Christ 265
  ruling power 235
  sanctifying power 234
  successors of apostles 234
  teaching power 234, 270
Blessed palms 58
Buddhists, good 104-105

C

Cafeteria Catholics 269
Cardinals 236
Catechism of the Catholic Church
  cross-references to 3
  description 16
  proposal of 14
  release of 14
  to quell dissent within Church 274
Catechism, Roman 18
Catechumenate 40
Catholic (original meaning) 272
Chalice 126
Christ, saving work of (biblical)
  accepted 165
  finished 163
  once for all 167
Code of Canon Law 17
Confession (biblical)
  cases when required before others 80
  directly to God 80-81
Confirmation 334
  received immediately following adult baptism 45
Contrition, Act of 73, 77
Contrition, perfect, note 82
Council of Carthage 351
Council of Ephesus 191-192

initially received through
baptism 26-28
justifying grace 28
making partakers of the divine
nature 63
quality of the soul 63
restored through penance 76
sacraments instrumental causes
of 57
state of 56
Great Schism 254
Gregory the Great 258, 297

H

Hail Mary 79, 206, 215
Hail, Holy Queen 205
Heaven (Catholic)
deserved by those who die in
grace 102
increase of glory in, merited
reward 99
must atone for temporal
punishment before entering 92
must be earned 103
must die in state of grace to
reach 91
Holy Orders, sacrament of 171, 335
Holy Spirit, gifts of 28
Holy water 58
Host 54, 149
Humanae Vitae 269

I

Idolatry
biblical meaning of 222-223
Images (biblical)
forbidden by Exodus 20:4-5 279
Images (Catholic)
interpretation of Exodus 20:4-5
279-280, note 465
Immolation 151
distinguished from death 169
unbloody 151, 169
Imprimatur 18
Indulgences 94-95
definition 94
for praying Rosary 206
plenary 95
Infallibility
collectively, of bishops 267
collectively, of Catholic faithful
299
of pope 267-268

J

John Paul II
devotion to Mary 200
Judgment, general 99
Judgment, particular 91-92
Judgment, universal 99
Justification (biblical) *(see also
Salvation)*
by faith 29-30
cannot increase 66
definition 29
divine act 65, 105
faith only requirement for 48
includes positive reckoning of
righteousness 30, 65
Justification (Catholic) *(see also
Salvation)*
baptism means of 25-27
definition 28
extensive preparation required
for adults 37
faith alone insufficient for 47
faith necessary for 31
forfeited through mortal sin 76
furthered by participation in
Eucharist 130
increased through good works
66
infant 324, 327, 329
merited by Christ 28
restored through penance 76

L

Last Supper (Catholic) 127-128
first Eucharist 128
Mass instituted at 127
Lent 44
Leo the Great 257
Limbo 26-27
Liturgy *(see also Rites)*
authority of 17-18, note 7
of the Eucharist 125-127, 145-148
Lord's Supper (biblical)
bread and wine sufficient 137
figurative interpretation
consistent with spiritual worship
138

M

Maccabees, Second 337
abridgement of another's
writings 109
primary evidence for purgatory
from 107-108
Maccabeus, Judas 107

Also from the author of
The Gospel According to Rome:

Catholicism:
Crisis of Faith

This fast-moving video documentary examines the post-Vatican II Roman Catholic Church through interviews with former and practicing priests and nuns. It is an ideal resource for churches, Bibles schools, mission agencies, or anyone interested in understanding modern Roman Catholicism. Gentle enough to share with Catholic friends and neighbors, *Catholicism: Crisis of Faith* is also a proven evangelistic tool. Available in English, Spanish, Portuguese, Polish, and Korean. To purchase, contact your local Christian video distributor, or write to:

Good News for Catholics
P.O. Box 595
Cupertino, CA 95015 USA

Other Good Harvest House Reading

ONCE A CATHOLIC
by *Tony Coffey*

This powerful book is the clearest and simplest presentation of the differences between Roman Catholic tradition and the teachings of Scripture. *Once a Catholic* is a sensitive, thoroughly biblical guidebook for personal reference or for use as a gift to Catholic family members, coworkers, or friends.

PROTESTANTS AND CATHOLICS:
Do They Now Agree?
by *John Ankerberg and John Weldon*

Can Protestants and Catholics truly unite? Ankerberg and Weldon answer that question by expertly evaluating the current teachings of the Catholic church in the light of God's Word. Christians will find this book a valuable source of discernment and guidance as they determine how to respond to today's efforts to unite Catholics and Protestants.

A WOMAN RIDES THE BEAST
by *Dave Hunt*

A Woman Rides the Beast is an eye-opening book about prophecy, Catholicism, and the last days from the best-selling author of *Global Peace and the Rise of Antichrist*. Prophecy expert Dave Hunt sifts through biblical truth and global events to present a well-defined portrait of the woman and her powerful place in the Antichrist's future empire. Eight remarkable clues in Revelation 17 and 18 prove the woman's identity beyond any reasonable doubt.

THE FACTS ON ROMAN CATHOLICISM
by *John Ankerberg and John Weldon*

Authors Ankerberg and Weldon offer a biblical examination of Catholic doctrine and provide important insight into this influential religion.

New Inductive Study Bible
Kay Arthur

Every feature of *The New Inductive Study Bible* is designed to help you gain a more intimate understanding of God and His Word. With the help of clear, easy-to-use instructions, you'll discover how to mine the treasures of Scripture in a way so personal, so memorable, that every insight you discover can be yours for life.

The Daily Bible
F. LaGard Smith

This quality softcover edition of the Narrated Bible skillfully divides the New International Version into 365 daily readings in chronological order. Devotional narrative guides you as God's plan for creation unfolds before you in uninterrupted sequence.

How to Study Your Bible
Kay Arthur

This exciting book equips you with tools that will help you interact directly with Scripture itself. A dynamic, step-by-step guide on studying the Bible book by book, chapter by chapter, and verse by verse.